# SP4RX

## WREN MCDONALD

NOBROW

LONDON - NEW YORK

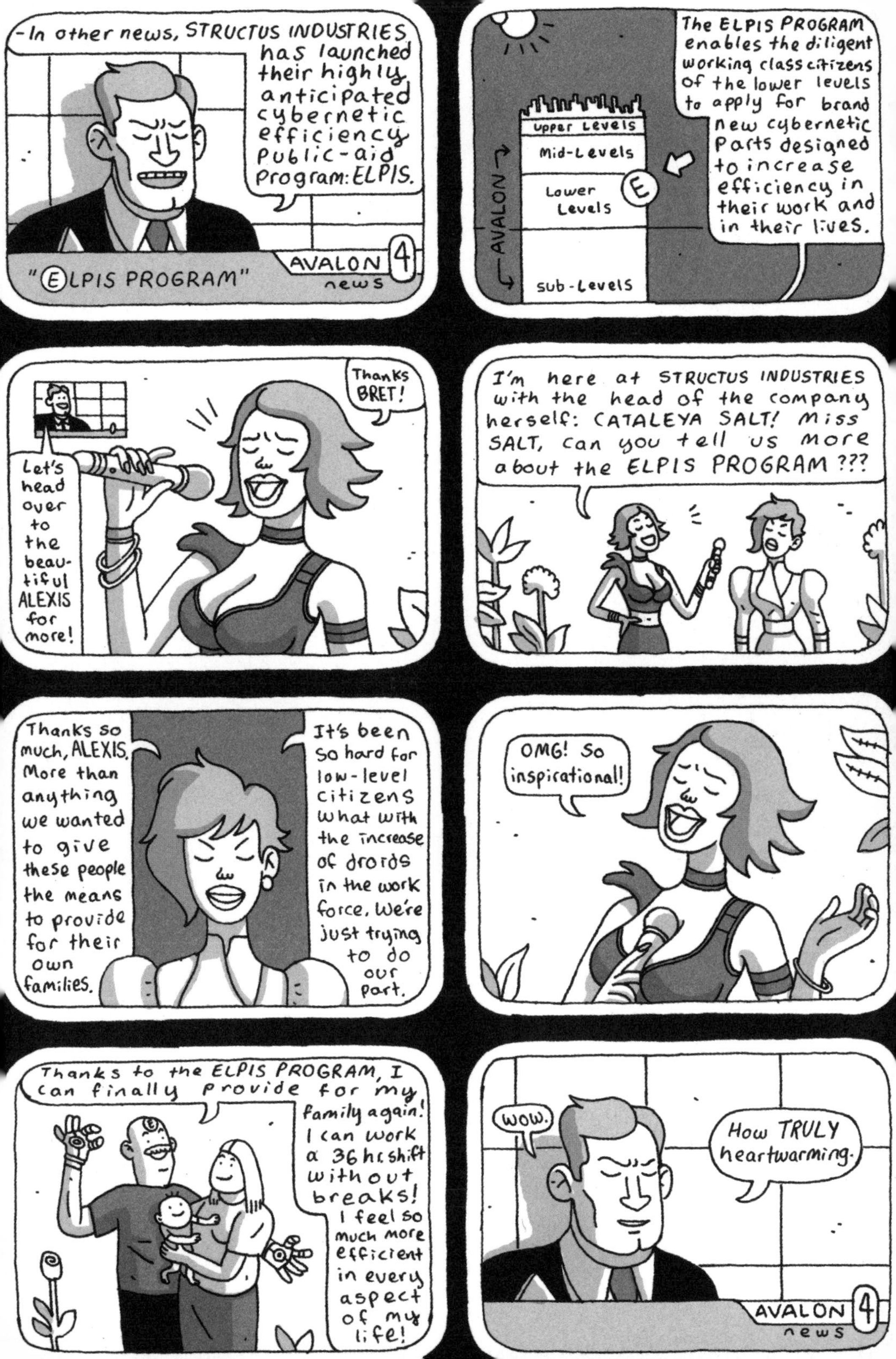

-In other news, STRUCTUS INDUSTRIES has launched their highly anticipated cybernetic efficiency public-aid program: ELPIS.
"ELPIS PROGRAM"
AVALON 4 news
The ELPIS PROGRAM enables the diligent working class citizens of the lower levels to apply for brand new cybernetic parts designed to increase efficiency in their work and in their lives.
Upper Levels
Mid-Levels
Lower Levels
Sub-Levels
AVALON
E
Let's head over to the beautiful ALEXIS for more!
Thanks BRET!
I'm here at STRUCTUS INDUSTRIES with the head of the company herself: CATALEYA SALT! Miss SALT, can you tell us more about the ELPIS PROGRAM???
Thanks so much, ALEXIS. More than anything we wanted to give these people the means to provide for their own families.
It's been so hard for low-level citizens what with the increase of droids in the work force. We're just trying to do our part.
OMG! So inspirational!
Thanks to the ELPIS PROGRAM, I can finally provide for my family again! I can work a 36 hr. shift without breaks! I feel so much more efficient in every aspect of my life!
WOW.
How TRULY heartwarming.
AVALON 4 news

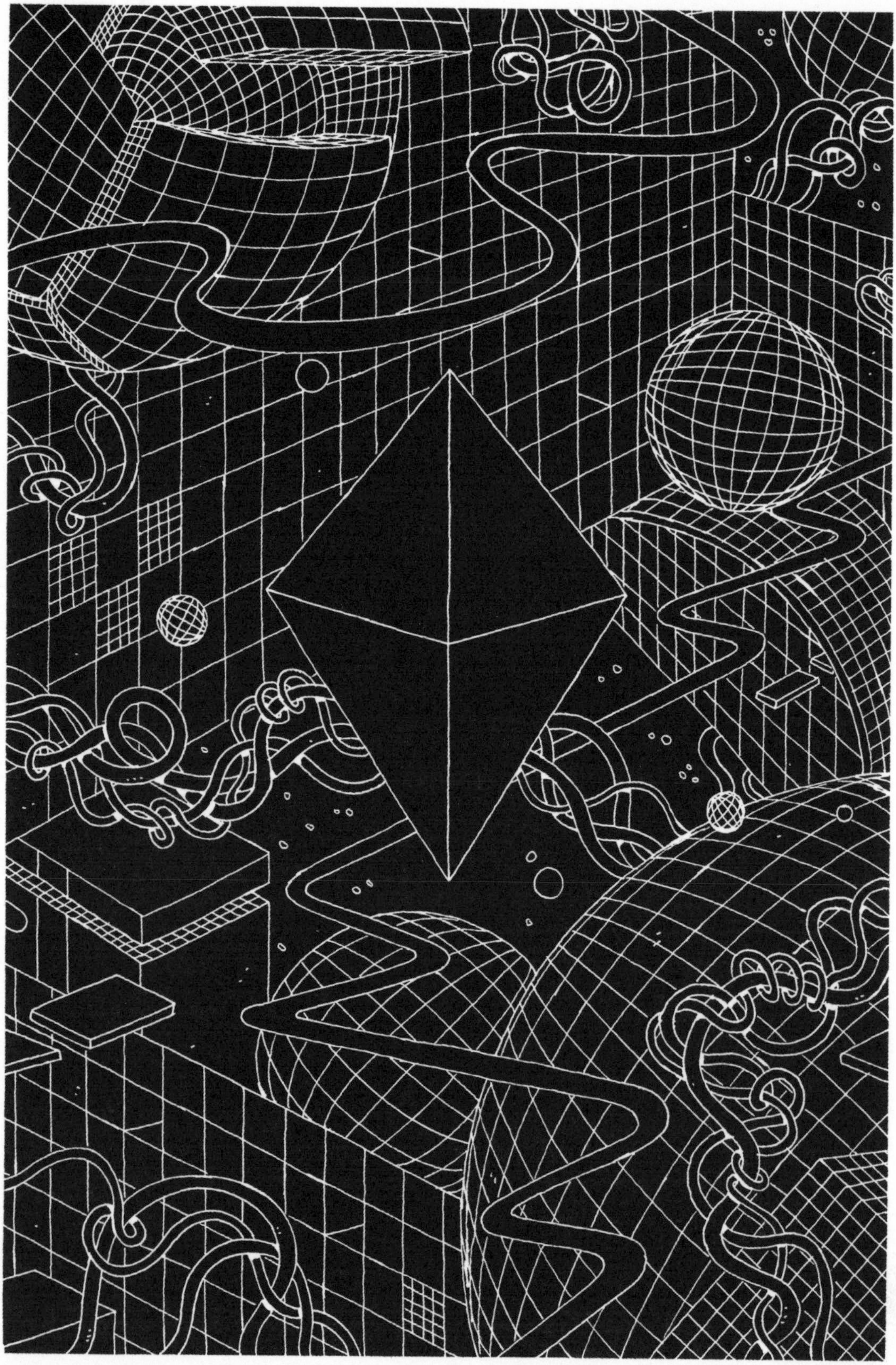

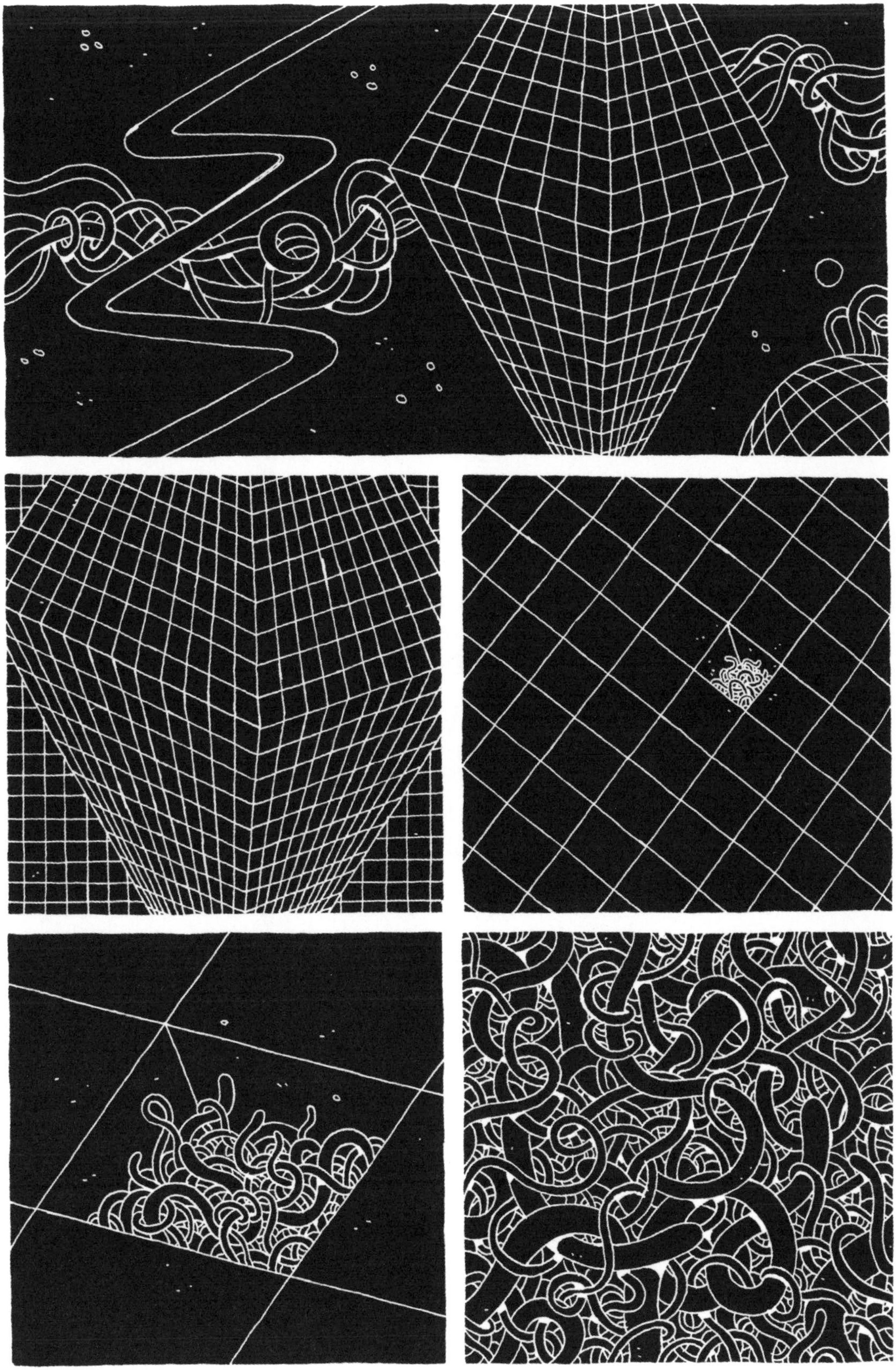

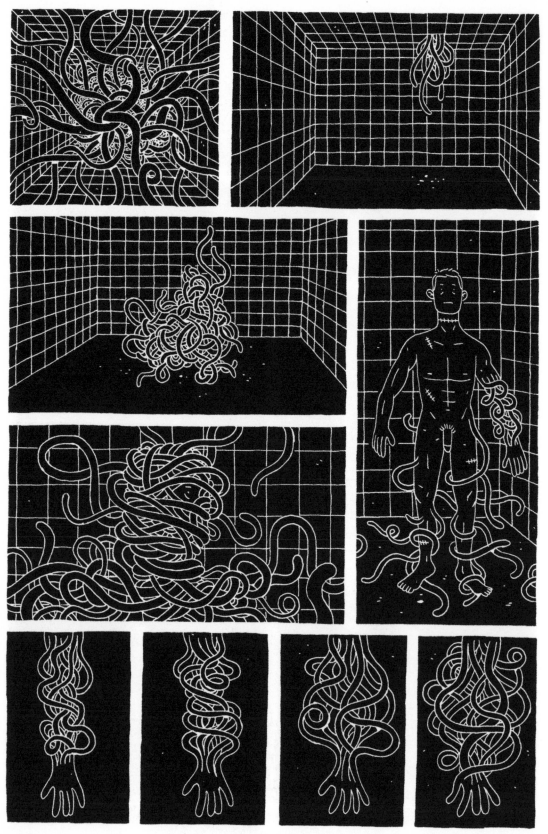

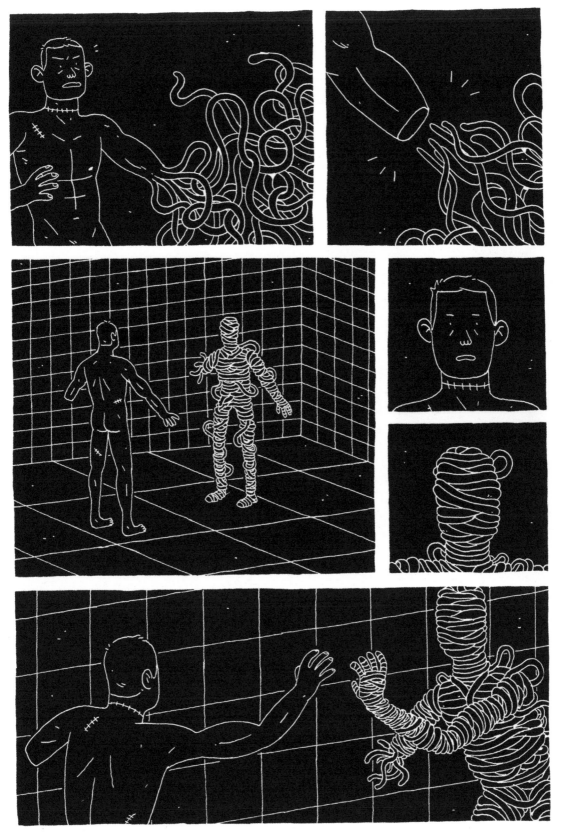

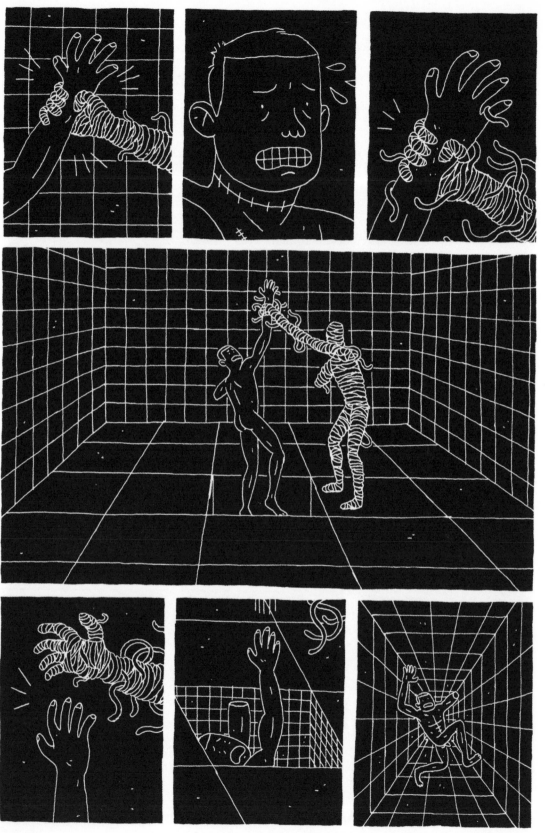

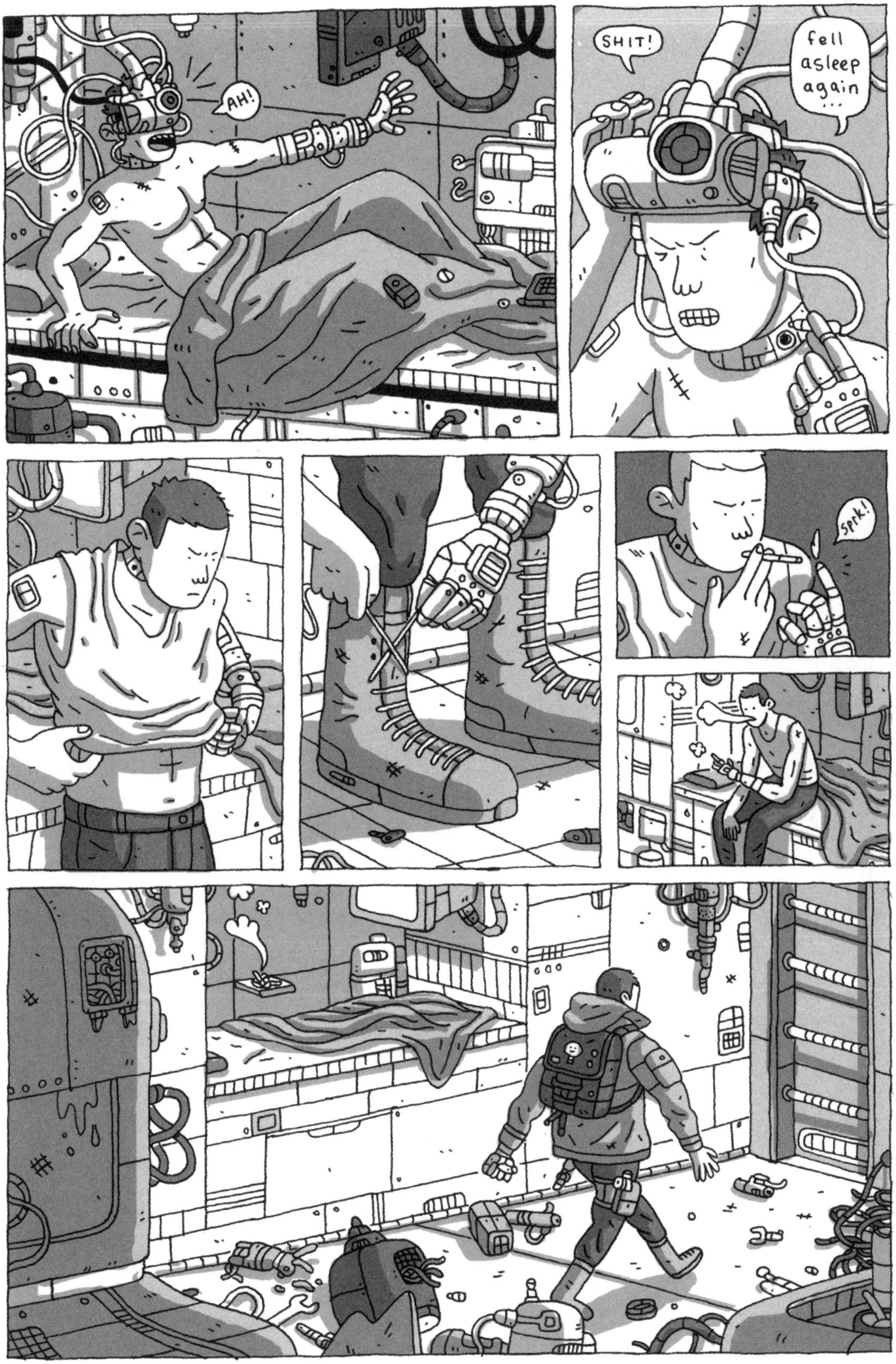
AH!
SHIT!
fell asleep again ...
sprk!

HALT!

ERROR: 07822, HOMO SAPIENS NOT PERMITTED ON SUB-LEVELS. COMMENCING EXTERMINATION...

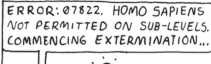

WHIRRRR

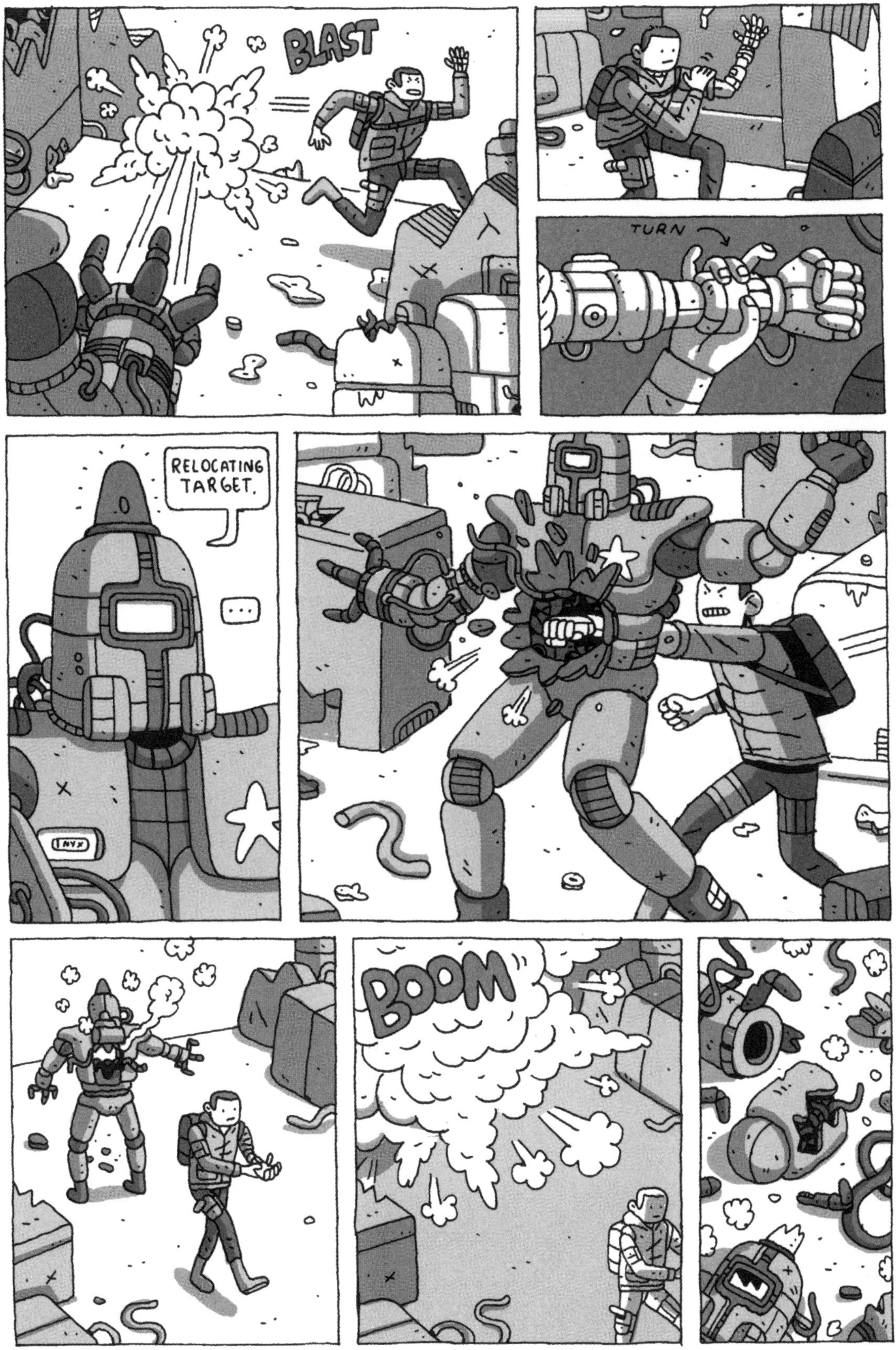
BLAST
TURN
RELOCATING TARGET.
...
NYX
BOOM

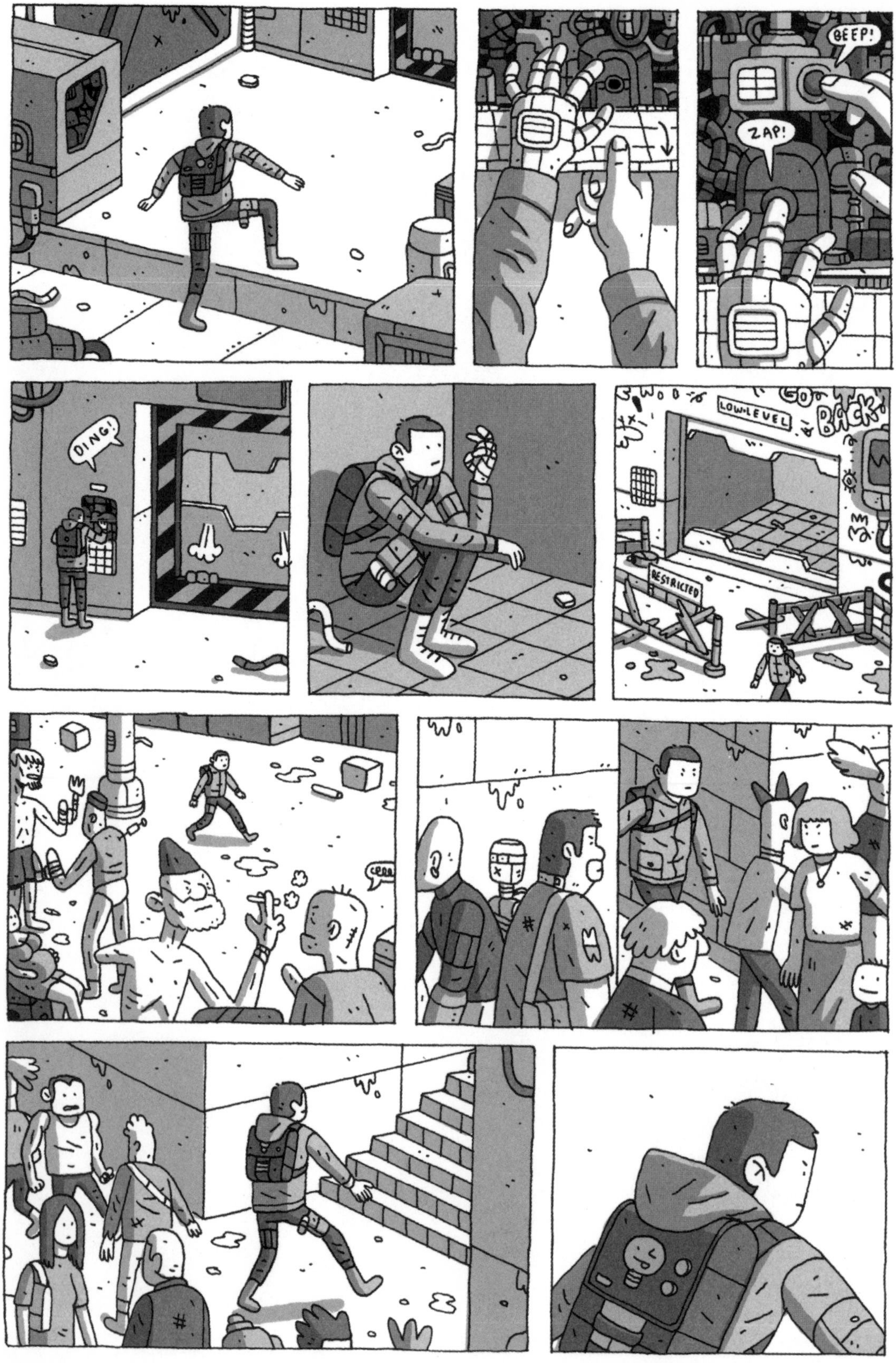
BEEP!
ZAP!
DING!
LOW-LEVEL
GO BACK
RESTRICTED

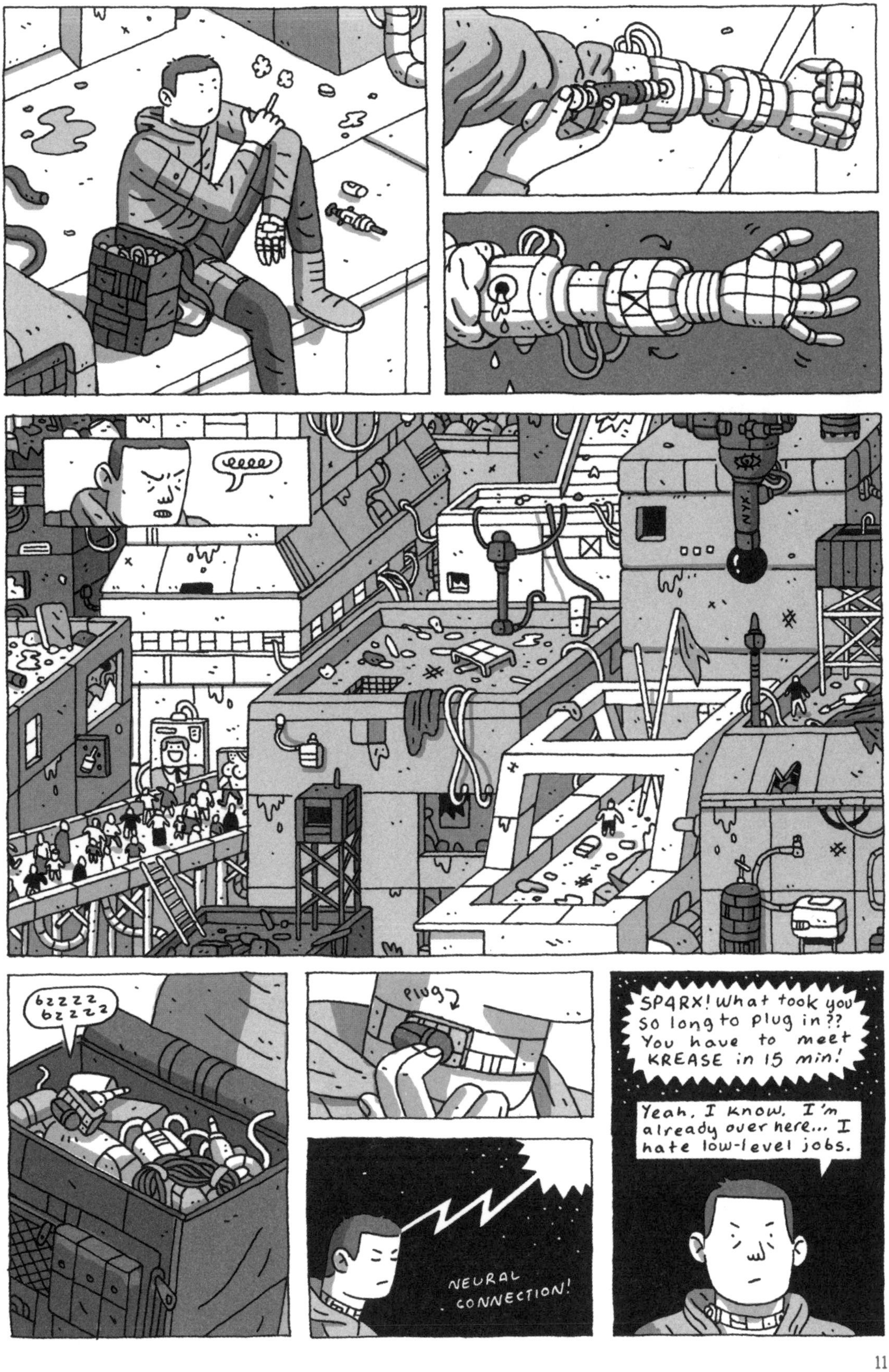

NYX
bzzzz bzzzz
plug
NEURAL CONNECTION!
SPARX! What took you so long to plug in?? You have to meet KREASE in 15 min!
Yeah, I know. I'm already over here... I hate low-level jobs.

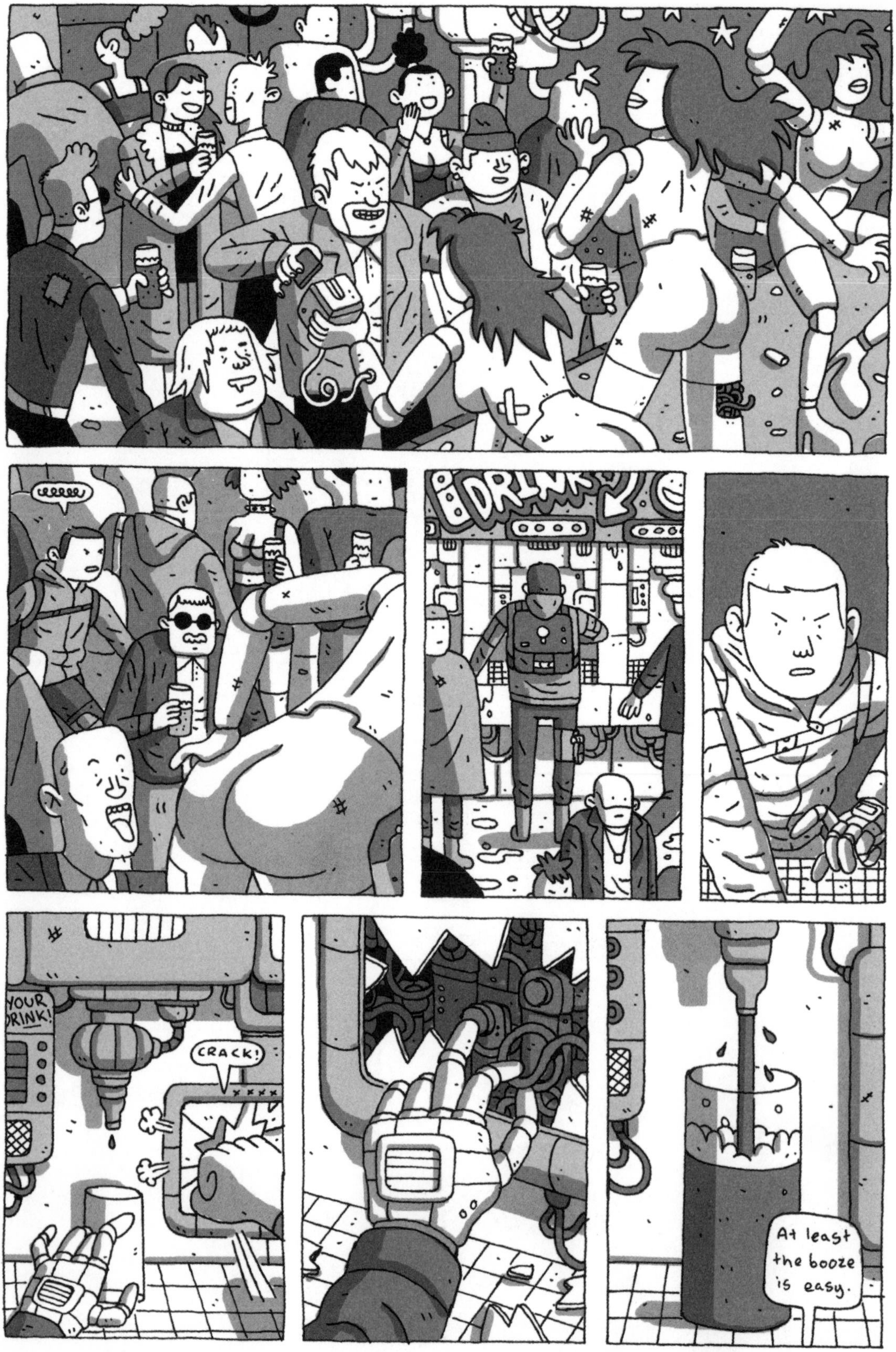
DRINK
YOUR DRINK!
CRACK!
At least the booze is easy.

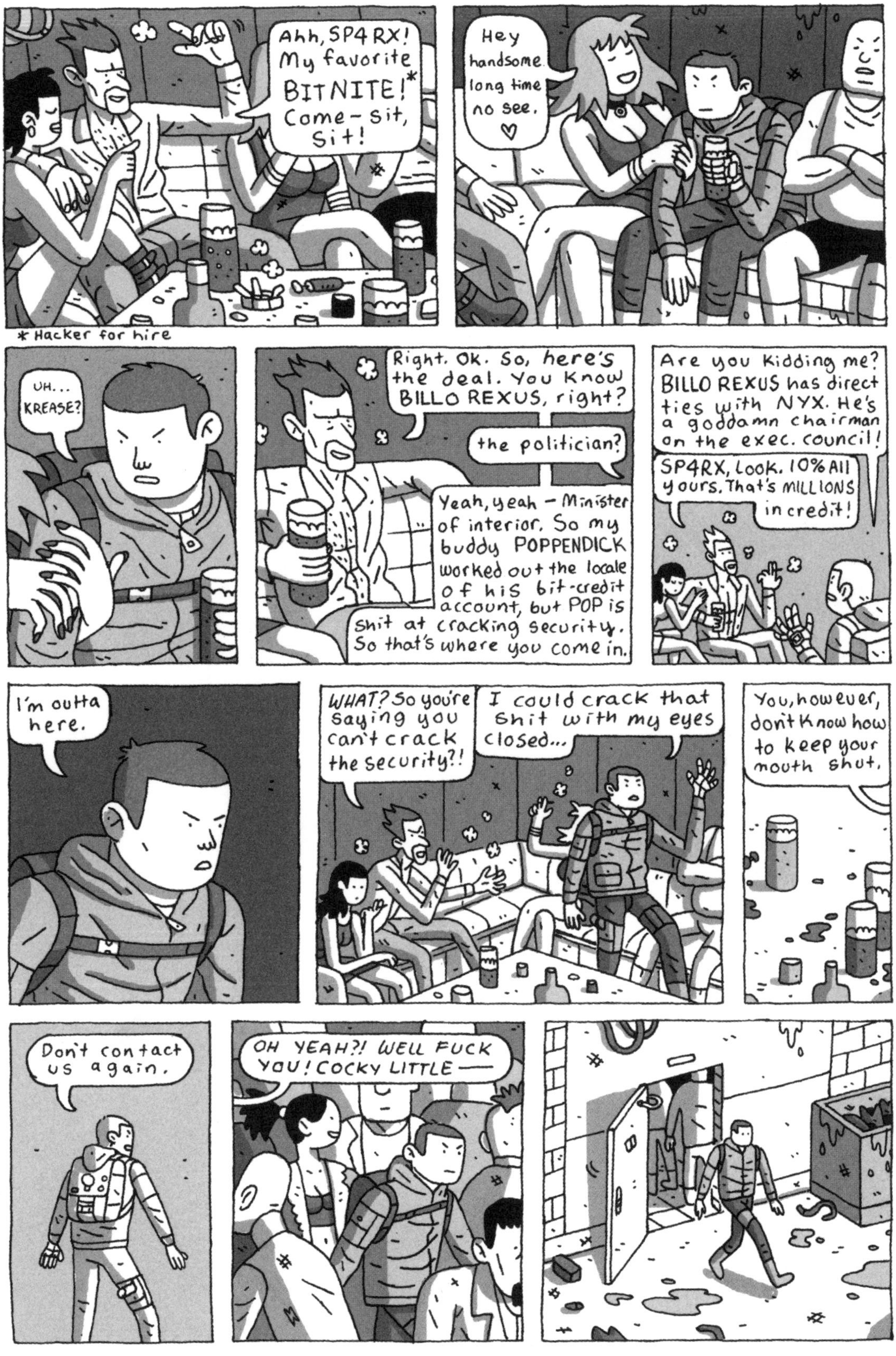

Ahh, SP4RX! My favorite BITNITE!* Come- sit, Sit!
Hey handsome. long time no see. ♡
* Hacker for hire
UH... KREASE?
Right. Ok. So, here's the deal. You Know BILLO REXUS, right?
the politician?
Yeah, yeah - Minister of interior. So my buddy POPPENDICK worked out the locale of his bit-credit account, but POP is shit at cracking security. So that's where you come in.
Are you kidding me? BILLO REXUS has direct ties with NYX. He's a goddamn chairman on the exec. council!
SP4RX, look. 10% All yours. That's MILLIONS in credit!
I'm outta here.
WHAT? So you're saying you can't crack the security?!
I could crack that shit with my eyes closed...
You, however, don't Know how to keep your mouth shut.
Don't contact us again.
OH YEAH?! WELL FUCK YOU! COCKY LITTLE—

catch →

Yo. Where'd you guys find this?

How the heck did an OBD-0.3 end up on this level?

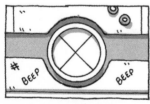

BEEP        BEEP

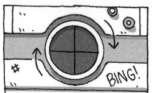

BING!

got it.

blip blip

blip blip blip

14

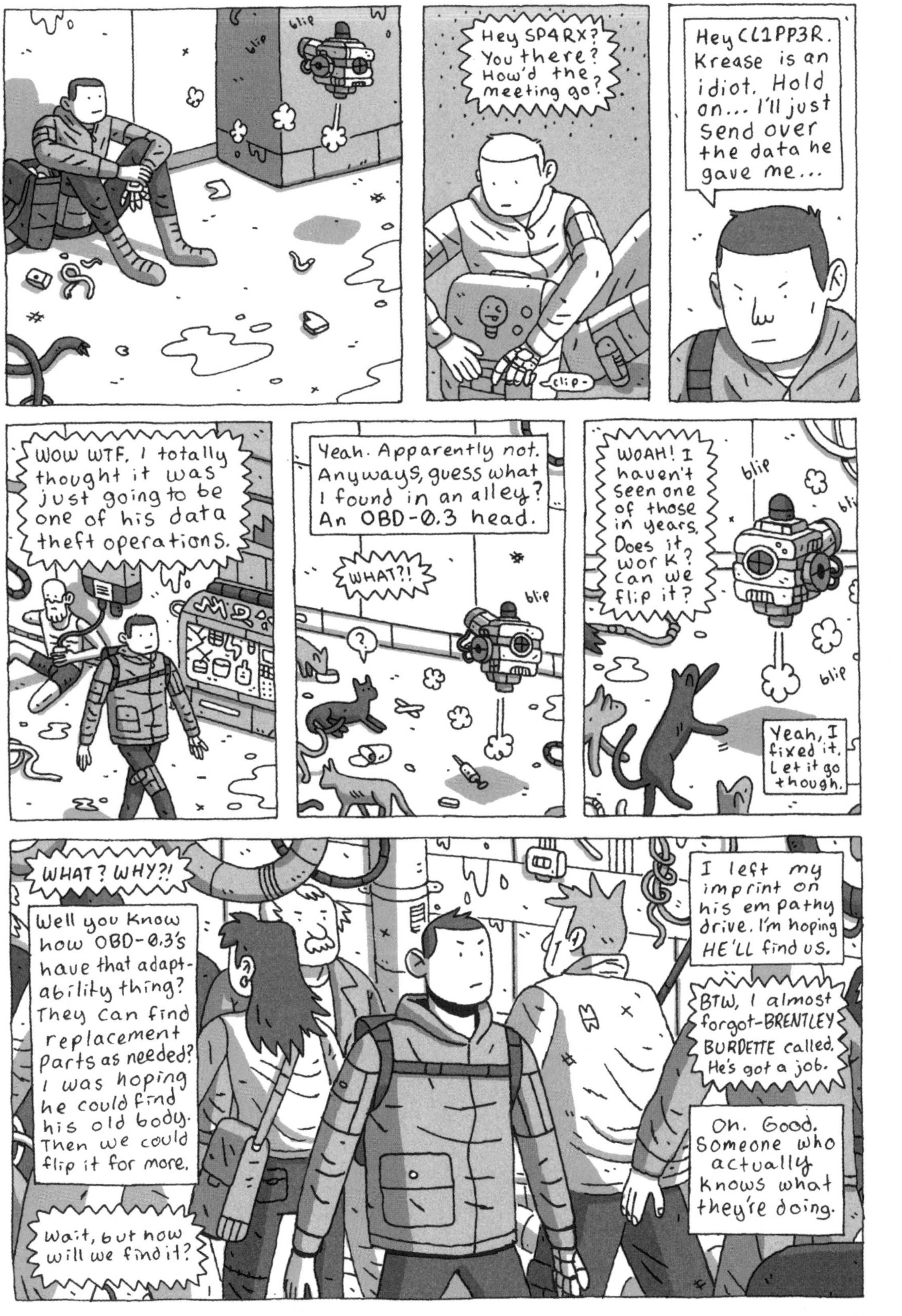

blip
blip
Hey SP4RX? You there? How'd the meeting go?
clip
Hey CL1PP3R. Krease is an idiot. Hold on... I'll just send over the data he gave me...
WOW WTF. I totally thought it was just going to be one of his data theft operations.
Yeah. Apparently not. Anyways, guess what I found in an alley? An OBD-0.3 head.
WHAT?!
blip
?
WOAH! I haven't seen one of those in years. Does it work? Can we flip it?
blip
blip
blip
Yeah, I fixed it. Let it go though.
WHAT? WHY?!
Well you know how OBD-0.3's have that adaptability thing? They can find replacement parts as needed? I was hoping he could find his old body. Then we could flip it for more.
Wait, but now will we find it?
I left my imprint on his empathy drive. I'm hoping HE'LL find us.
BTW, I almost forgot—BRENTLEY BURDETTE called. He's got a job.
Oh. Good. Someone who actually knows what they're doing.

CHANGING THE COURSE OF HISTORY
ONE STEP AT A TIME
WITH INNOVATIVE DESIGN
AND INSPIRATIONAL VISION
MAKING THE WORLD A BETTER PLACE
THROUGH EFFICIENCY & PROGRESS
TOGETHER, WE STAND AS ONE...
THE
ELPIS
PROGRAM
© STRUCTUS INDUSTRIES

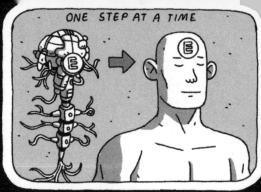

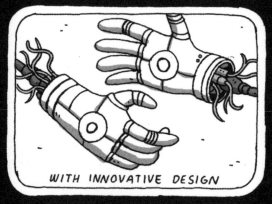

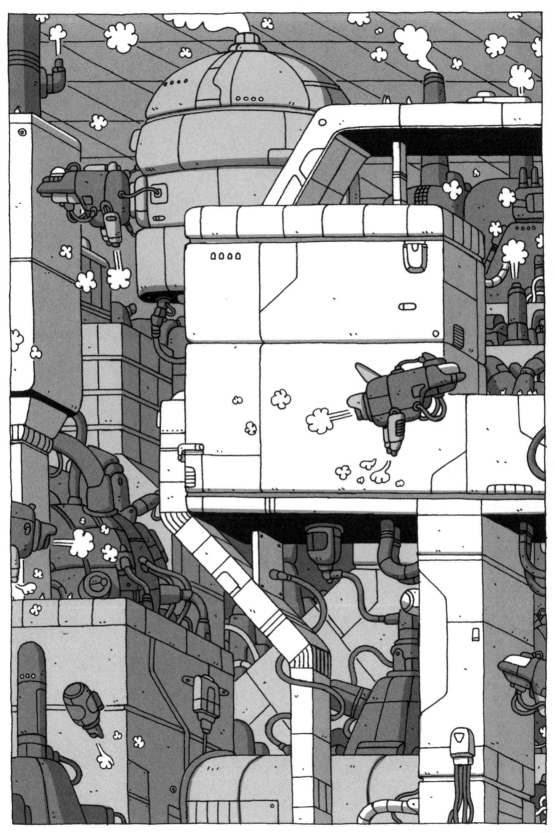

You've got 15 seconds.

Nice. OK. 2 rights then a left.

Just push it open. I disabled the lock and alarm on my end.

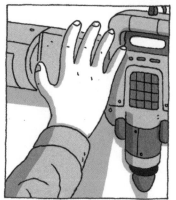

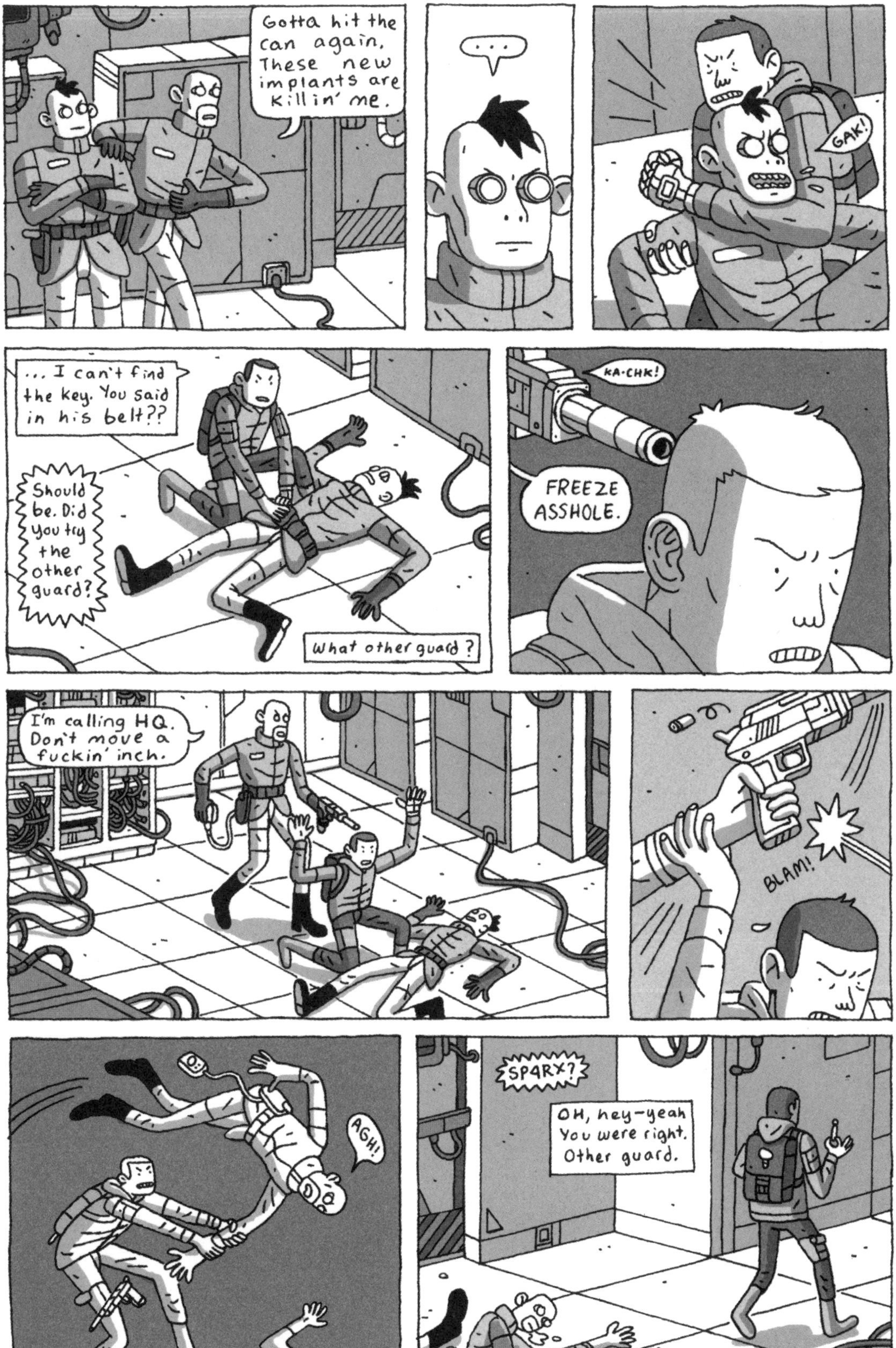
Gotta hit the can again. These new implants are killin' me.
. . .
GAK!
... I can't find the key. You said in his belt??
Should be. Did you try the other guard?
What other guard?
KA-CHK!
FREEZE ASSHOLE.
I'm calling HQ. Don't move a fuckin' inch.
BLAM!
AGH!
SP4RX?
OH, hey-yeah You were right. Other guard.

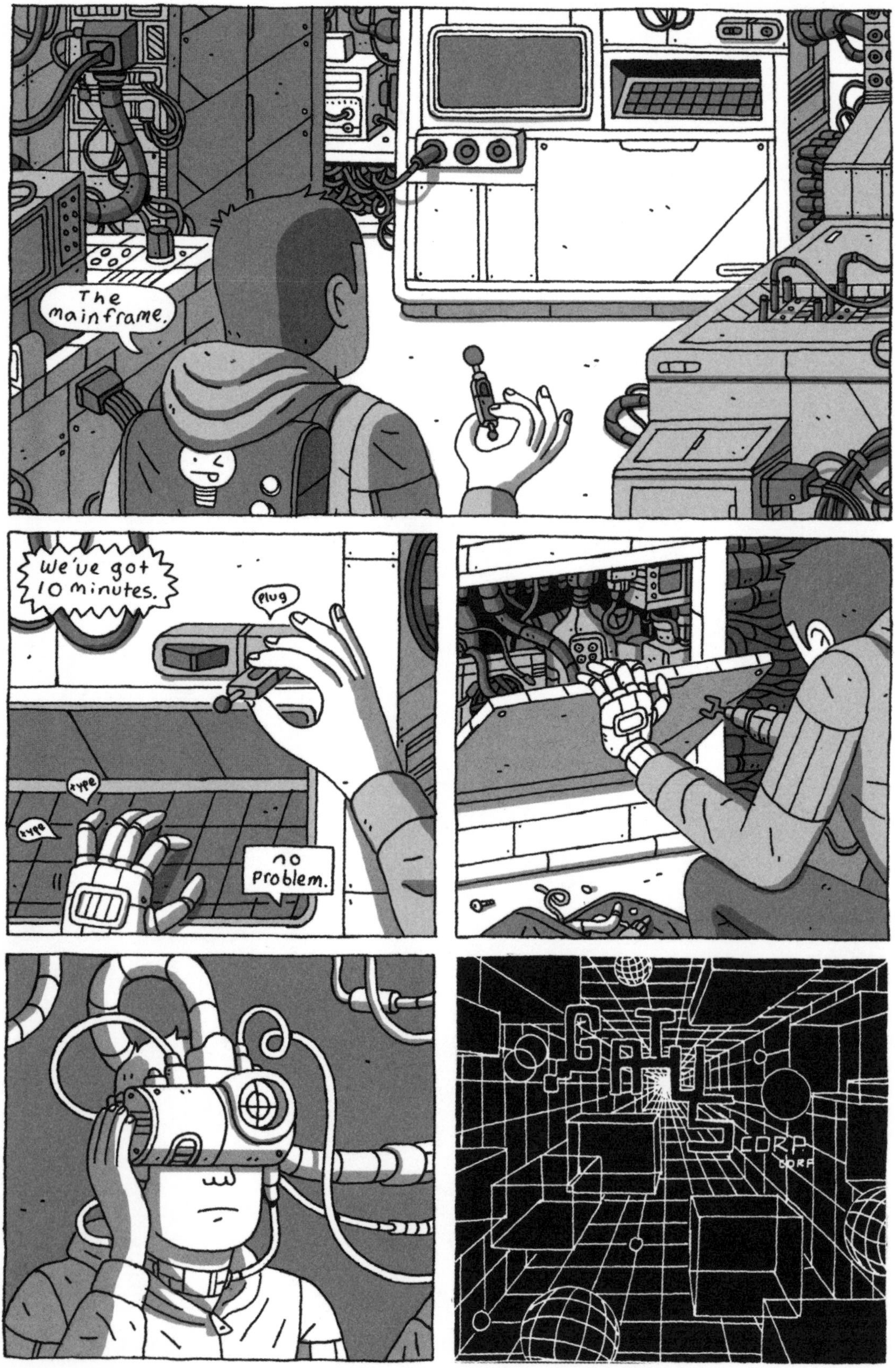
The mainframe.
We've got 10 minutes.
plug
type
type
no problem.
CORP.
CORP

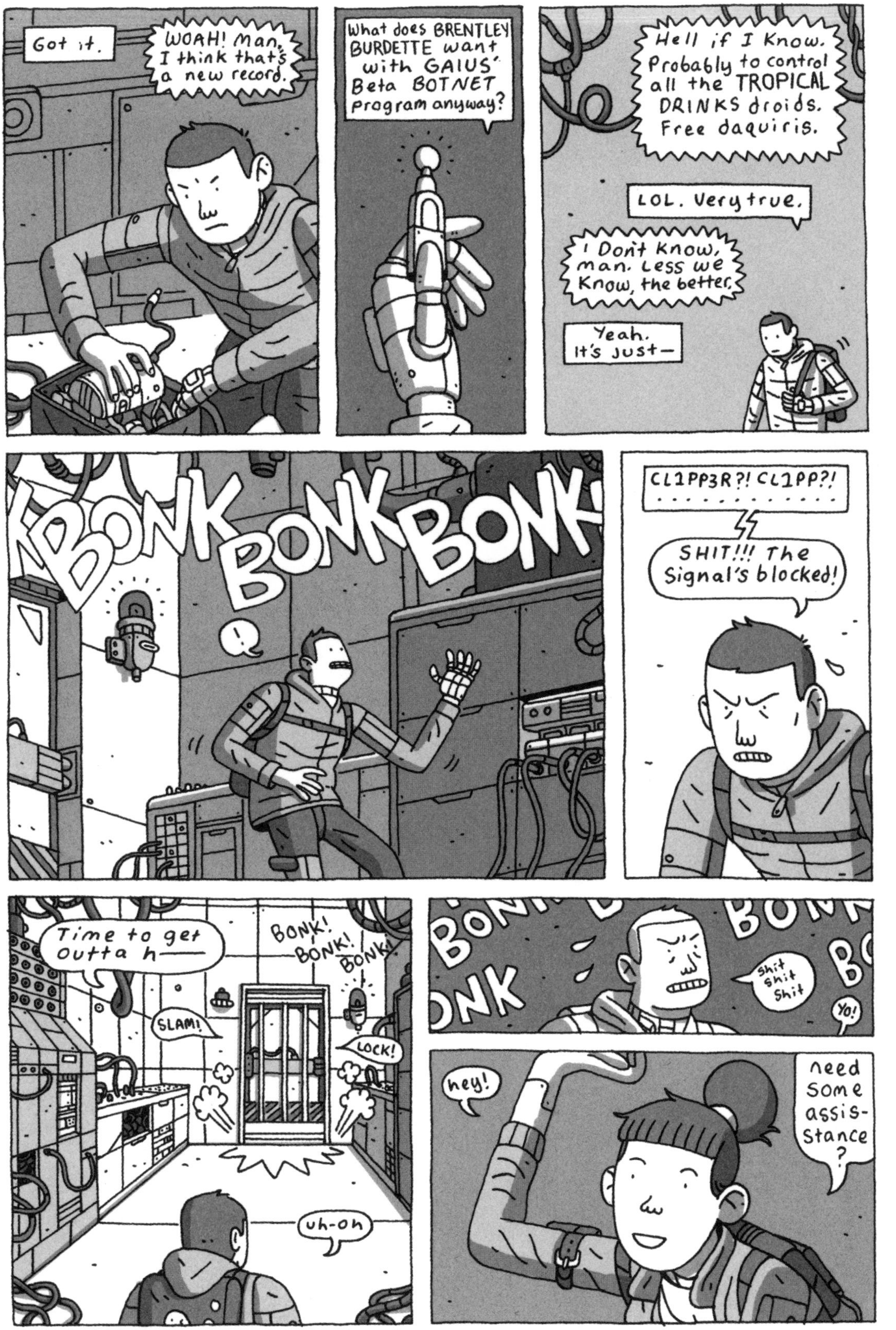
Got it.
WOAH! Man, I think that's a new record.
What does BRENTLEY BURDETTE want with GAIUS' Beta BOTNET program anyway?
Hell if I Know. Probably to control all the TROPICAL DRINKS droids. Free daquiris.
LOL. Very true.
I Don't Know, man. Less we Know, the better.
Yeah. It's just—
BONK BONK BONK
!
CL1PP3R?! CL1PP?!
. . . . . . . . . . .
SHIT!!! The Signal's blocked!
Time to get outta h—
BONK! BONK! BONK!
SLAM!
LOCK!
uh-oh
Shit Shit Shit
Yo!
hey!
need some assis-stance?

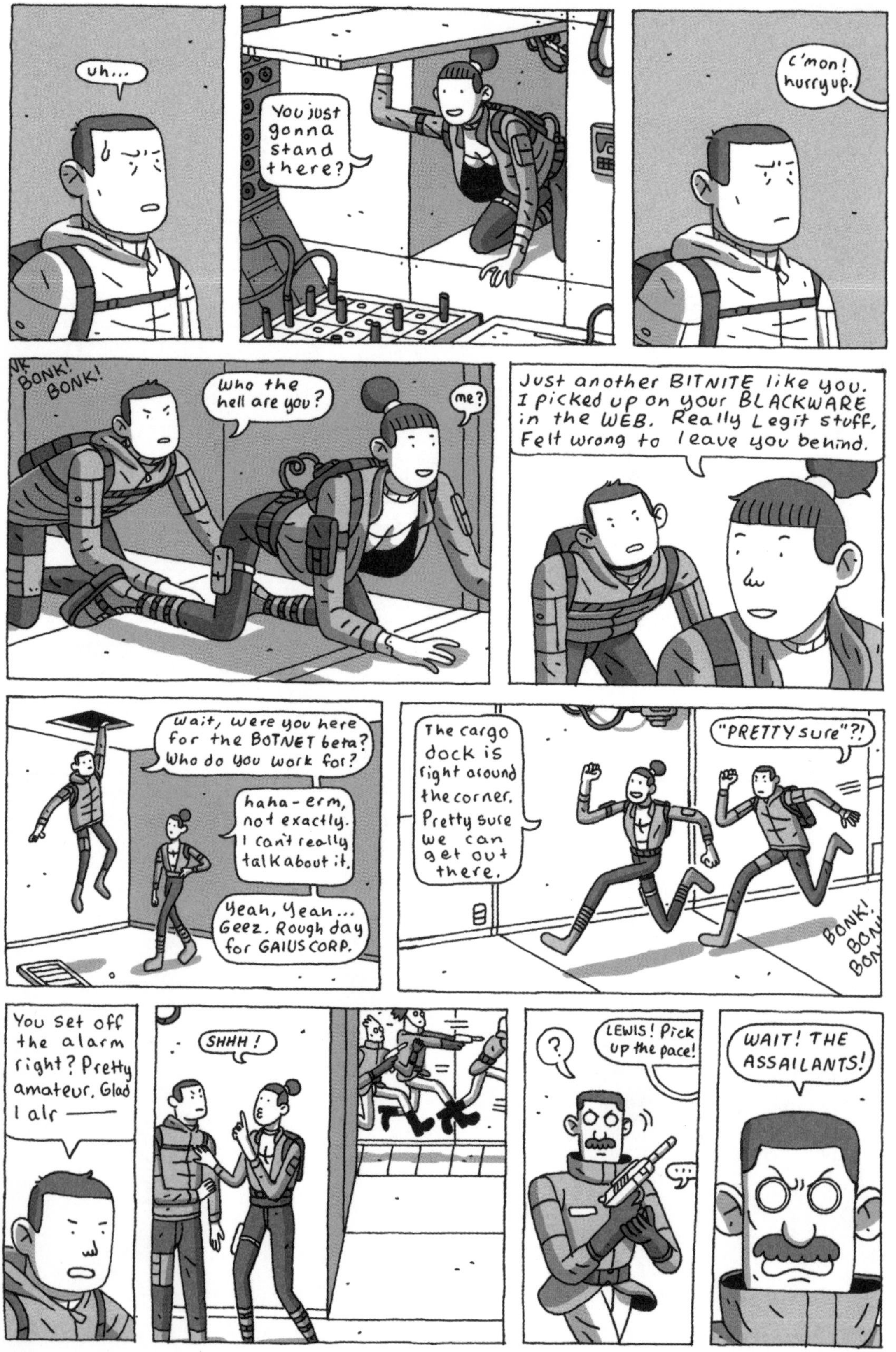
uh...
You just gonna stand there?
c'mon! hurryup.
BONK! BONK!
Who the hell are you?
me?
Just another BITNITE like you. I picked up on your BLACKWARE in the WEB. Really Legit stuff. Felt wrong to leave you behind.
wait, were you here for the BOTNET beta? Who do you work for?
haha-erm, not exactly. I can't really talk about it.
Yeah, Yeah... Geez. Rough day for GAIUS CORP.
The cargo dock is right around the corner. Pretty sure we can get out there.
"PRETTY sure"?!
BONK!
You set off the alarm right? Pretty amateur. Glad I alr —
SHHH!
?
LEWIS! Pick up the pace!
...
WAIT! THE ASSAILANTS!

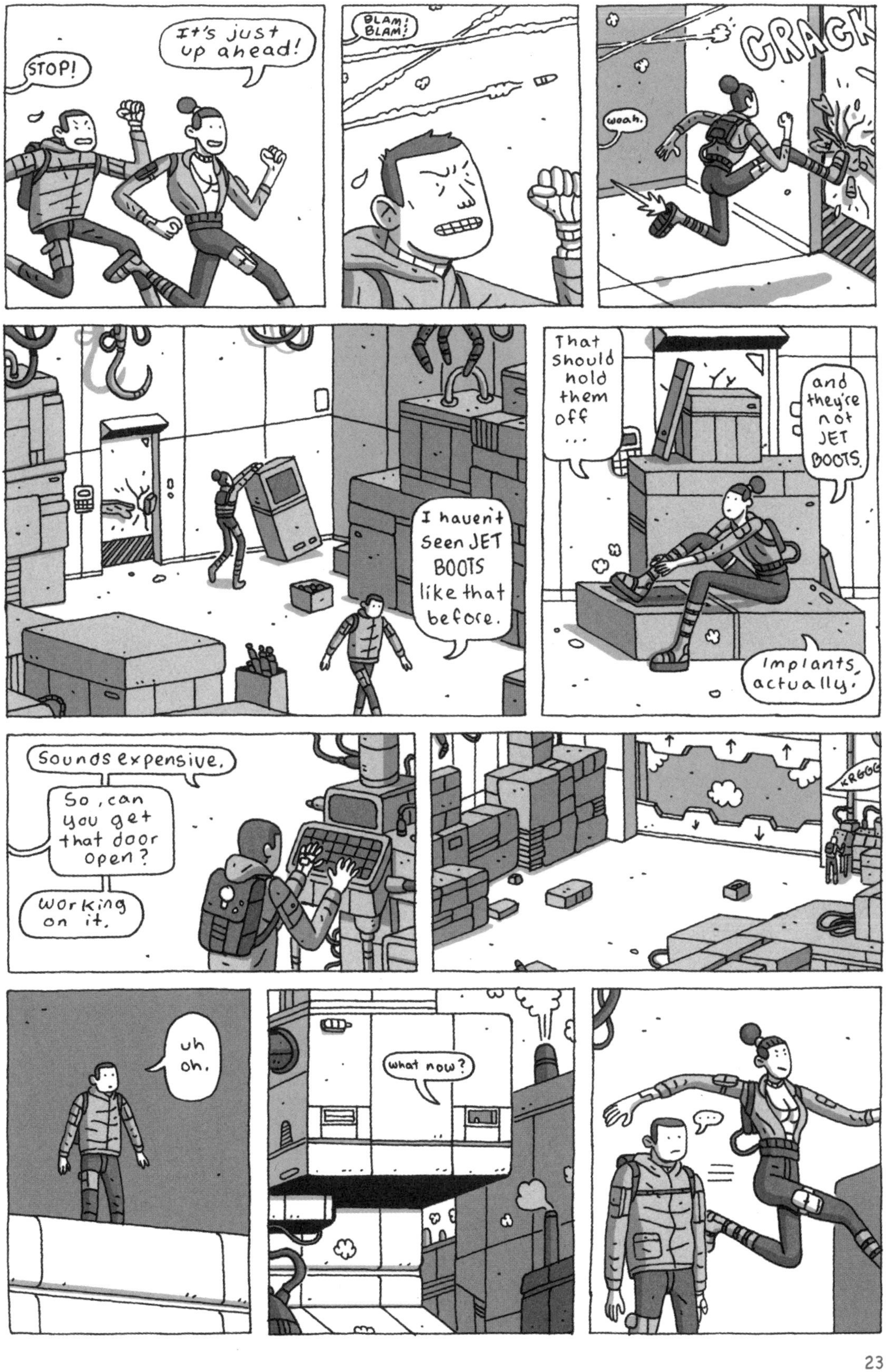
STOP!
It's just up ahead!
BLAM! BLAM!
woah.
CRACK
I haven't seen JET BOOTS like that before.
That should hold them off ...
and they're not JET BOOTS.
Implants, actually.
Sounds expensive.
So, can you get that door open?
Working on it.
KRGGG
uh oh.
what now?
...

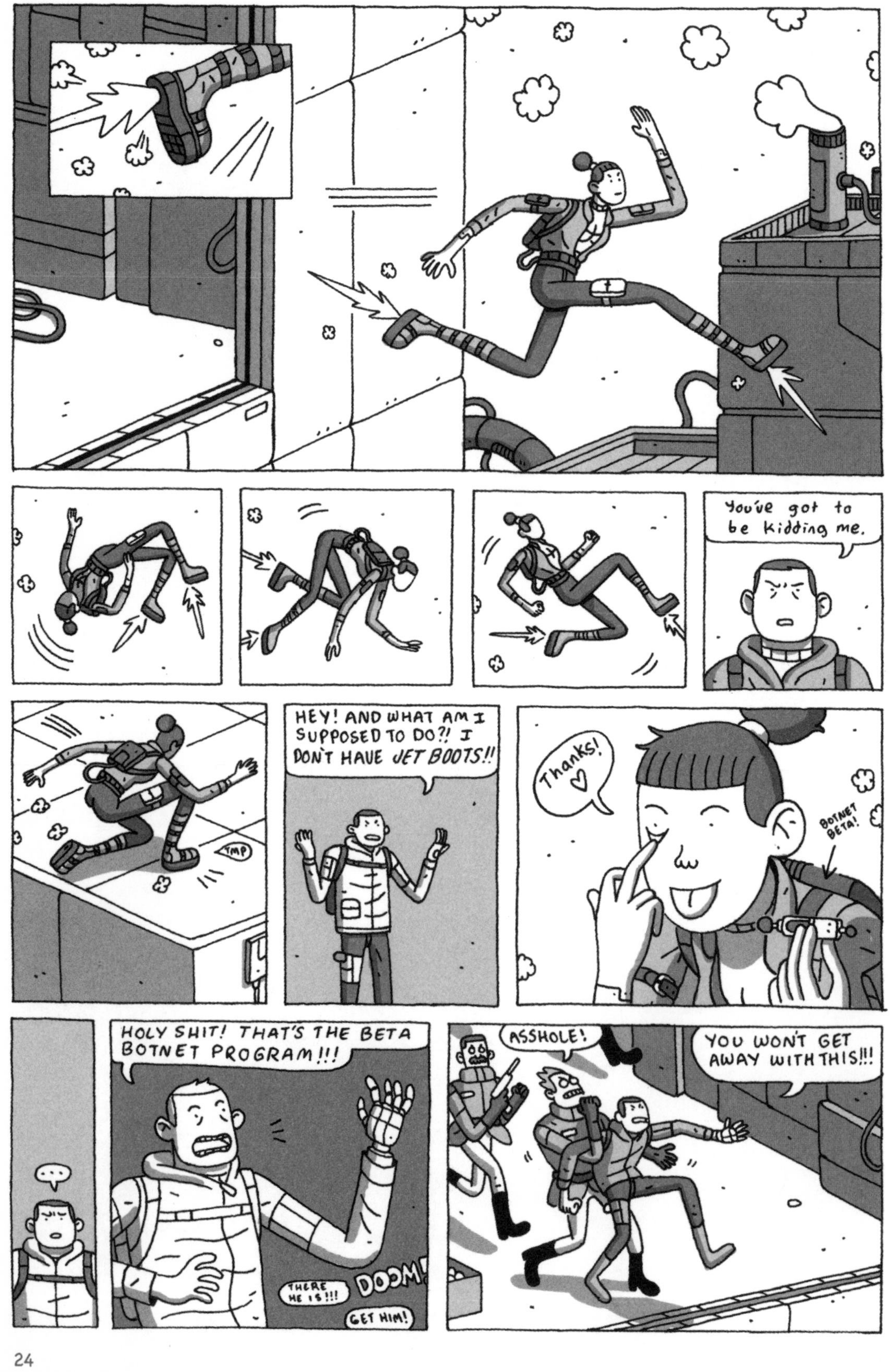
You've got to be kidding me.
HEY! AND WHAT AM I SUPPOSED TO DO?! I DON'T HAVE JET BOOTS!!
TMP
Thanks! ♡
BOTNET BETA!
...
HOLY SHIT! THAT'S THE BETA BOTNET PROGRAM!!!
THERE HE IS!!!
DOOM!
GET HIM!
ASSHOLE!
YOU WON'T GET AWAY WITH THIS!!!

A full cavity search was made. The BOTNET BETA could not be located.

unacceptable

UN-FUCKING-ACCEPTABLE You don't seem to understand the MONEY these ASSHOLES have cost us! FIND HIS ACCOMPLICE AND GET THE PROGRAM BACK! NOW!

Sir..

We've given him a neural relaxer. He claims to not have known the girl, but in an hour or 2, we'll go in and find out ourselves.

Hmph. JUST FIND IT!

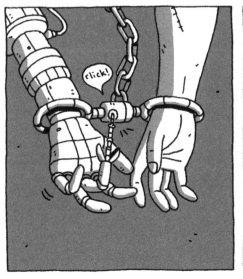

click!

That bitch...

25

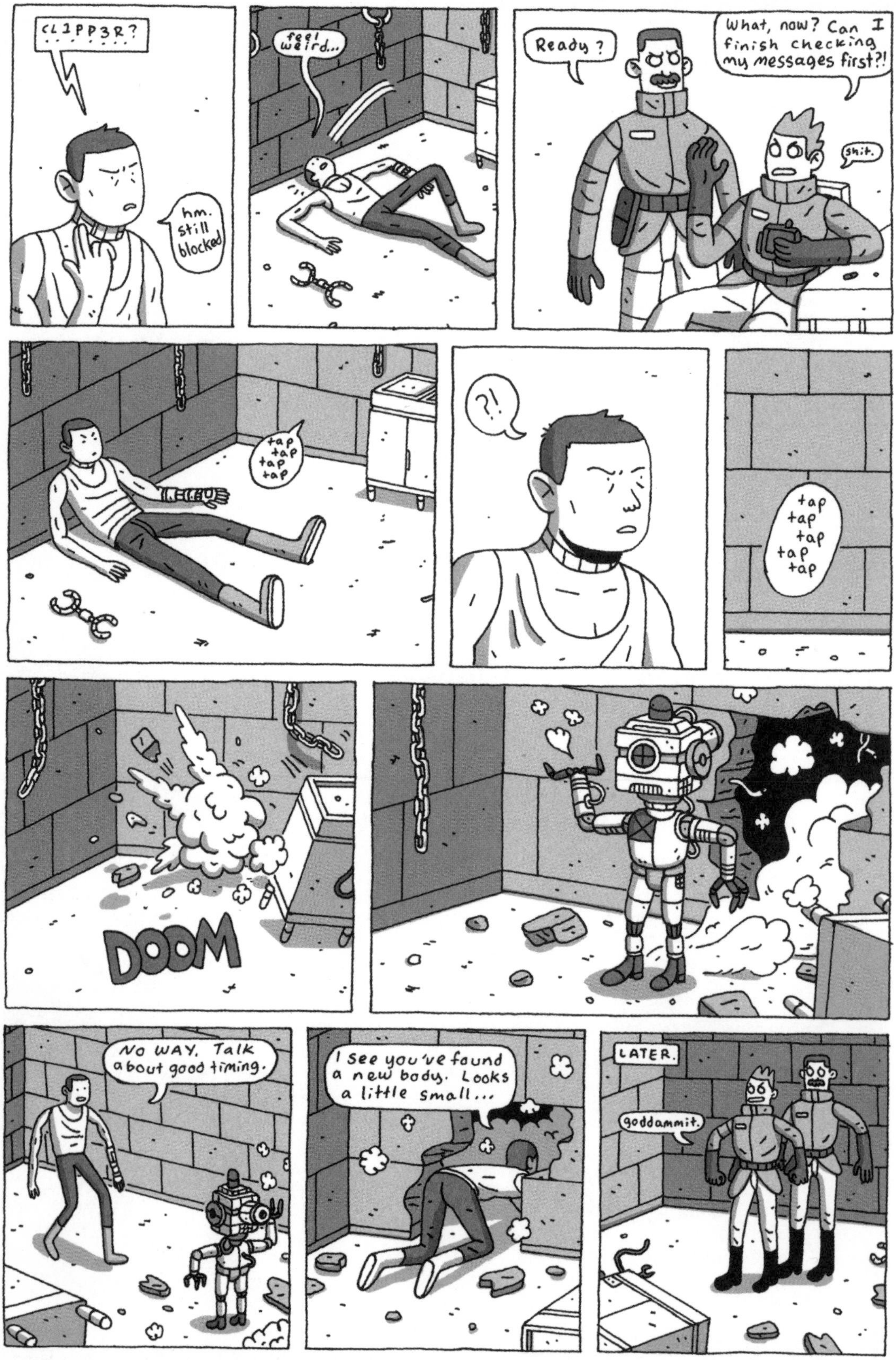
CL1PP3R?
hm. still blocked
feel weird...
Ready?
What, now? Can I finish checking my messages first?!
shit.
tap tap tap tap
?!
tap tap tap tap tap
DOOM
NO WAY. Talk about good timing.
I see you've found a new body. Looks a little small...
LATER.
goddammit.

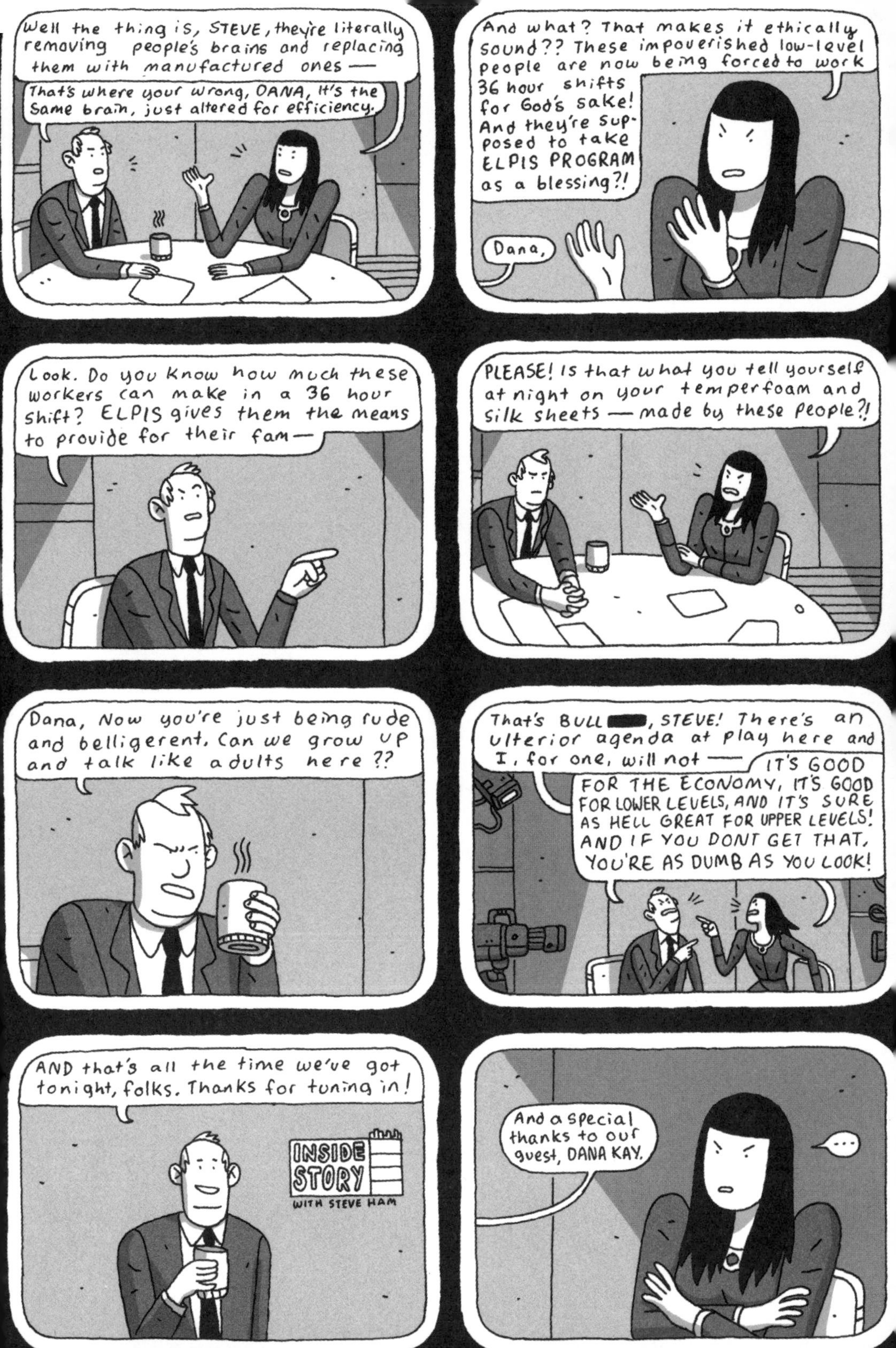
Well the thing is, STEVE, they're literally removing people's brains and replacing them with manufactured ones —
That's where your wrong, DANA, it's the Same brain, just altered for efficiency.
And what? That makes it ethically sound?? These impoverished low-level people are now being forced to work 36 hour shifts for God's sake! And they're supposed to take ELPIS PROGRAM as a blessing?!
Dana,
Look. Do you know how much these workers can make in a 36 hour shift? ELPIS gives them the means to provide for their fam—
PLEASE! Is that what you tell yourself at night on your temperfoam and silk sheets — made by these people?!
Dana, Now you're just being rude and belligerent. Can we grow up and talk like adults here??
That's BULL[redacted], STEVE! There's an ulterior agenda at play here and I, for one, will not —
IT'S GOOD FOR THE ECONOMY, IT'S GOOD FOR LOWER LEVELS, AND IT'S SURE AS HELL GREAT FOR UPPER LEVELS! AND IF YOU DONT GET THAT, YOU'RE AS DUMB AS YOU LOOK!
AND that's all the time we've got tonight, folks. Thanks for tuning in!
INSIDE STORY
WITH STEVE HAM
And a special thanks to our guest, DANA KAY.
...

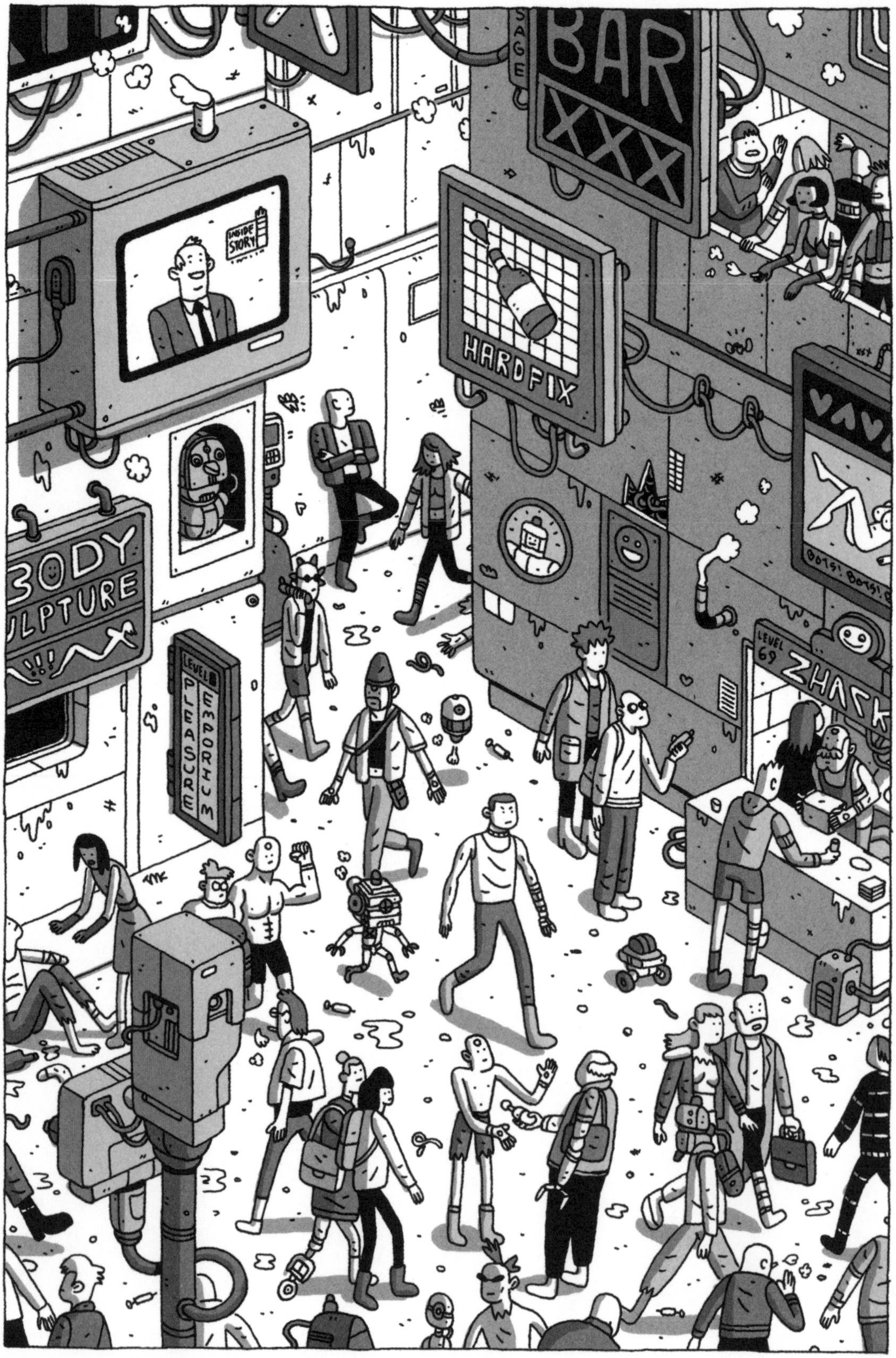
BAR
XXX
INSIDE STORY
HARDFIX
ULPTURE
LEVEL
PLEASURE
EMPORIUM
LEVEL 69

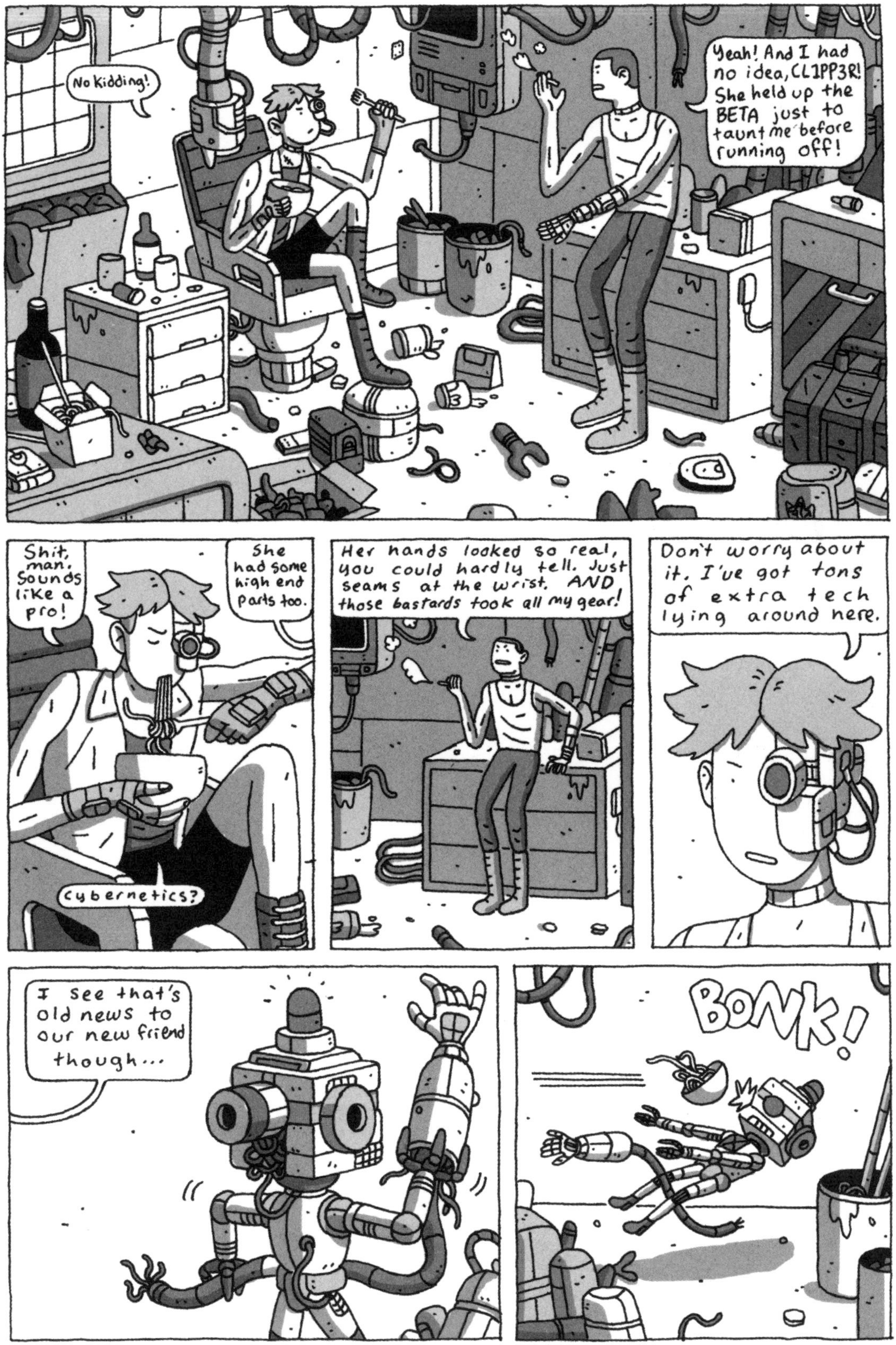
No Kidding!
Yeah! And I had no idea, CL1PP3R! She held up the BETA just to taunt me before running off!
Shit, man. Sounds like a pro!
Cybernetics?
She had some high end parts too.
Her hands looked so real, you could hardly tell. Just seams at the wrist. AND those bastards took all my gear!
Don't worry about it. I've got tons of extra tech lying around here.
I see that's old news to our new friend though...
BONK!

Aw C'mon! Give the little guy a break. He totally saved my ass!

Yeah? Well IT will have to do more than that 'cause we're definitely NOT getting that bit-credit from BRENTLEY BURDETTE.

I'm plugging in to see if there's any trace of the BOT-NET BETA...

This place is gross, I don't know why you still live here... You should move to the sublevels, It's total freedom down there.

Yeah, If you call running from extermination bots every time you leave your place "freedom,"

Now shut up. You're distracting me.

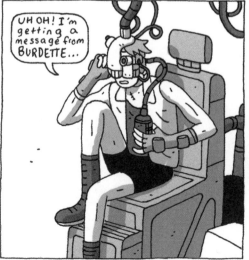

UH OH! I'm getting a message from BURDETTE...

He wants you to go to his place. He's expecting the BETA.

shit.

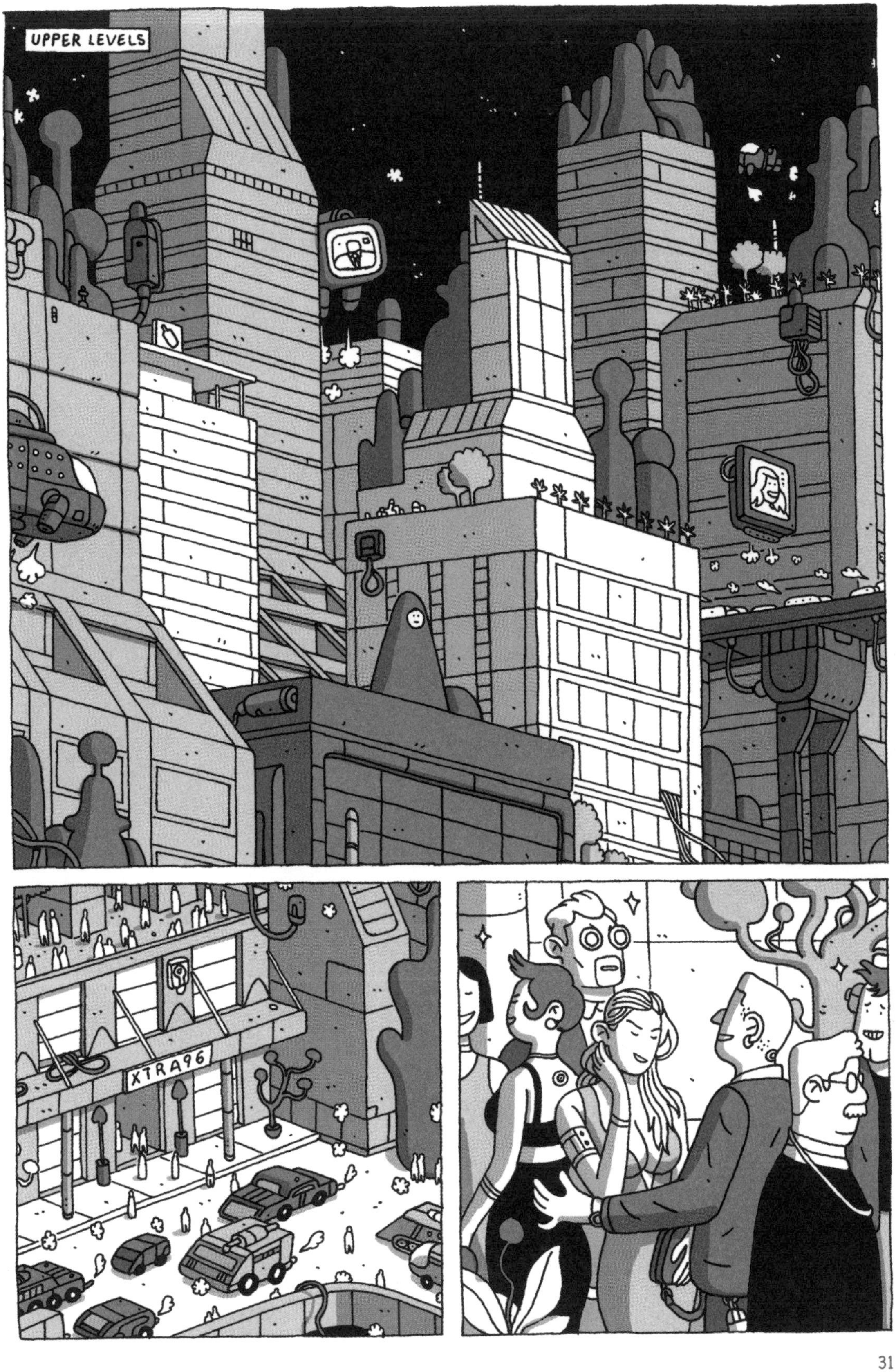
UPPER LEVELS
XTRA96

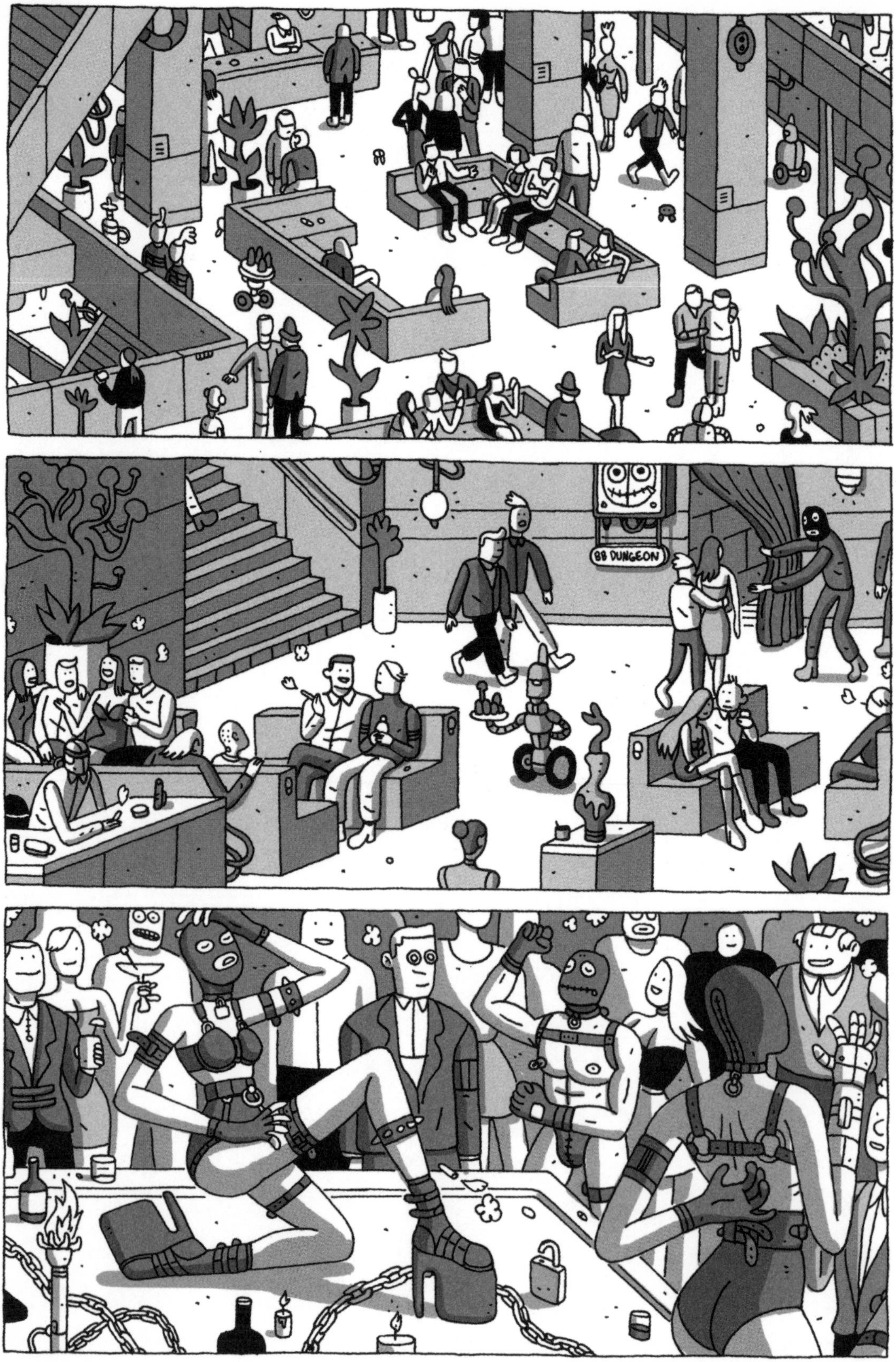
88 DUNGEON

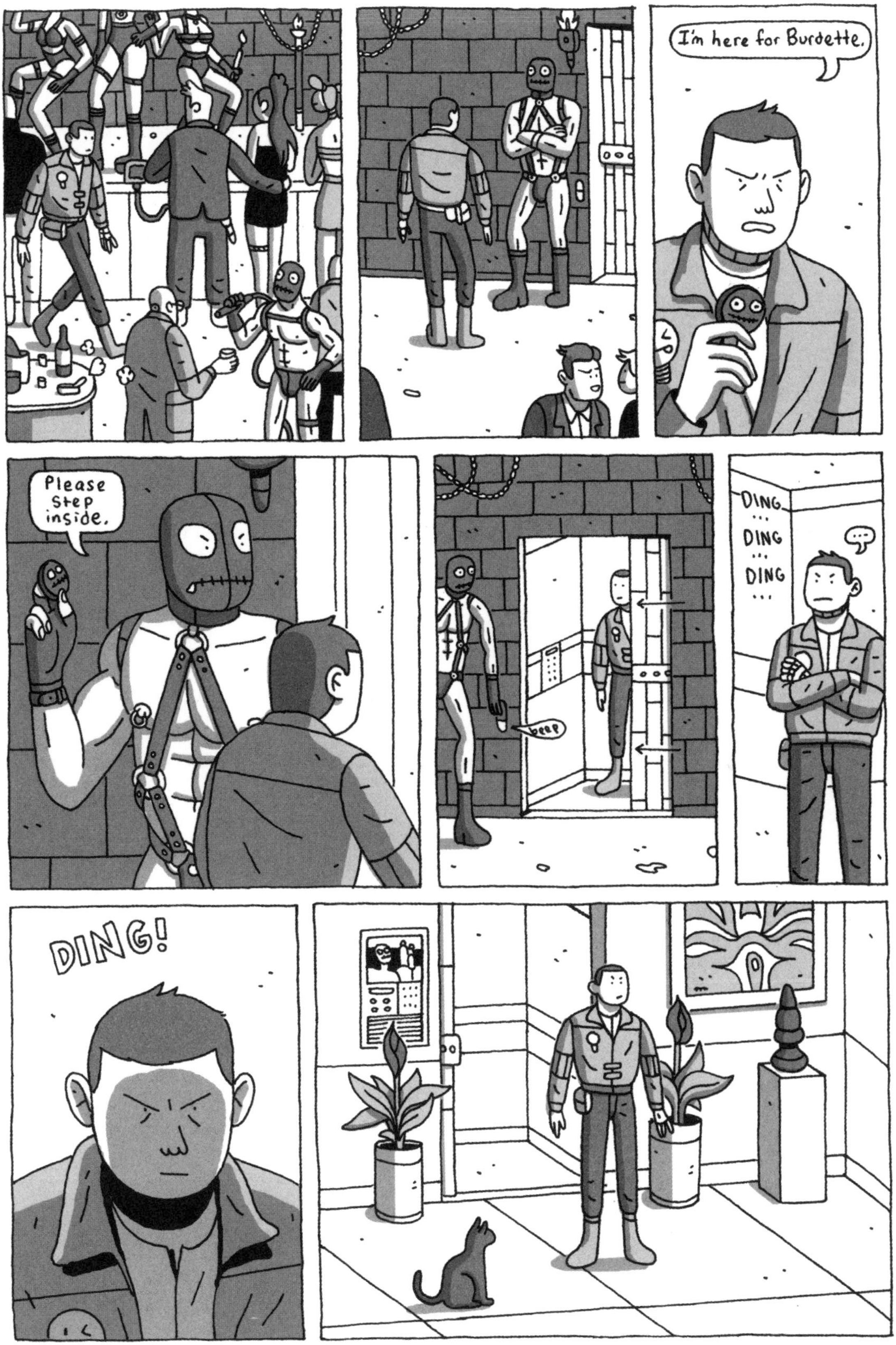
I'm here for Burdette.
Please step inside.
beep
DING... DING... DING...
...
DING!

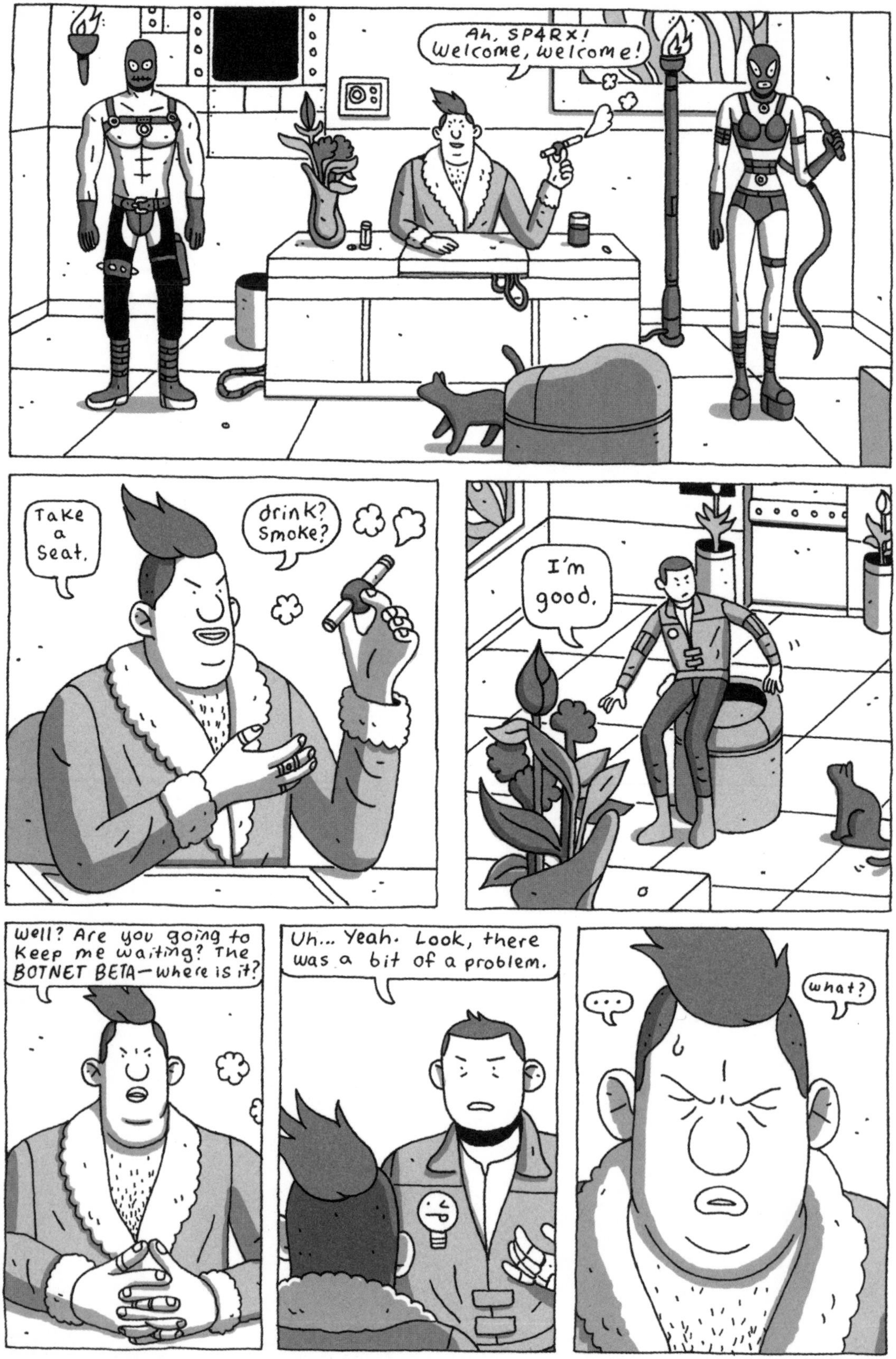

Ah, SP4RX! Welcome, welcome!
Take a seat.
drink? Smoke?
I'm good.
Well? Are you going to keep me waiting? The BOTNET BETA—where is it?
Uh... Yeah. Look, there was a bit of a problem.
...
what?

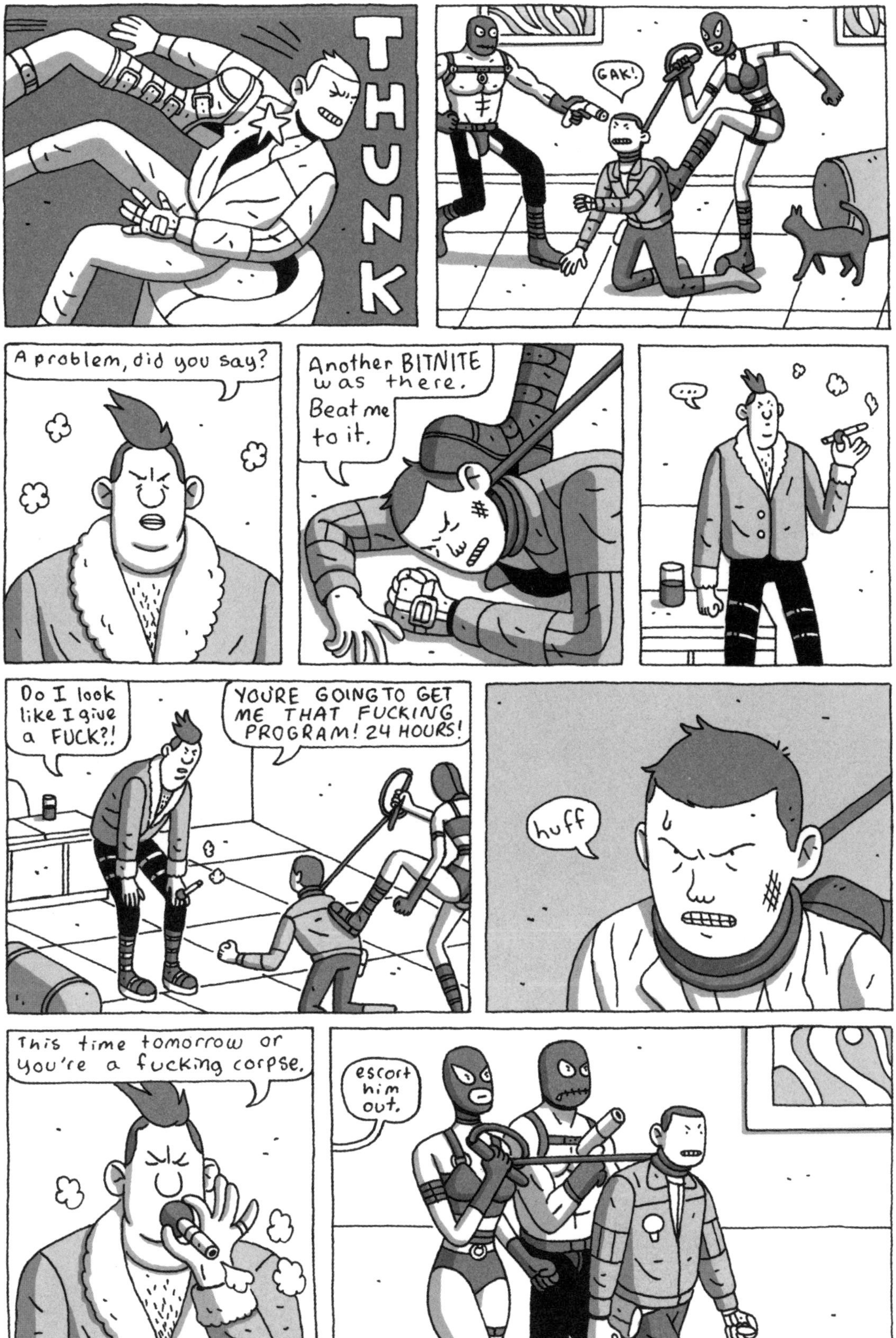
THUNK
GAK!
A problem, did you say?
Another BITNITE was there. Beat me to it.
...
Do I look like I give a FUCK?!
YOU'RE GOING TO GET ME THAT FUCKING PROGRAM! 24 HOURS!
huff
This time tomorrow or you're a fucking corpse.
escort him out.

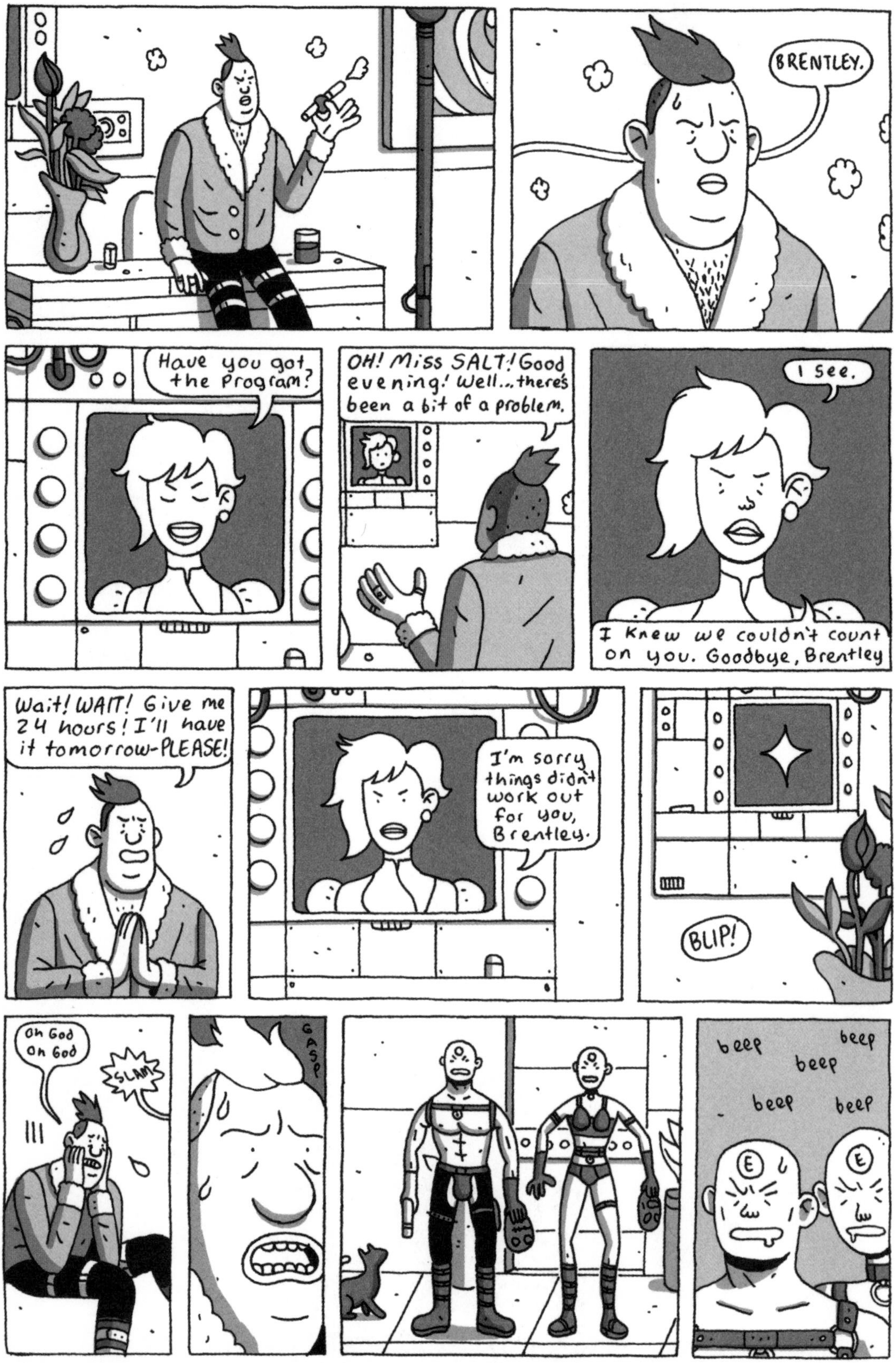
BRENTLEY.
Have you got the Program?
OH! Miss SALT! Good evening! Well... there's been a bit of a problem.
I see.
I knew we couldn't count on you. Goodbye, Brentley
Wait! WAIT! Give me 24 hours! I'll have it tomorrow-PLEASE!
I'm sorry things didn't work out for you, Brentley.
BLIP!
Oh God Oh God
SLAM
GASP
beep
beep
beep
beep
beep

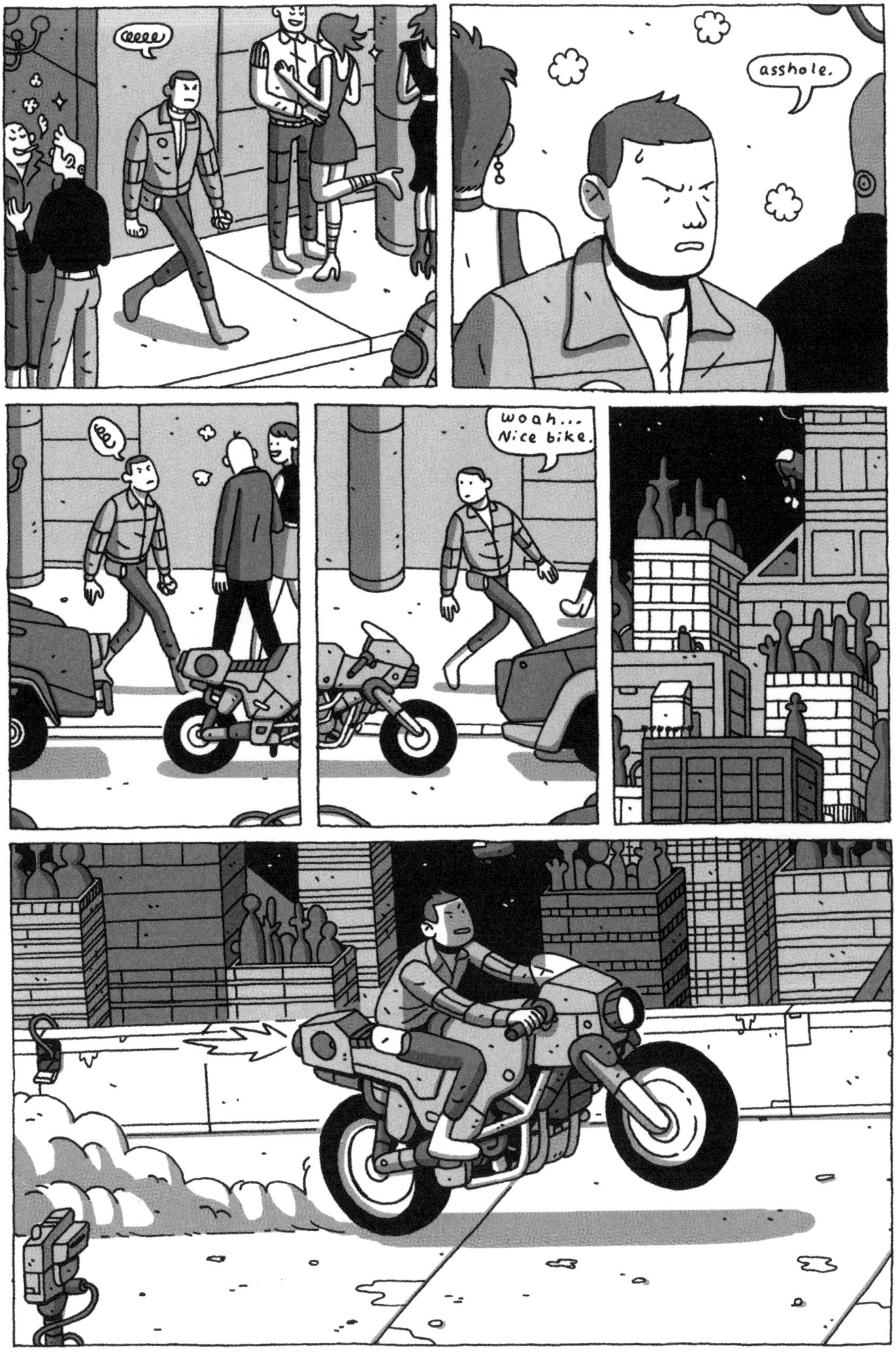
asshole.
woah...
Nice bike.

WEEKEND UPDATE
SPORTZ
WOW! A spectacular hit from rookie Ray Garreth! Unfortunately he's been suspended due to use of ELPIS cybernetics, which are still pending approval from the SBC.*
Now you may be asking, "What is a superstar like Garreth doing with cybernetics aimed at low level citizens?" Well, Garreth only recently became an upper level citizen when he was drafted earlier this season.
Upper Level
Lower Level
*Spike Ball Committee
Hopefully the SBC will resolve this issue quickly so that we can get this heavy hitter off the bench and back on the field, cracking skulls, where he belongs!
YAHHH

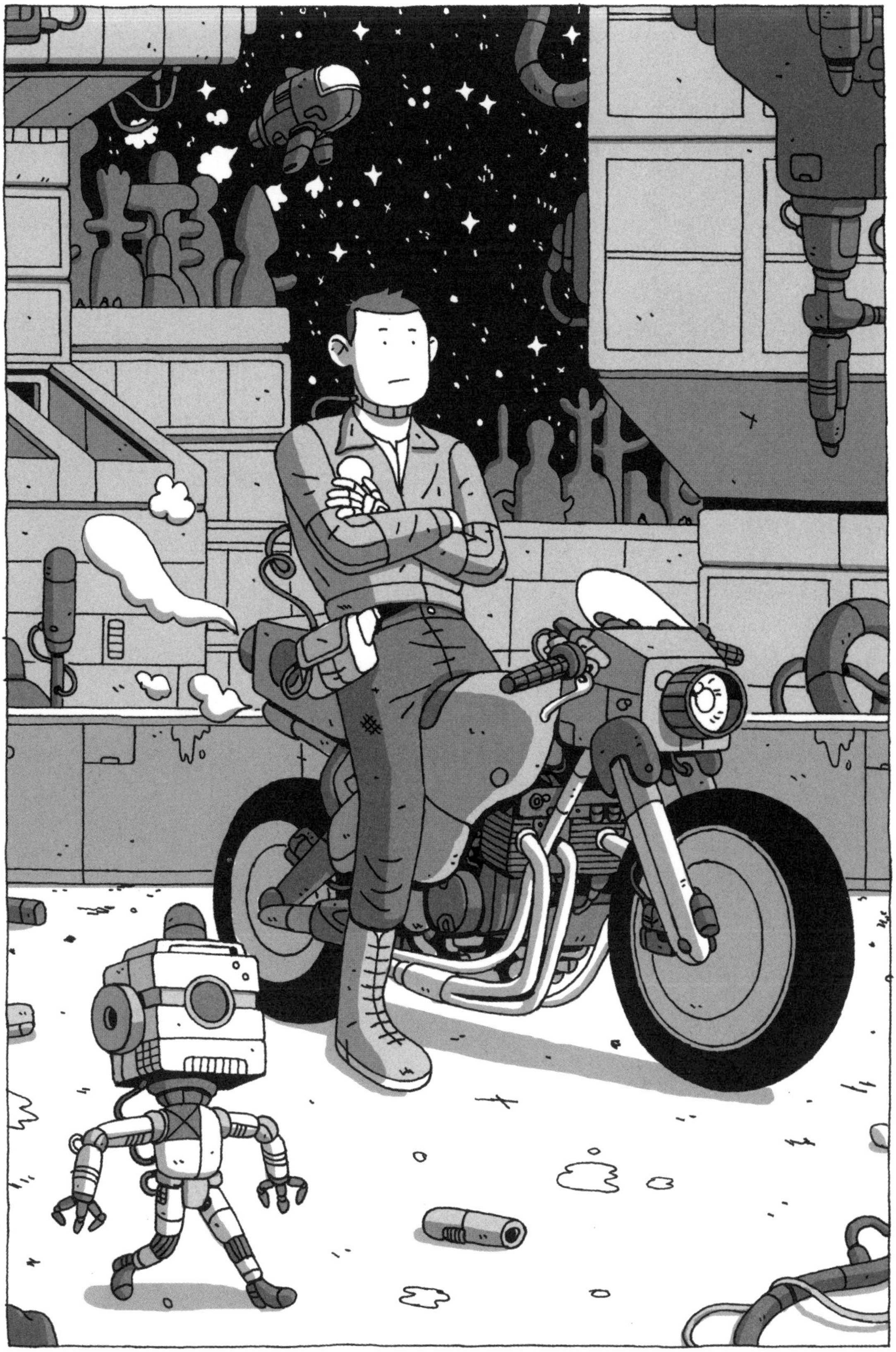

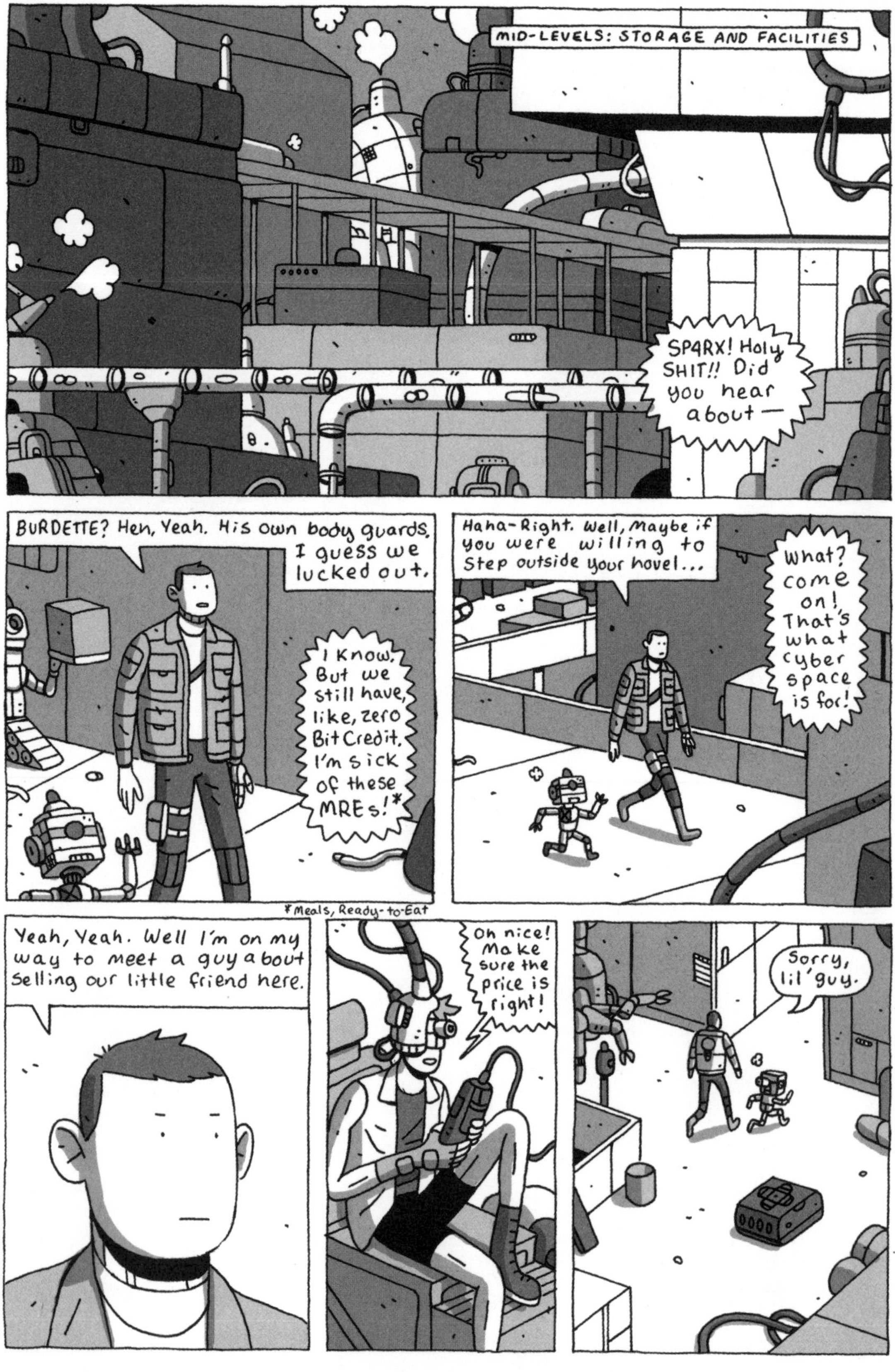
MID-LEVELS: STORAGE AND FACILITIES
SP4RX! Holy SHIT!! Did you hear about—
BURDETTE? Heh, Yeah. His own body guards. I guess we lucked out.
I know. But we still have, like, zero BitCredit. I'm sick of these MREs!*
Haha-Right. Well, maybe if you were willing to step outside your hovel...
What? come on! That's what cyber space is for!
*Meals, Ready-to-Eat
Yeah, Yeah. Well I'm on my way to meet a guy about selling our little friend here.
Oh nice! Make sure the price is right!
Sorry, lil' guy.

So how much do you think we can get??

I'm not sure.

I've heard about one going for 40K, but that was before the crash... DO YOU THINK WE COULD GET 40K?!!

We could relocate to COSMOCOLONY 6 with that kind of credit! Leave this shithole behind!!!

Haha. Don't get your hopes up. Besides, there's something not quite right about living in space.

Yeah? Well there's "Something not quite right" about living in fucking Avalon.

well...

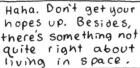

That's true, but—

WAIT! DAMMIT! Where's the OBD-0.3!

WHAT?! SP4RX?

P4RX?! id you u find the SP4R

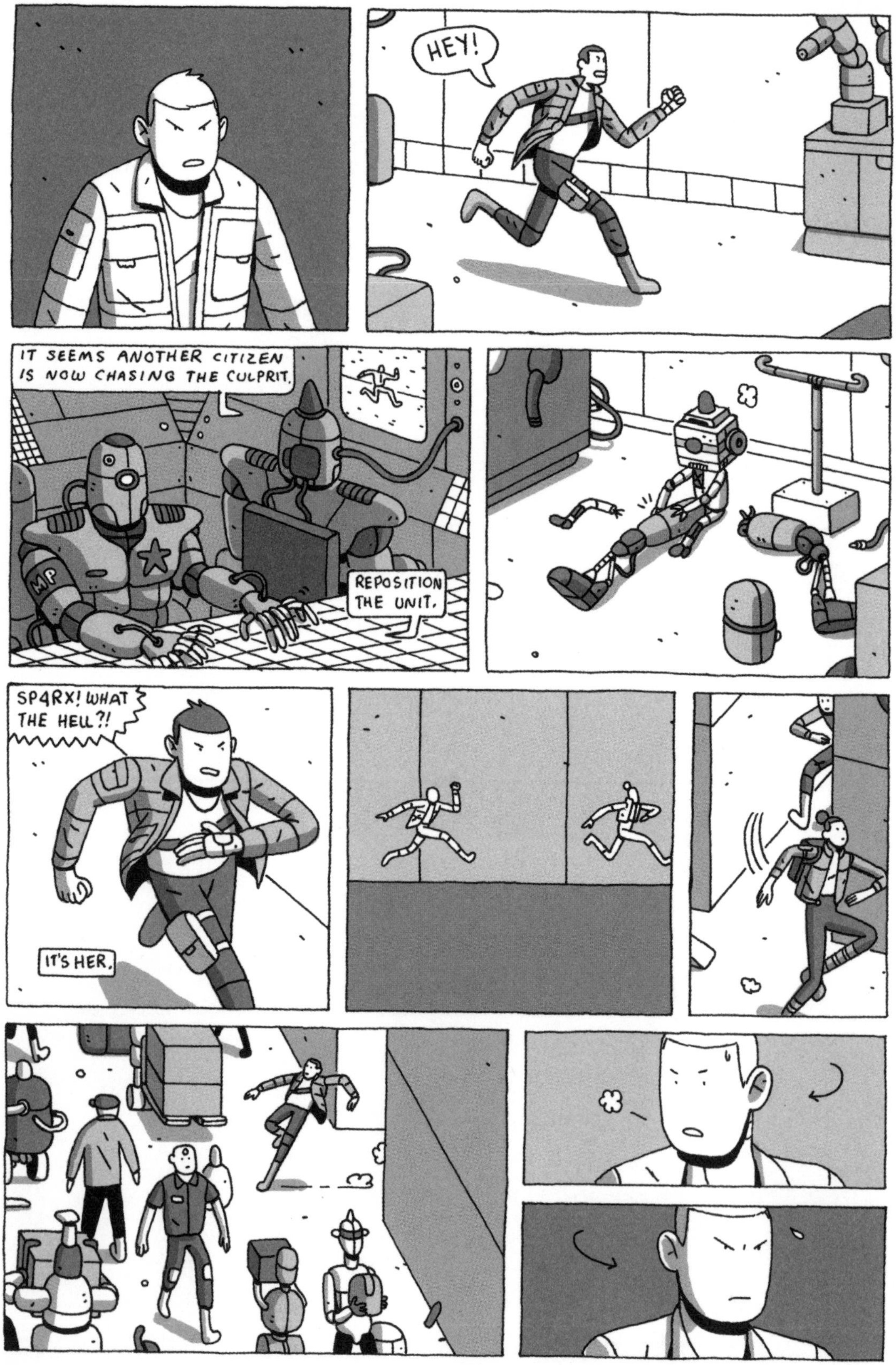
HEY!
IT SEEMS ANOTHER CITIZEN IS NOW CHASING THE CULPRIT.
REPOSITION THE UNIT.
SP4RX! WHAT THE HELL?!
IT'S HER.

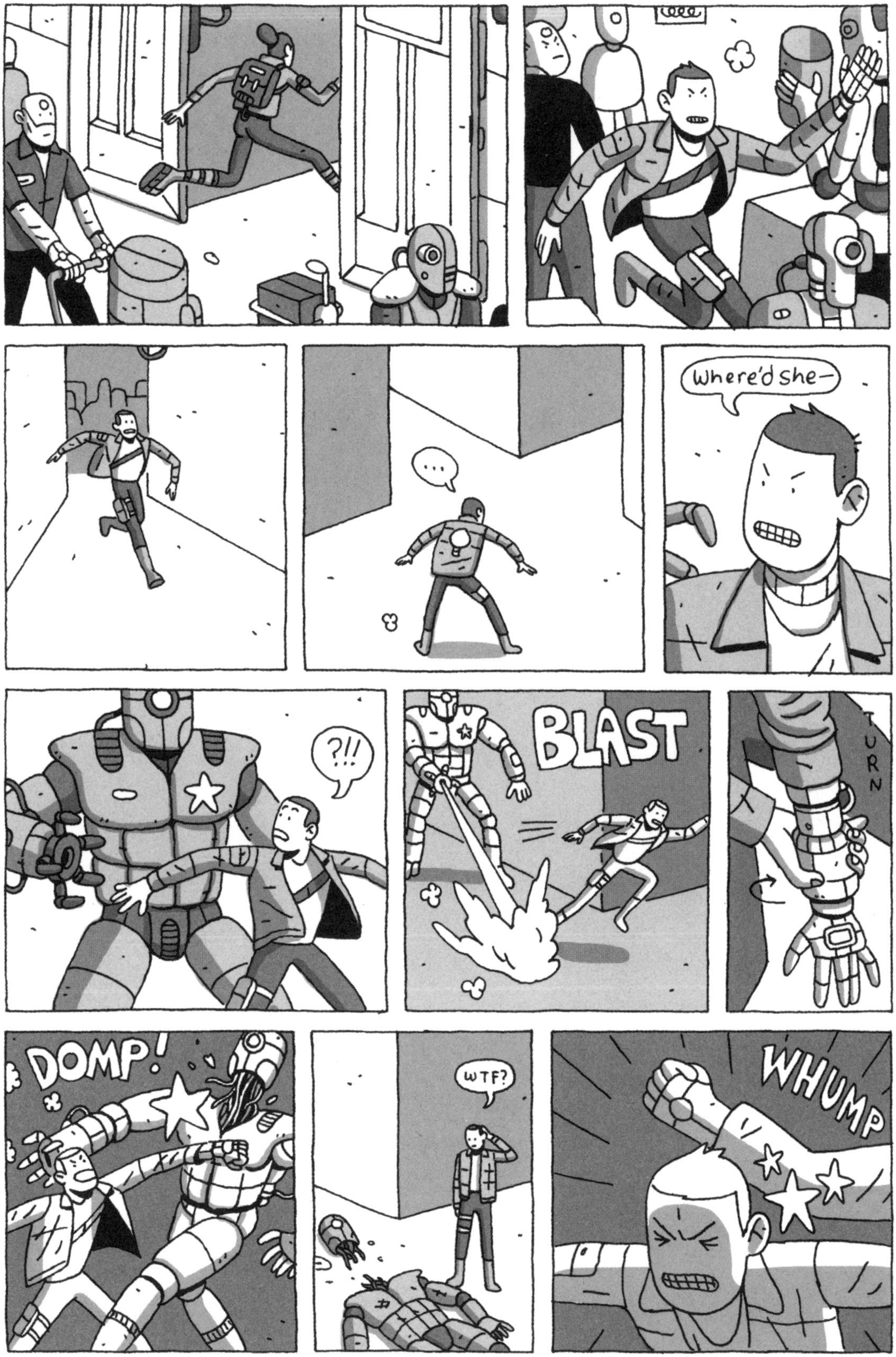

Where'd she-
...
?!!
BLAST
TURN
DOMP!
WTF?
WHUMP

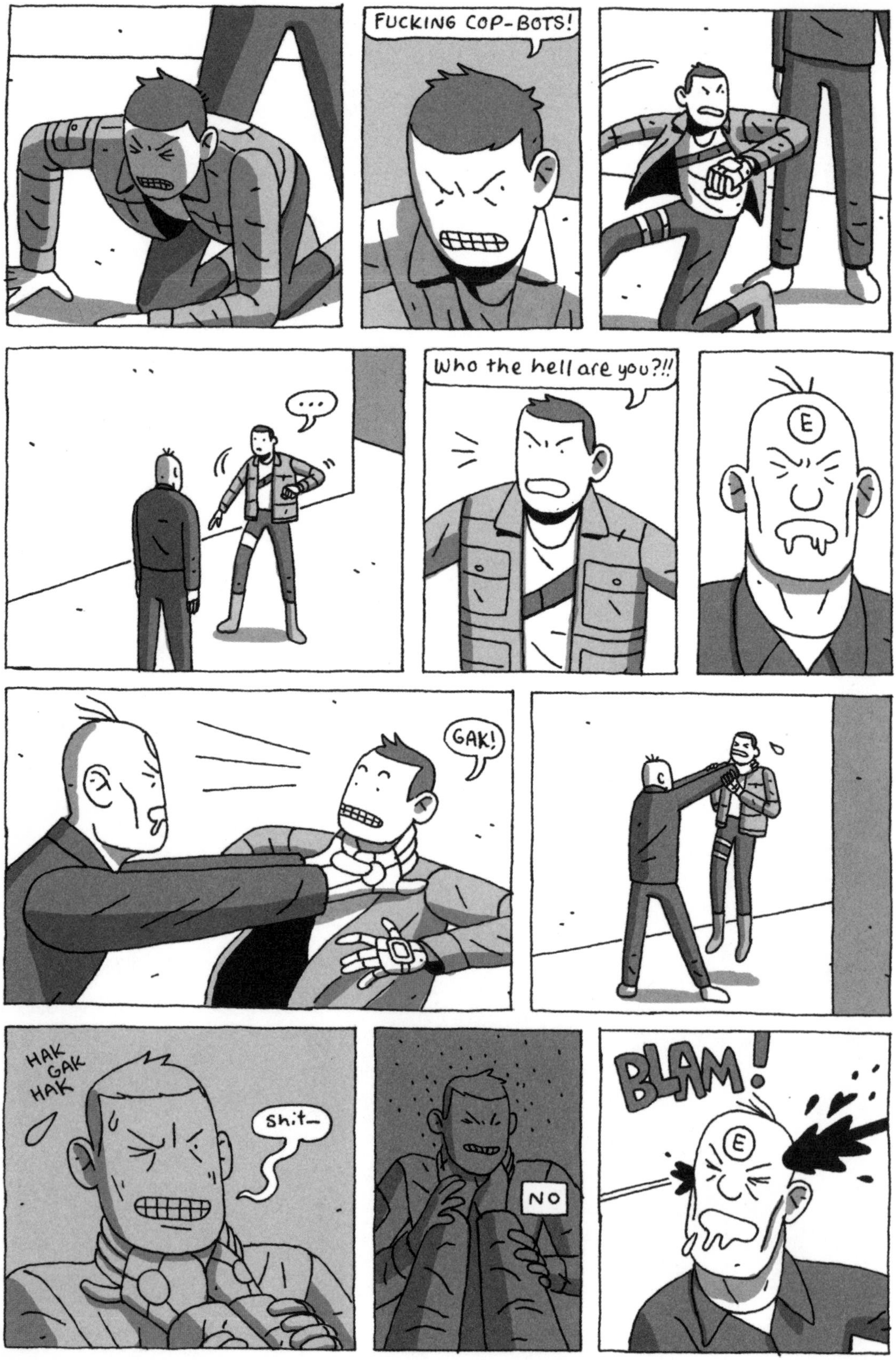
FUCKING COP-BOTS!
...
Who the hell are you?!!
E
GAK!
HAK
GAK
HAK
shit_
NO
BLAM!
E

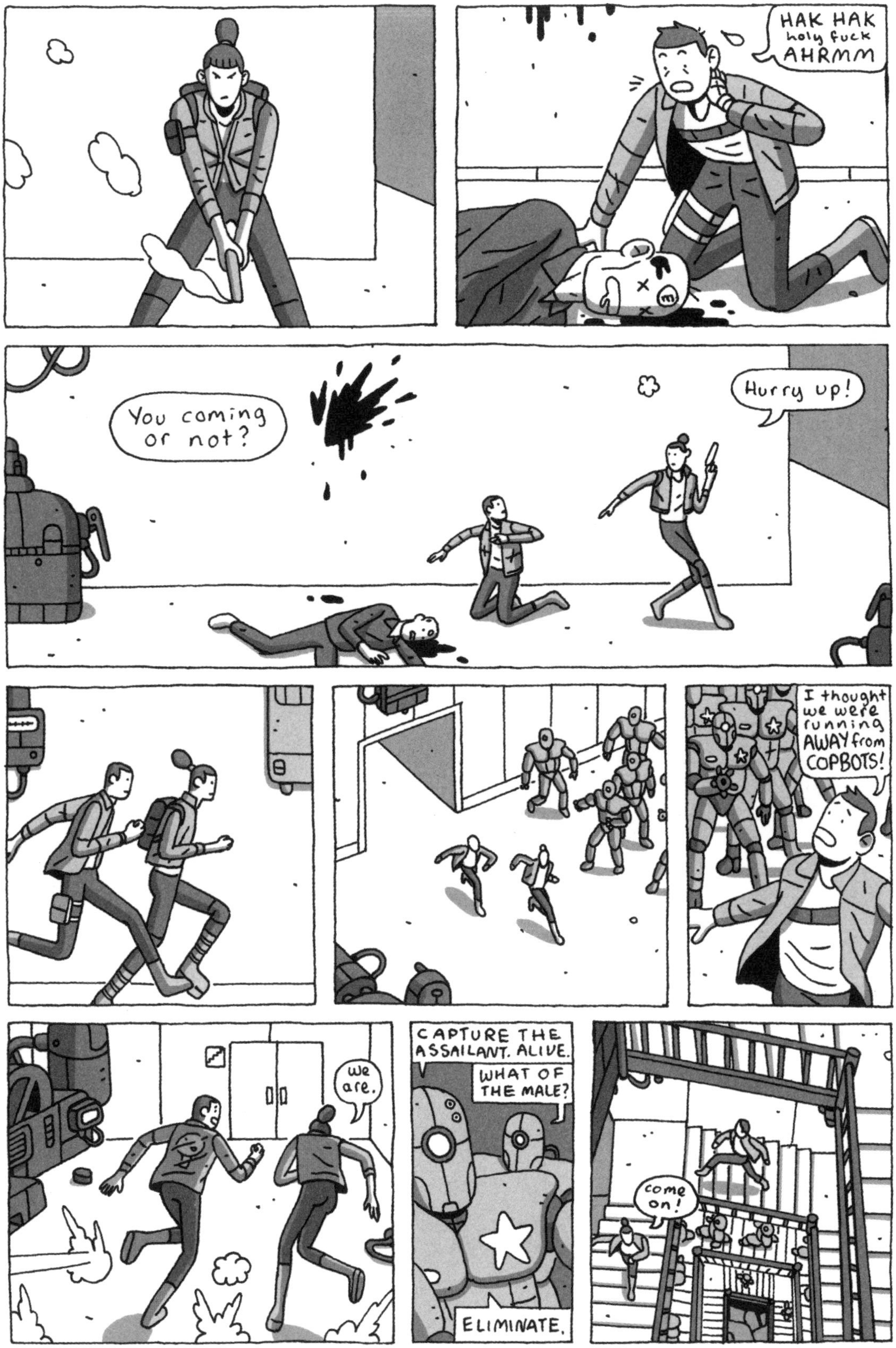
HAK HAK
holy fuck
AHRMM
You coming or not?
Hurry up!
I thought we were running AWAY from COPBOTS!
We are.
CAPTURE THE ASSAILANT. ALIVE.
WHAT OF THE MALE?
ELIMINATE.
come on!

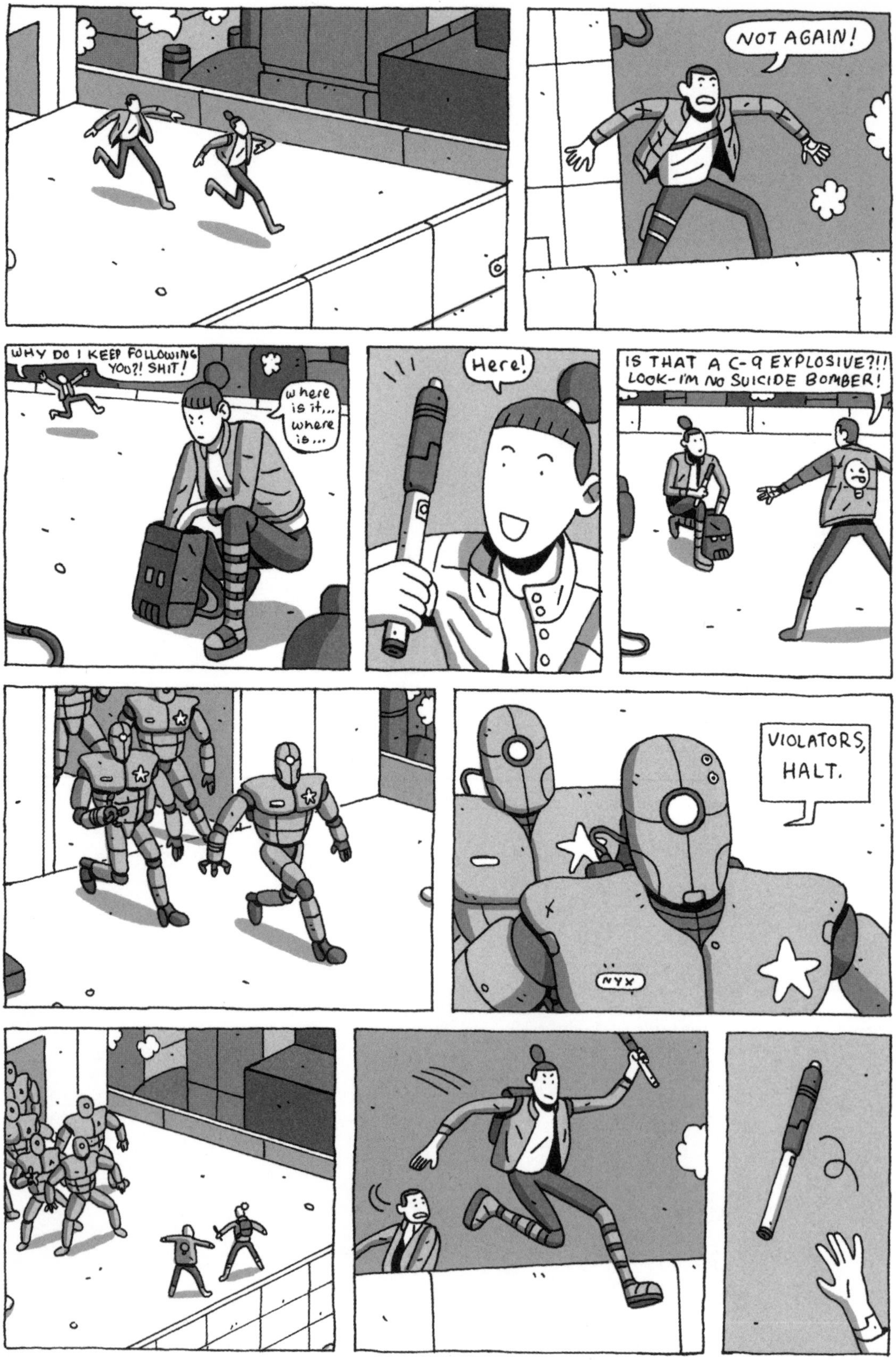
NOT AGAIN!
WHY DO I KEEP FOLLOWING YOU?! SHIT!
where is it,.. where is...
Here!
IS THAT A C-9 EXPLOSIVE?!! LOOK-I'M NO SUICIDE BOMBER!
VIOLATORS, HALT.
NYX

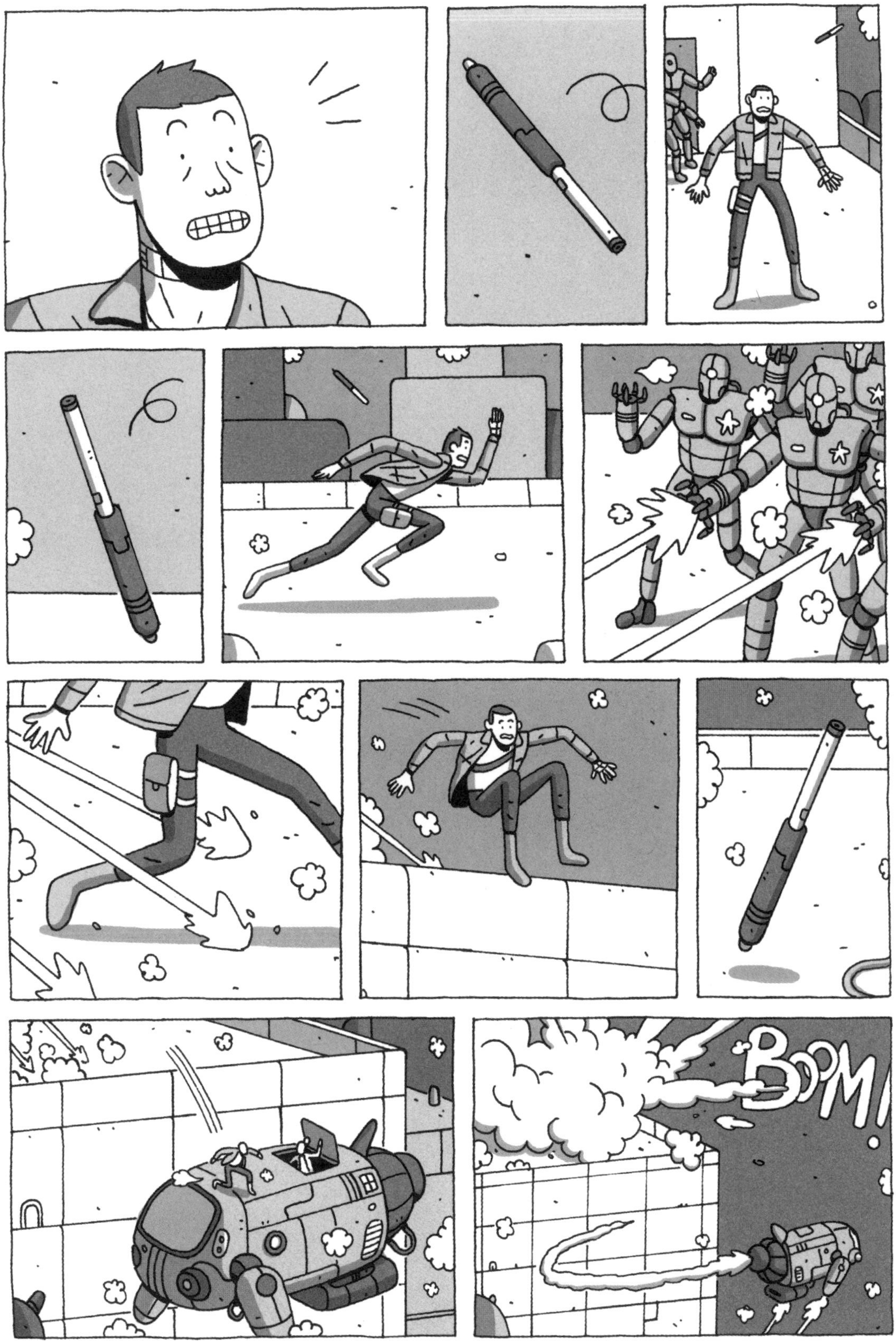
BOOM

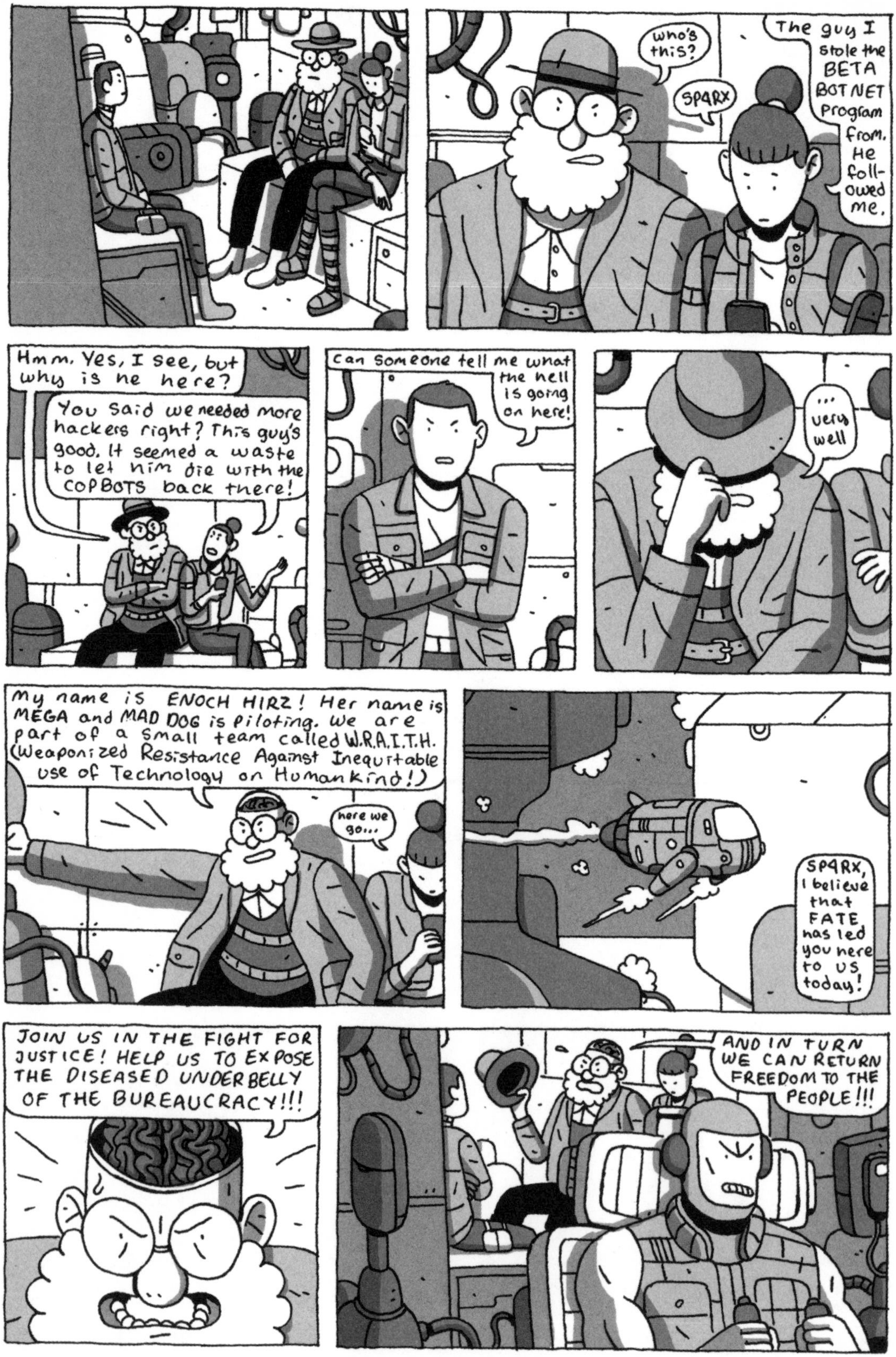
who's this?
SP4RX
The guy I stole the BETA BOTNET Program from. He followed me.
Hmm. Yes, I see, but why is he here?
You said we needed more hackers right? This guy's good. It seemed a waste to let him die with the COPBOTS back there!
Can someone tell me what the hell is going on here!
... very well
My name is ENOCH HIRZ! Her name is MEGA and MAD DOG is piloting. We are part of a small team called W.R.A.I.T.H. (Weaponized Resistance Against Inequitable use of Technology on Humankind!)
here we go...
SP4RX, I believe that FATE has led you here to us today!
JOIN US IN THE FIGHT FOR JUSTICE! HELP US TO EXPOSE THE DISEASED UNDERBELLY OF THE BUREAUCRACY!!!
AND IN TURN WE CAN RETURN FREEDOM TO THE PEOPLE!!!

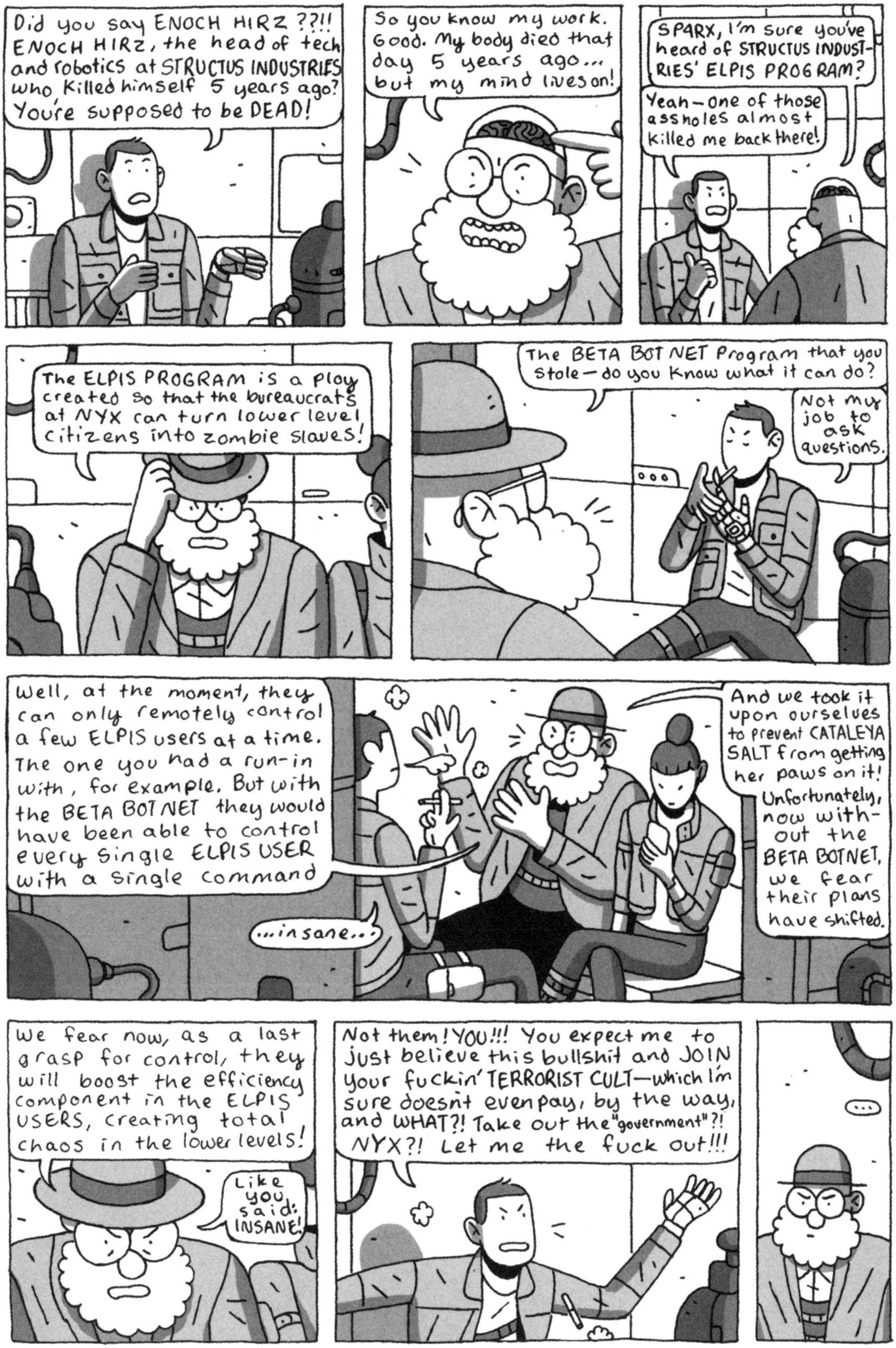
Did you say ENOCH HIRZ ??!! ENOCH HIRZ, the head of tech and robotics at STRUCTUS INDUSTRIES who Killed himself 5 years ago? You're supposed to be DEAD!
So you know my work. Good. My body died that day 5 years ago... but my mind lives on!
SPARX, I'm sure you've heard of STRUCTUS INDUSTRIES' ELPIS PROGRAM?
Yeah—one of those assholes almost killed me back there!
The ELPIS PROGRAM is a ploy created so that the bureaucrats at NYX can turn lower level citizens into zombie slaves!
The BETA BOT NET Program that you stole—do you know what it can do?
Not my job to ask questions.
Well, at the moment, they can only remotely control a few ELPIS users at a time. The one you had a run-in with, for example. But with the BETA BOTNET they would have been able to control every single ELPIS USER with a single command
...insane...
And we took it upon ourselves to prevent CATALEYA SALT from getting her paws on it! Unfortunately, now without the BETA BOTNET, we fear their plans have shifted.
We fear now, as a last grasp for control, they will boost the efficiency component in the ELPIS USERS, creating total chaos in the lower levels!
Like you said: INSANE!
Not them! YOU!!! You expect me to just believe this bullshit and JOIN your fuckin' TERRORIST CULT—which I'm sure doesn't even pay, by the way, and WHAT?! Take out the "government"?! NYX?! Let me the fuck out!!!
...

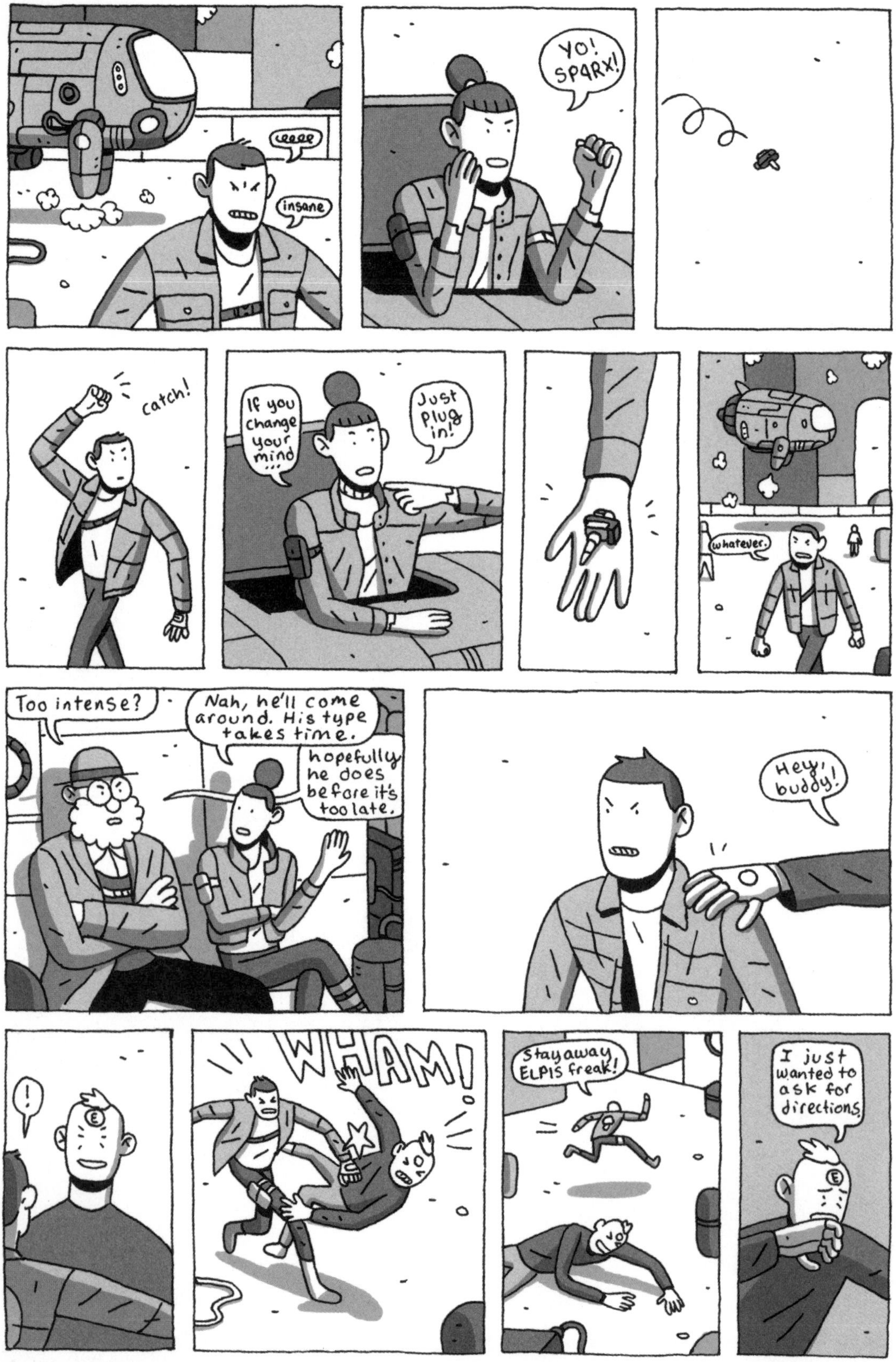
eeeee
insane
YO! SP4RX!
catch!
If you change your mind ...
Just plug in!
whatever.
Too intense?
Nah, he'll come around. His type takes time.
hopefully he does before it's too late.
Hey, buddy!
!
WHAM!
Stay away ELPIS freak!
I just wanted to ask for directions.

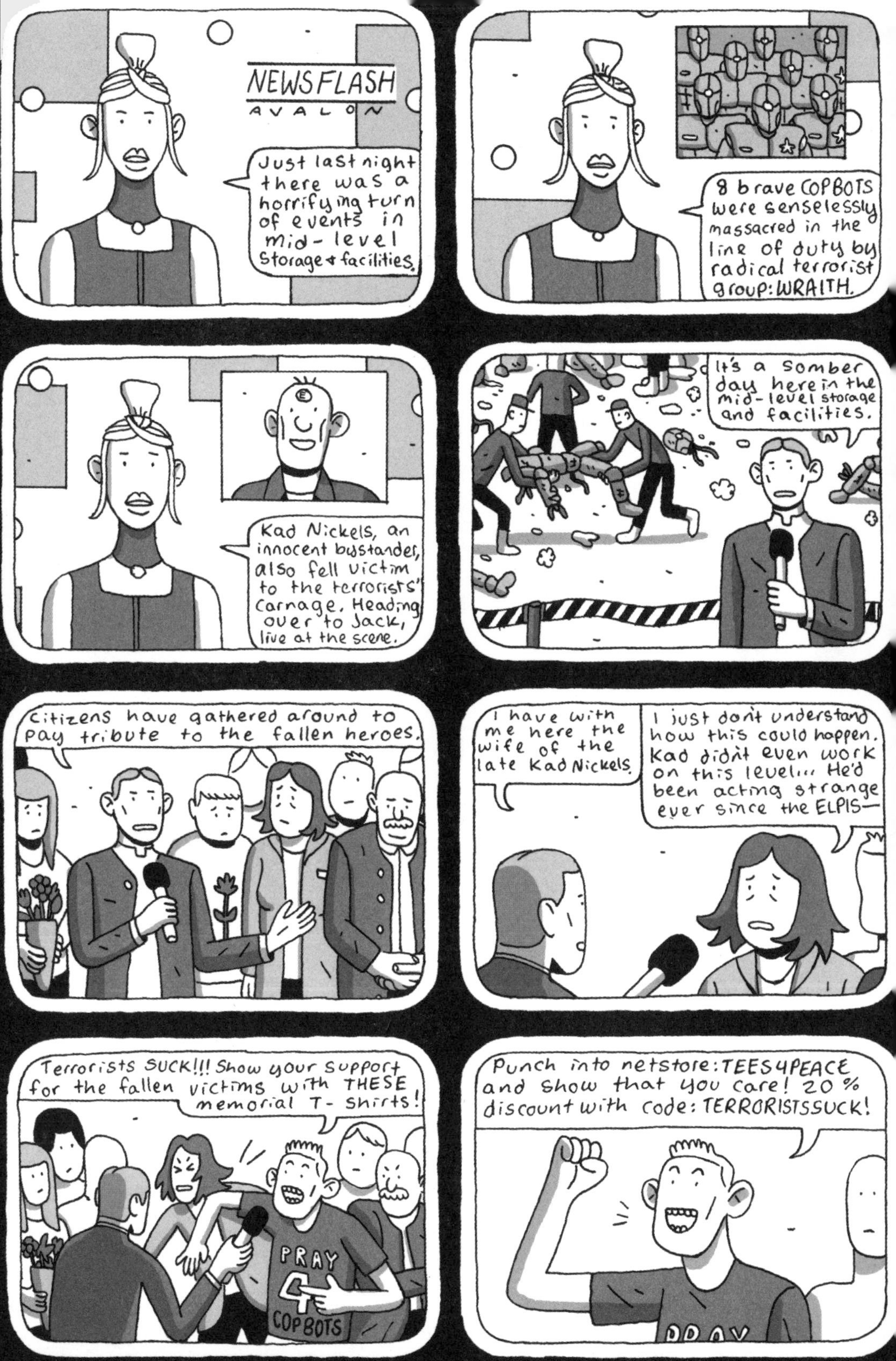
NEWSFLASH
AVALON
Just last night there was a horrifying turn of events in mid-level storage & facilities.
8 brave COPBOTS were senselessly massacred in the line of duty by radical terrorist group: WRAITH.
Kad Nickels, an innocent bystander, also fell victim to the terrorists' carnage. Heading over to Jack, live at the scene.
It's a somber day here in the mid-level storage and facilities.
Citizens have gathered around to pay tribute to the fallen heroes.
I have with me here the wife of the late Kad Nickels.
I just don't understand how this could happen. Kad didn't even work on this level... He'd been acting strange ever since the ELPIS—
Terrorists SUCK!!! Show your support for the fallen victims with THESE memorial T-shirts!
PRAY 4 COPBOTS
Punch into netstore: TEES4PEACE and show that you care! 20% discount with code: TERRORISTSSUCK!

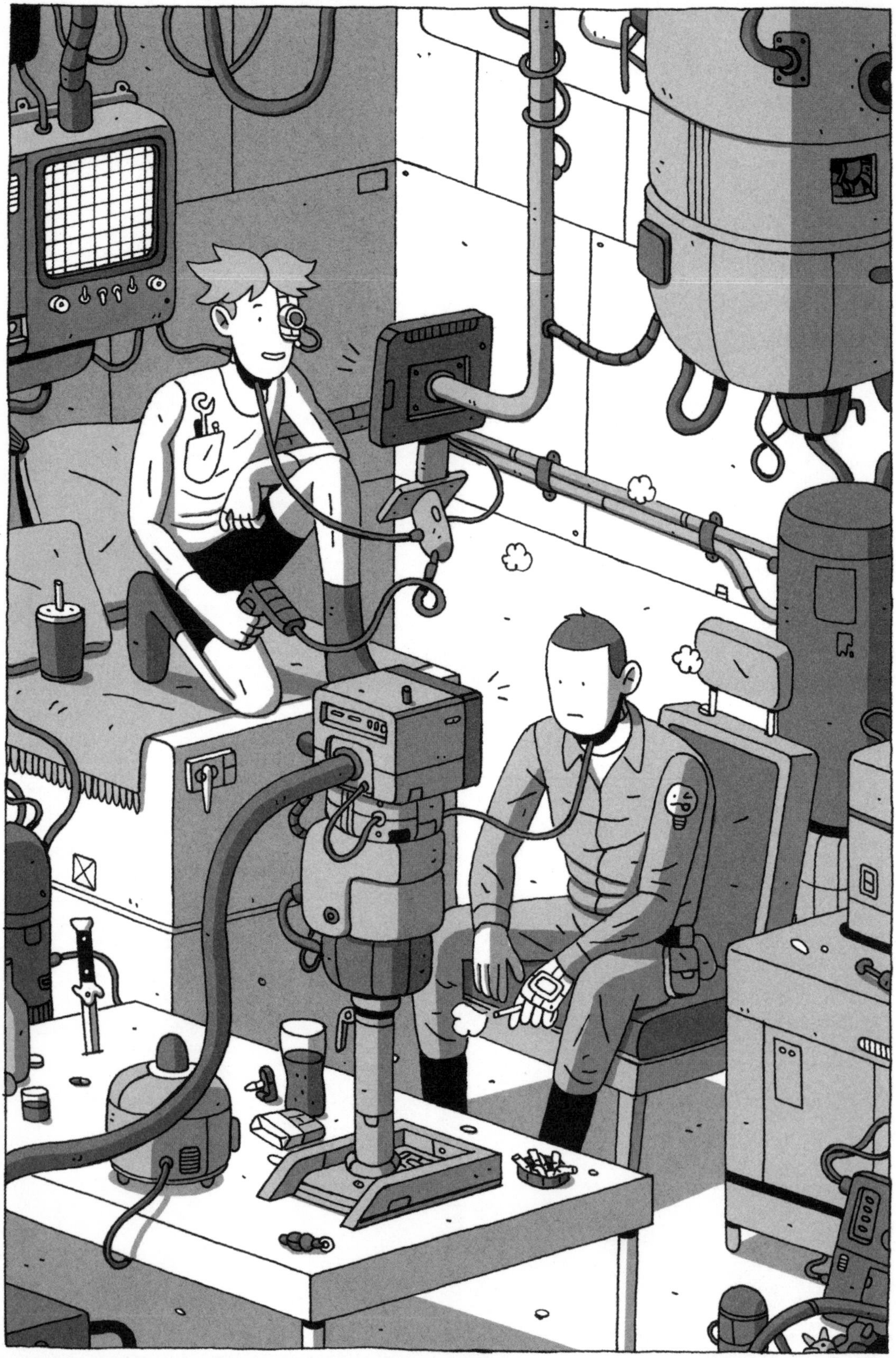

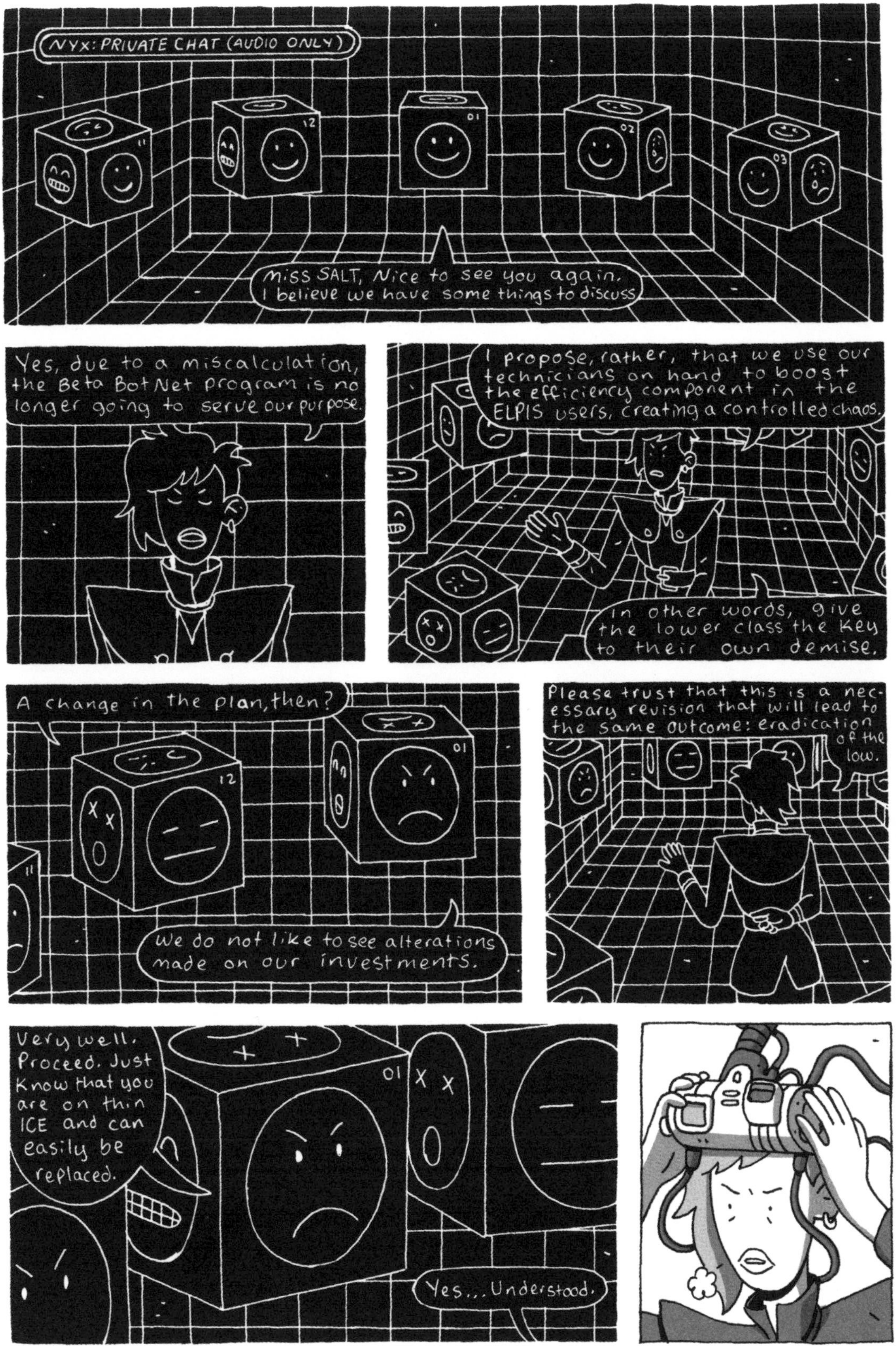
NYX: PRIVATE CHAT (AUDIO ONLY)
MISS SALT, Nice to see you again. I believe we have some things to discuss
Yes, due to a miscalculation, the Beta Bot Net program is no longer going to serve our purpose.
I propose, rather, that we use our technicians on hand to boost the efficiency component in the ELPIS users, creating a controlled chaos.
In other words, give the lower class the Key to their own demise.
A change in the plan, then?
We do not like to see alterations made on our investments.
Please trust that this is a necessary revision that will lead to the same outcome: eradication of the low.
Very well. Proceed. Just Know that you are on thin ICE and can easily be replaced.
Yes... Understood.

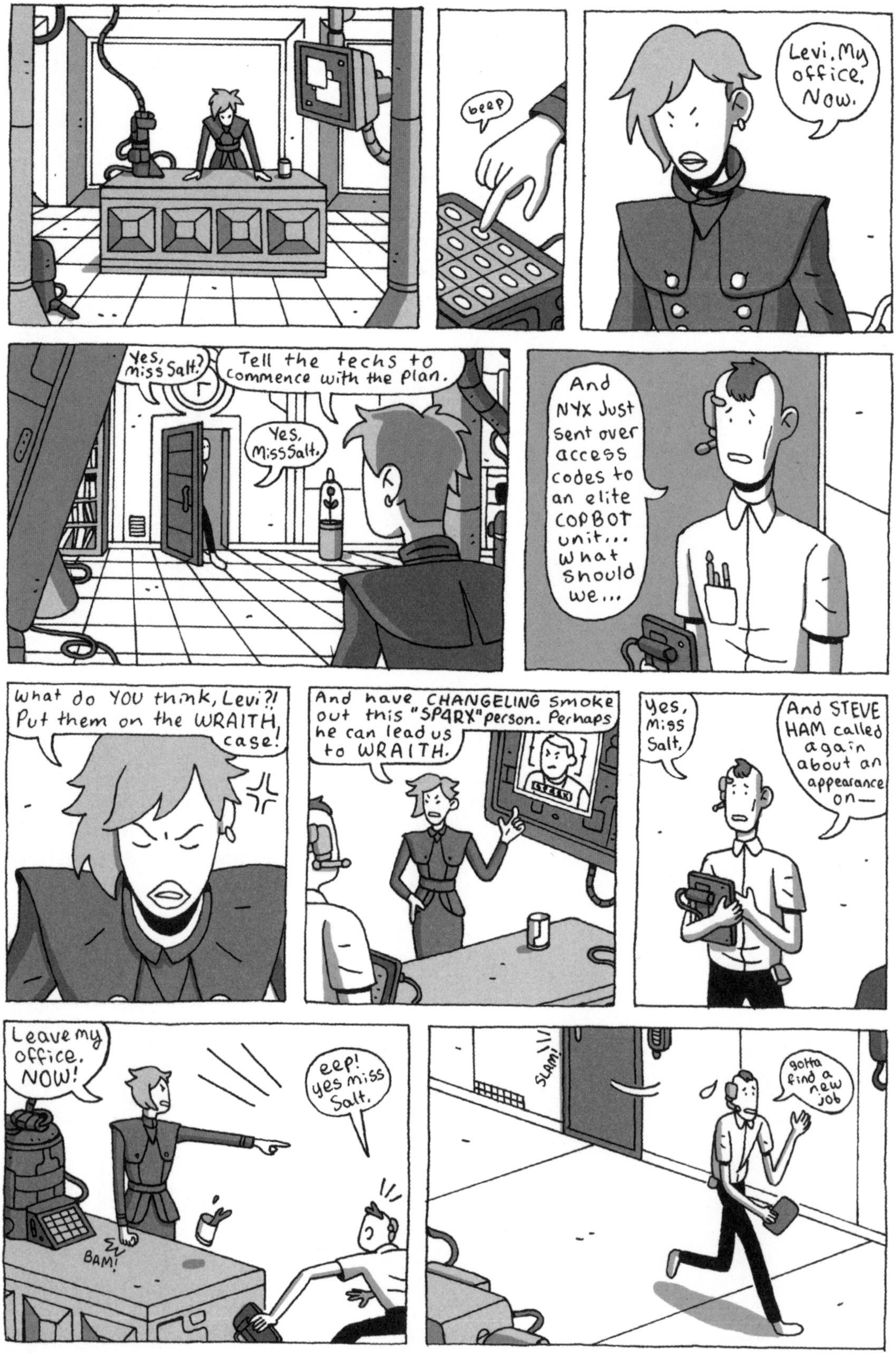
beep
Levi, My office. Now.
Yes, miss Salt?
Tell the techs to commence with the plan.
Yes, Miss Salt.
And NYX Just sent over access codes to an elite COPBOT unit... what should we...
What do YOU think, Levi?! Put them on the WRAITH case!
And have CHANGELING smoke out this "SPARX" person. Perhaps he can lead us to WRAITH.
Yes, Miss Salt.
And STEVE HAM called again about an appearance on—
Leave my office. NOW!
BAM!
eep! yes miss Salt.
SLAM!
gotta find a new job

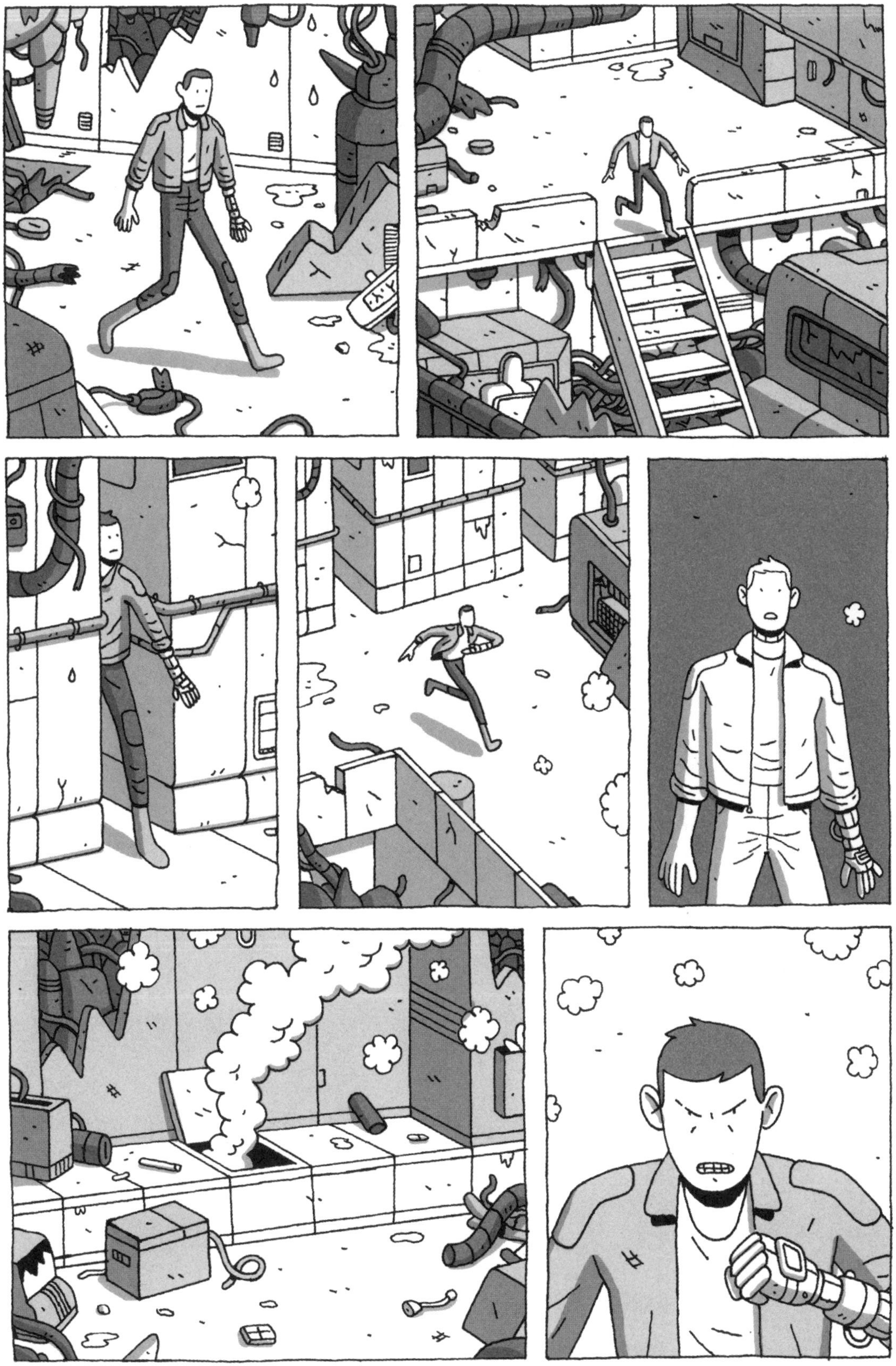

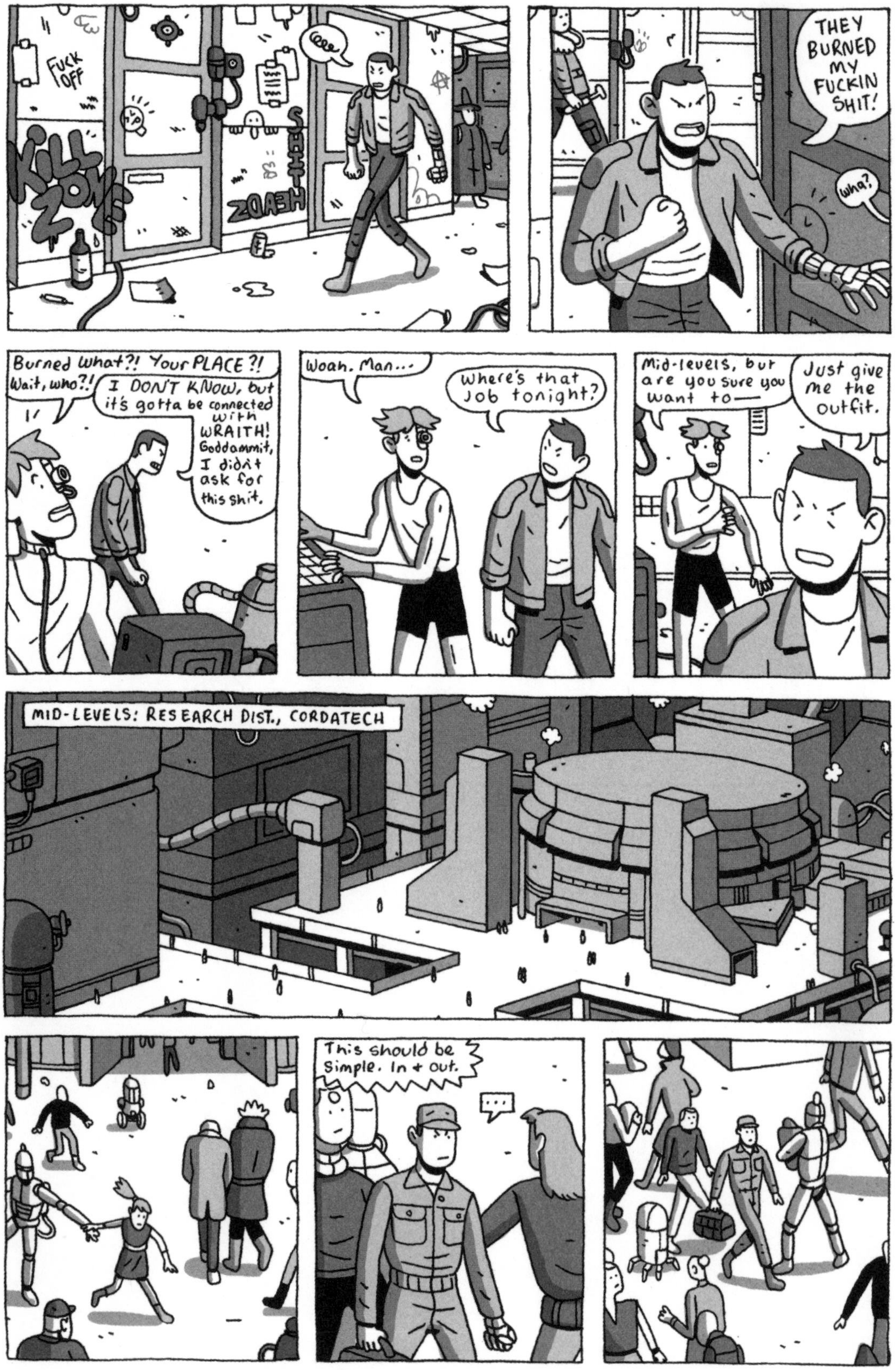
FUCK OFF
KILL ZONE
SHIT HEADZ
THEY BURNED MY FUCKIN SHIT!
Wha?
Burned what?! Your PLACE?! Wait, who?!
I DON'T KNOW, but it's gotta be connected with WRAITH! Goddammit, I didn't ask for this shit.
Woah. Man...
Where's that job tonight?
Mid-levels, but are you sure you want to—
Just give me the outfit.
MID-LEVELS: RESEARCH DIST., CORDATECH
This should be simple. In + out.
...

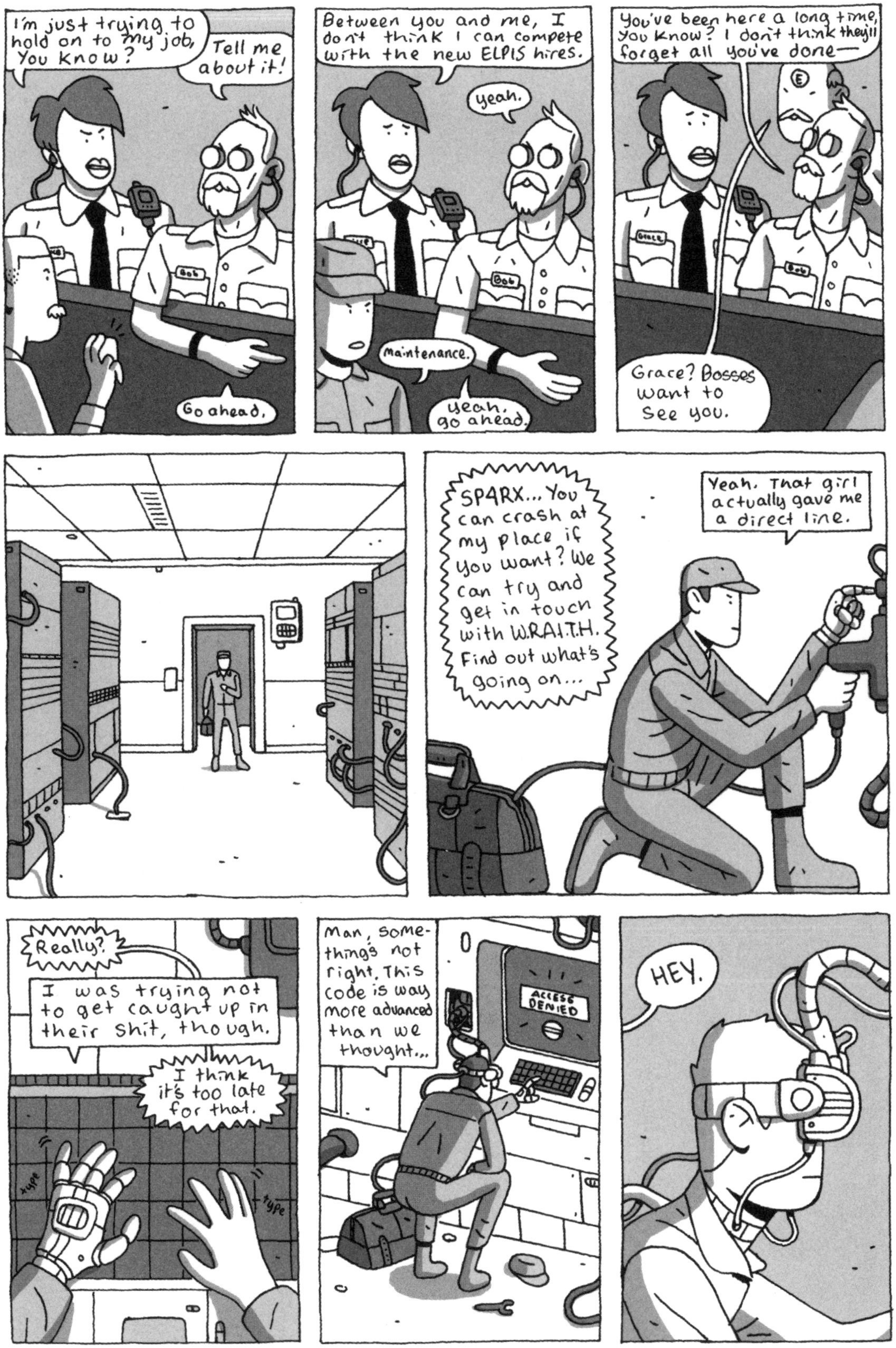
I'm just trying to hold on to my job, You know?
Tell me about it!
Go ahead.
Between you and me, I don't think I can compete with the new ELPIS hires.
yeah.
maintenance.
yeah. go ahead.
You've been here a long time, You know? I don't think they'll forget all you've done—
Grace? Bosses want to see you.
SP4RX... You can crash at my place if you want? We can try and get in touch with W.R.A.I.T.H. Find out what's going on...
Yeah. That girl actually gave me a direct line.
Really?
I was trying not to get caught up in their shit, though.
I think it's too late for that.
type
type
Man, something's not right. This code is way more advanced than we thought...
ACCESS DENIED
HEY.

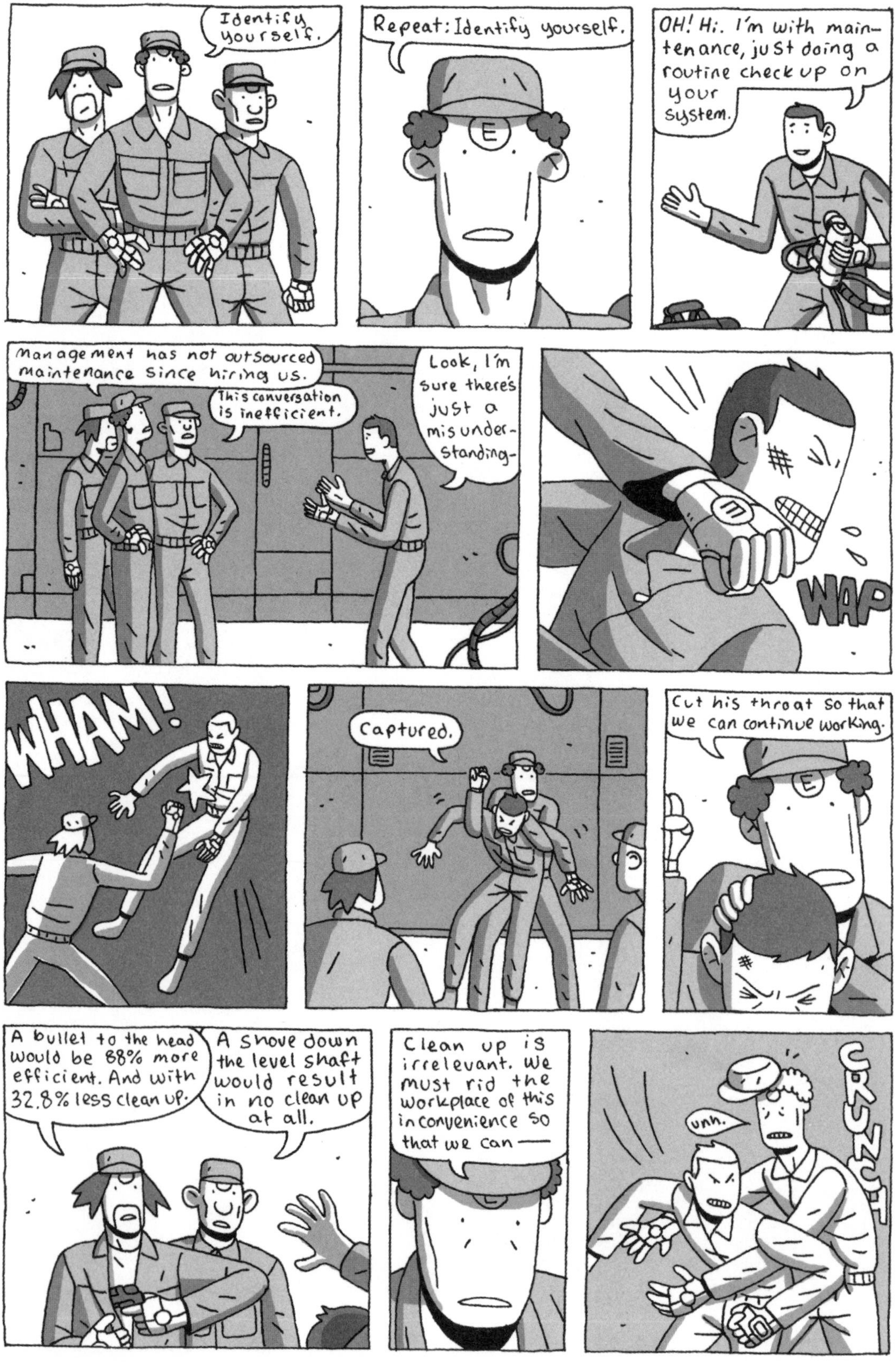
Identify yourself.
Repeat: Identify yourself.
OH! Hi. I'm with maintenance, just doing a routine check up on your system.
Management has not outsourced maintenance since hiring us.
This conversation is inefficient.
Look, I'm sure there's just a misunderstanding-
WAP
WHAM!
Captured.
Cut his throat so that we can continue working.
A bullet to the head would be 88% more efficient. And with 32.8% less clean up.
A shove down the level shaft would result in no clean up at all.
Clean up is irrelevant. We must rid the workplace of this inconvenience so that we can—
unh.
CRUNCH

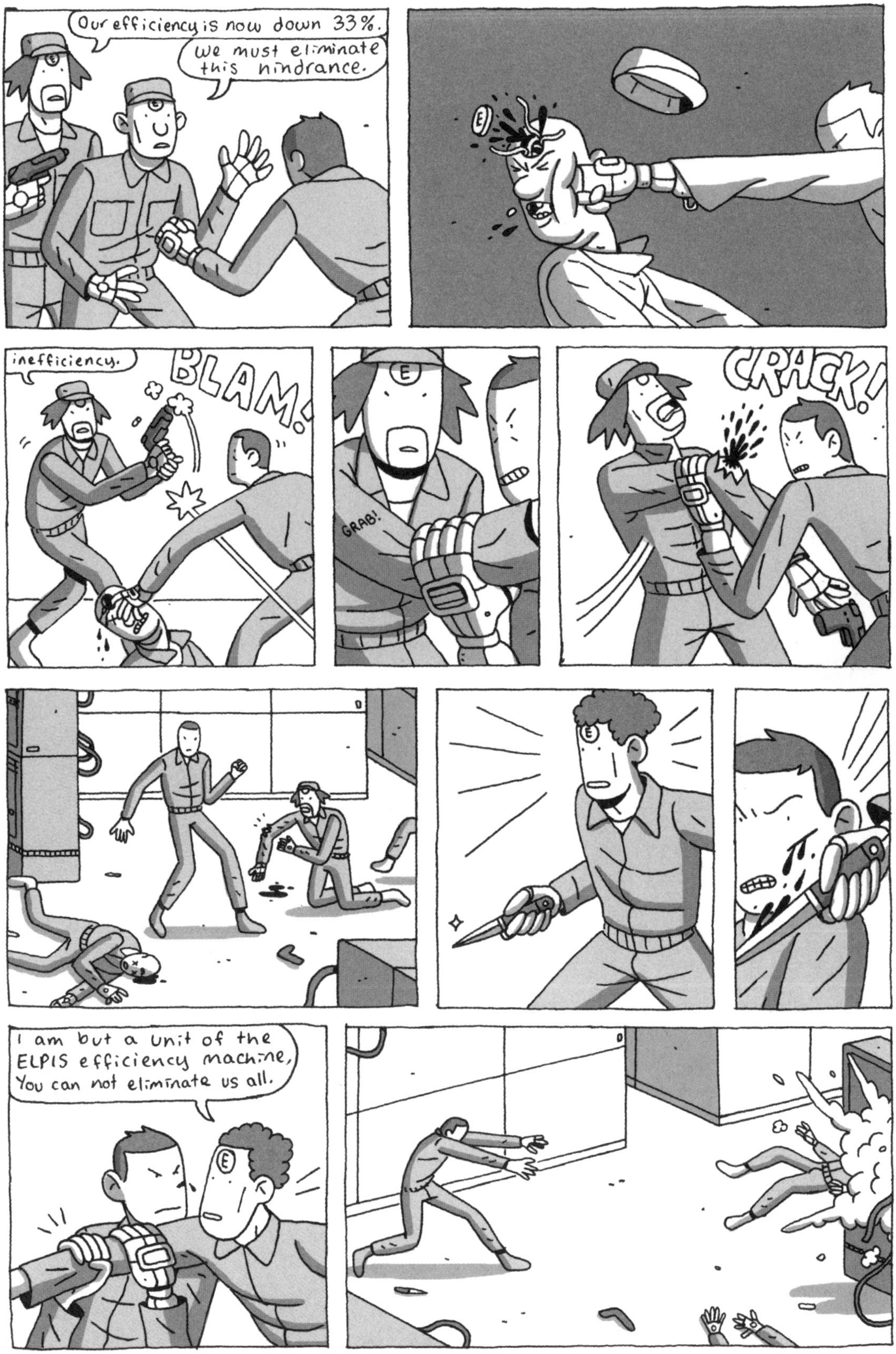
Our efficiency is now down 33%.
We must eliminate this hindrance.
inefficiency.
BLAM!
GRAB!
CRACK!
I am but a unit of the ELPIS efficiency machine, You can not eliminate us all.

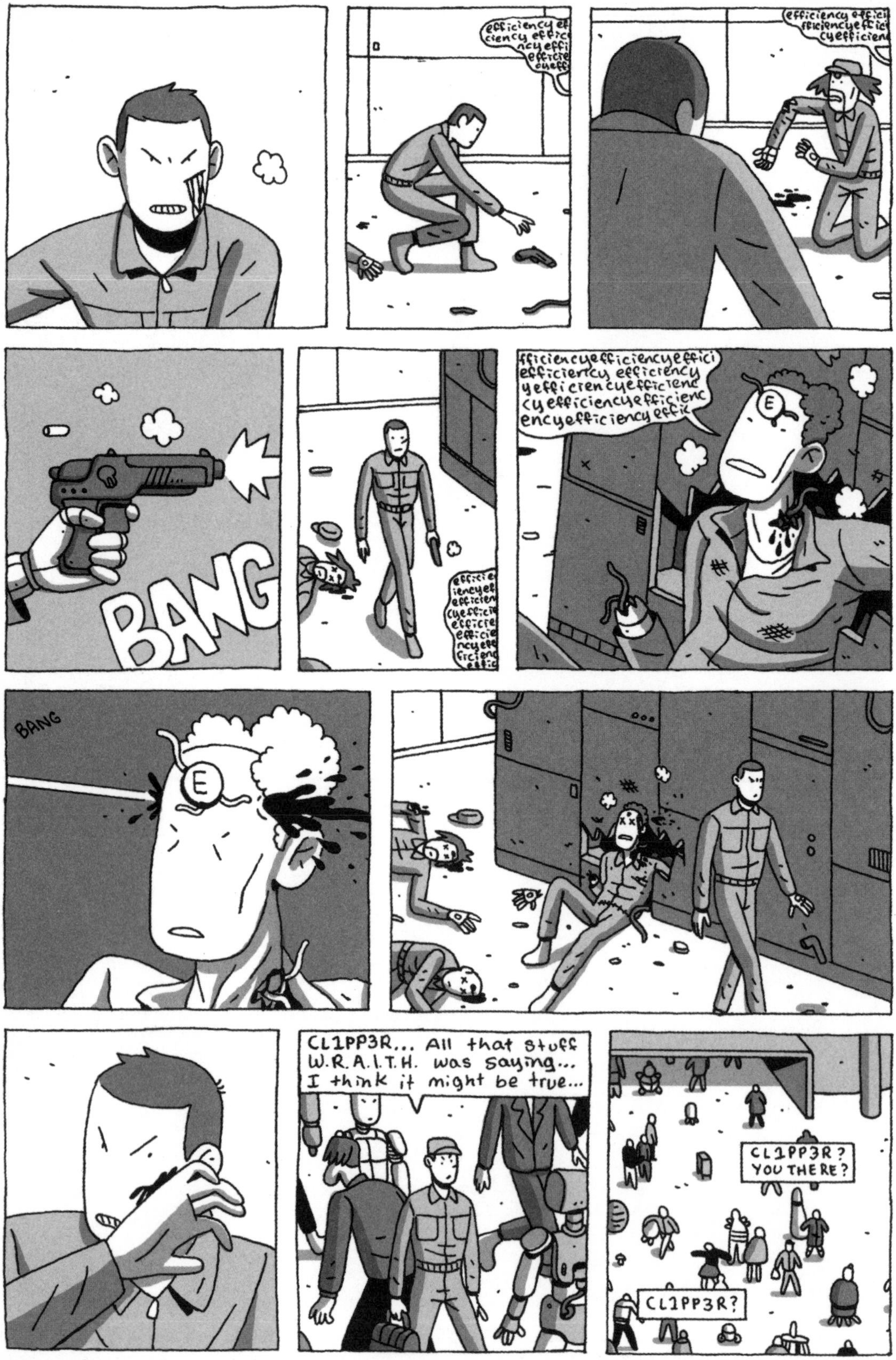

efficiency efficiency efficiency efficiency efficiency
efficiency efficiency efficiency
BANG
efficiency efficiency efficiency efficiency efficiency efficiency
efficiencyefficiencyefficiencyefficiencyefficiencyefficiencyefficiencyefficiency
BANG
CL1PP3R... All that stuff W.R.A.I.T.H. was saying... I think it might be true...
CL1PP3R? YOU THERE?
CL1PP3R?

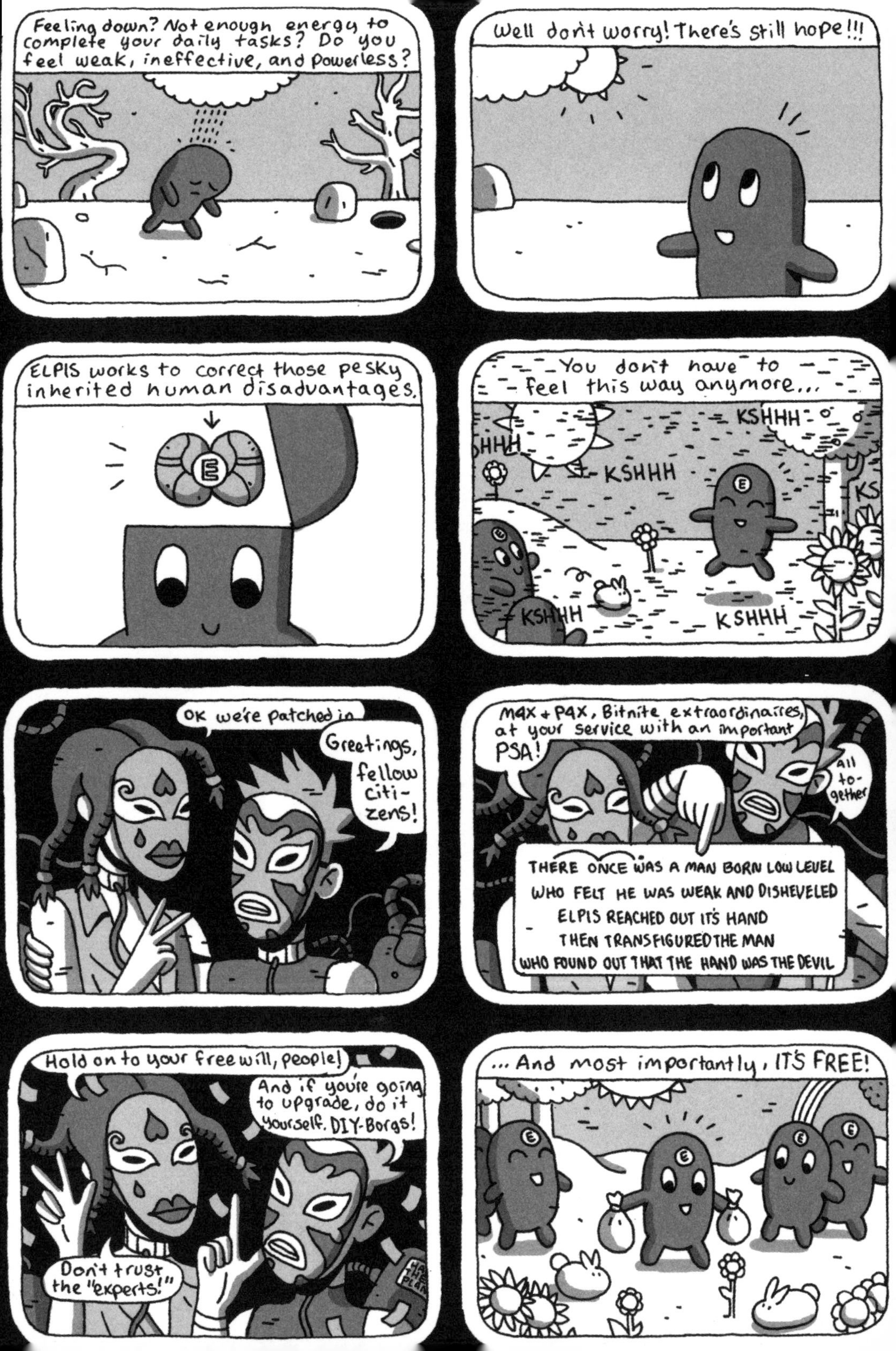
Feeling down? Not enough energy to complete your daily tasks? Do you feel weak, ineffective, and powerless?
Well don't worry! There's still hope!!!
ELPIS works to correct those pesky inherited human disadvantages.
E
You don't have to feel this way anymore...
KSHHH
KSHHH
KSHHH
KSHHH
OK we're patched in
Greetings, fellow citi-zens!
MAX + PAX, Bitnite extraordinaires, at your service with an important PSA!
all to-gether
THERE ONCE WAS A MAN BORN LOW LEVEL
WHO FELT HE WAS WEAK AND DISHEVELED
ELPIS REACHED OUT IT'S HAND
THEN TRANSFIGURED THE MAN
WHO FOUND OUT THAT THE HAND WAS THE DEVIL
Hold on to your free will, people!
And if you're going to upgrade, do it yourself. DIY-Borgs!
Don't trust the "experts!"
... And most importantly, IT'S FREE!

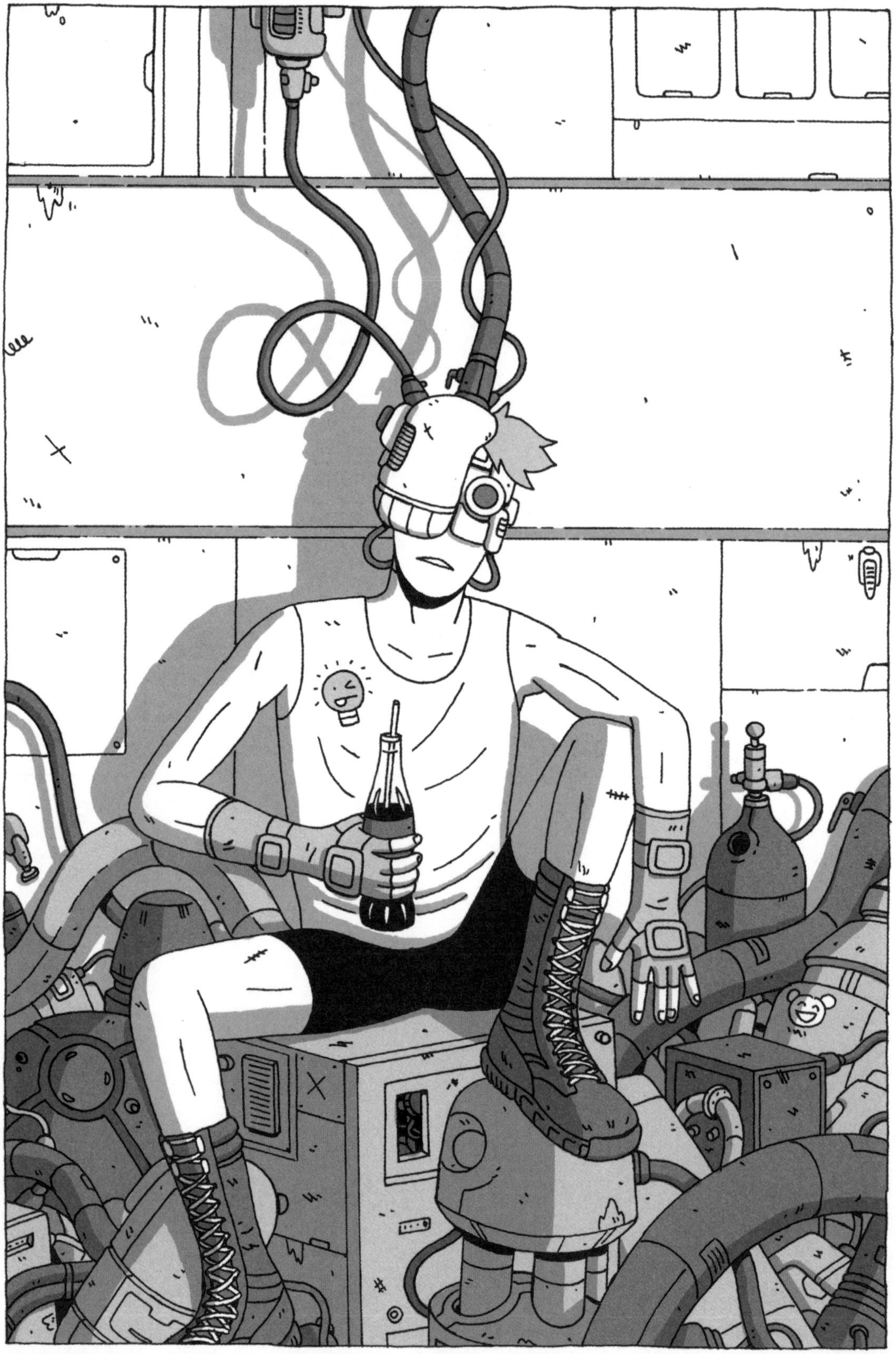

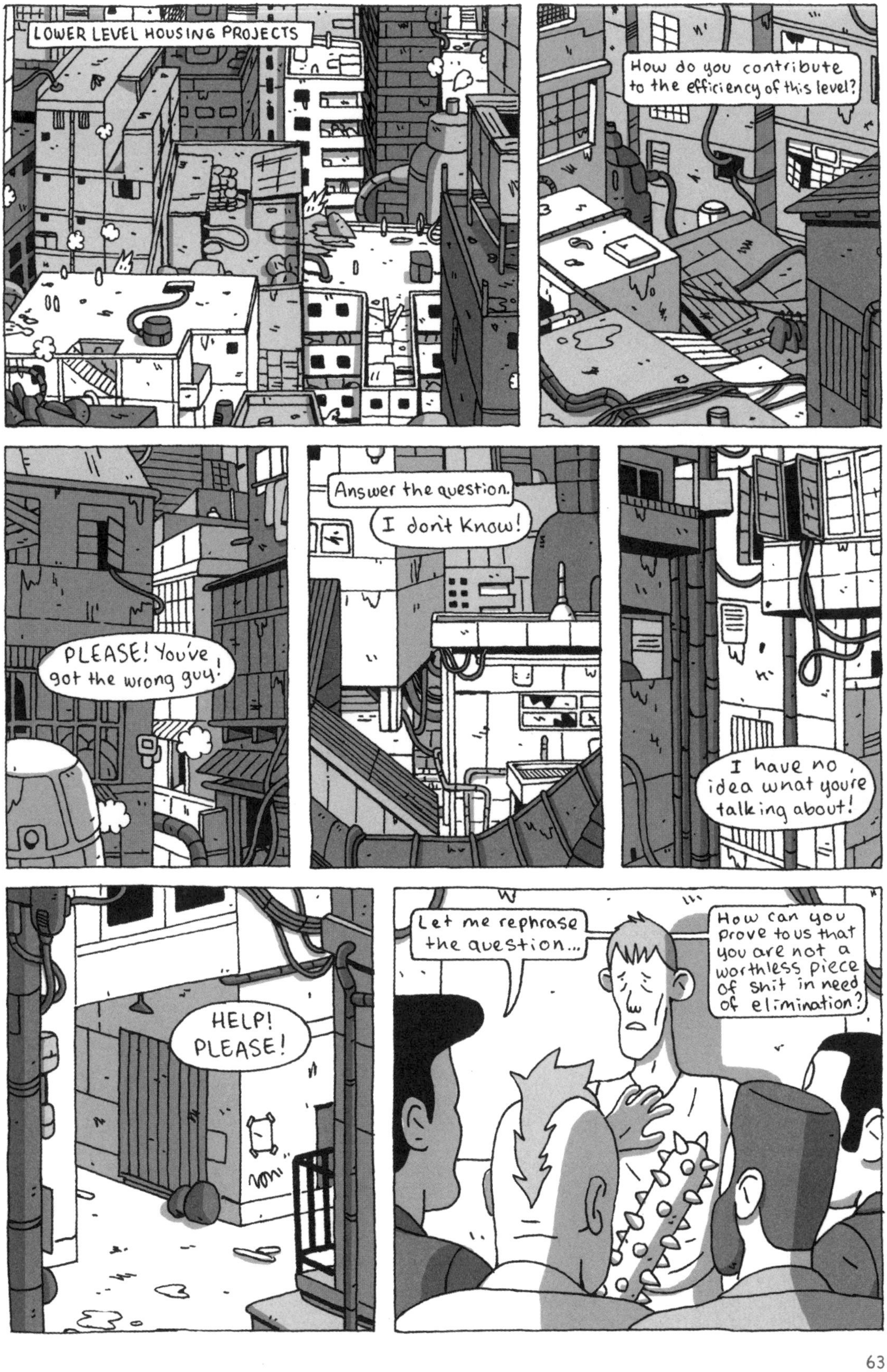
LOWER LEVEL HOUSING PROJECTS
How do you contribute to the efficiency of this level?
PLEASE! You've got the wrong guy!
Answer the question.
I don't Know!
I have no idea what you're talking about!
HELP! PLEASE!
Let me rephrase the question...
How can you prove to us that you are not a worthless piece of shit in need of elimination?

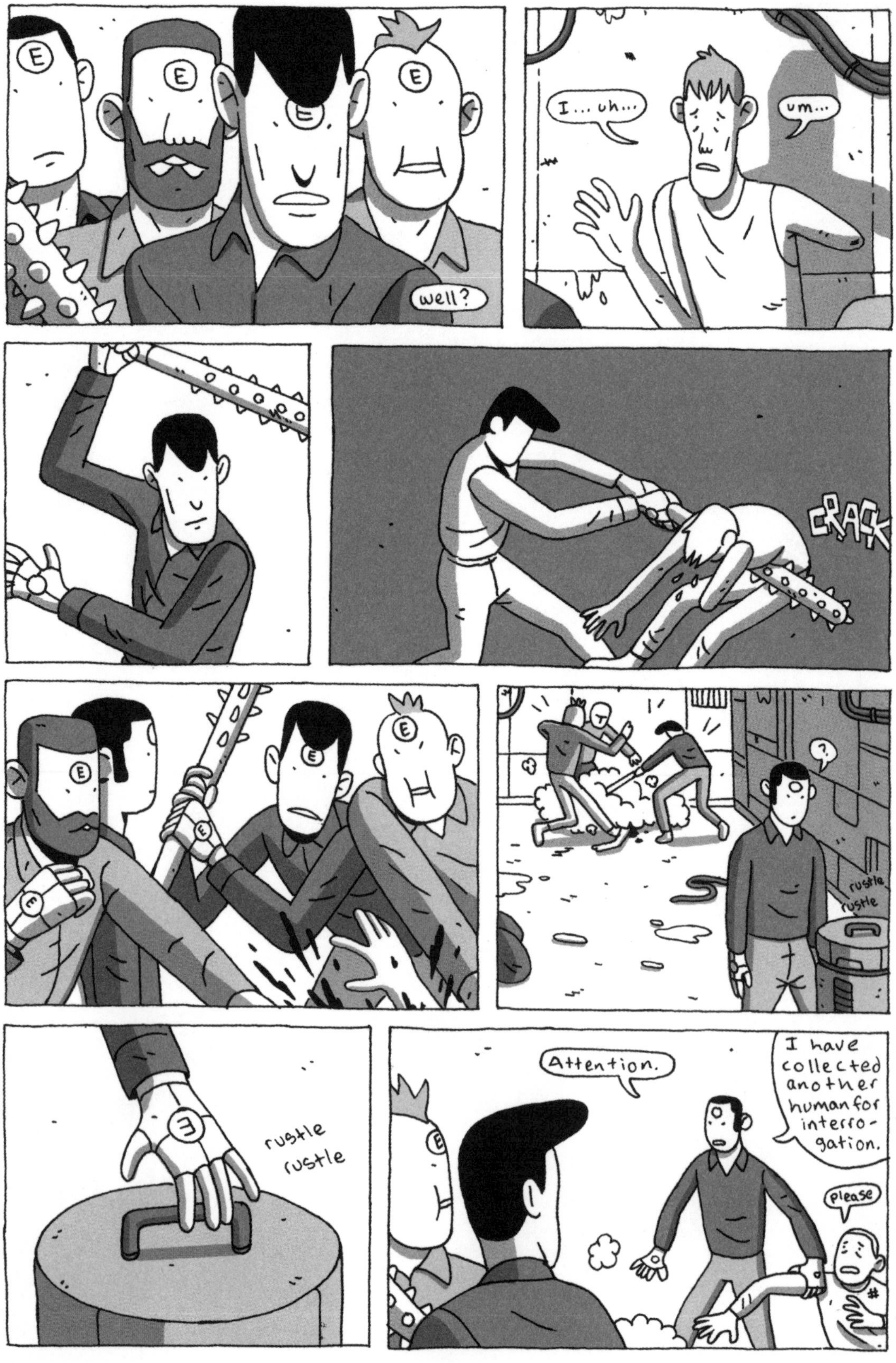
well?
I... uh...
um...
CRACK
?
rustle
rustle
rustle
rustle
Attention.
I have collected another human for interro-gation.
please

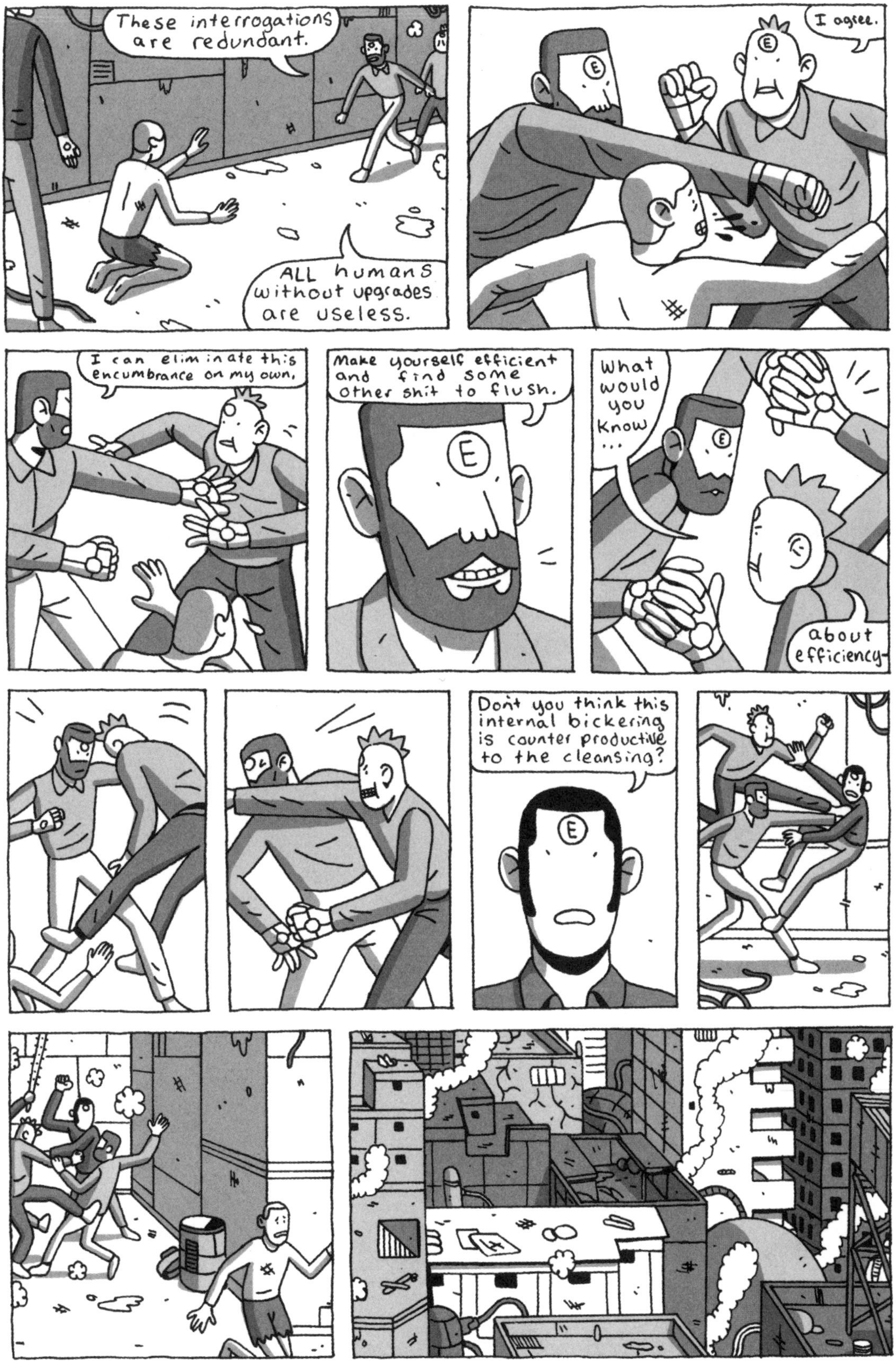
These interrogations are redundant.
ALL humans without upgrades are useless.
I agree.
I can eliminate this encumbrance on my own.
Make yourself efficient and find some other shit to flush.
What would you know...
about efficiency-
Don't you think this internal bickering is counter productive to the cleansing?

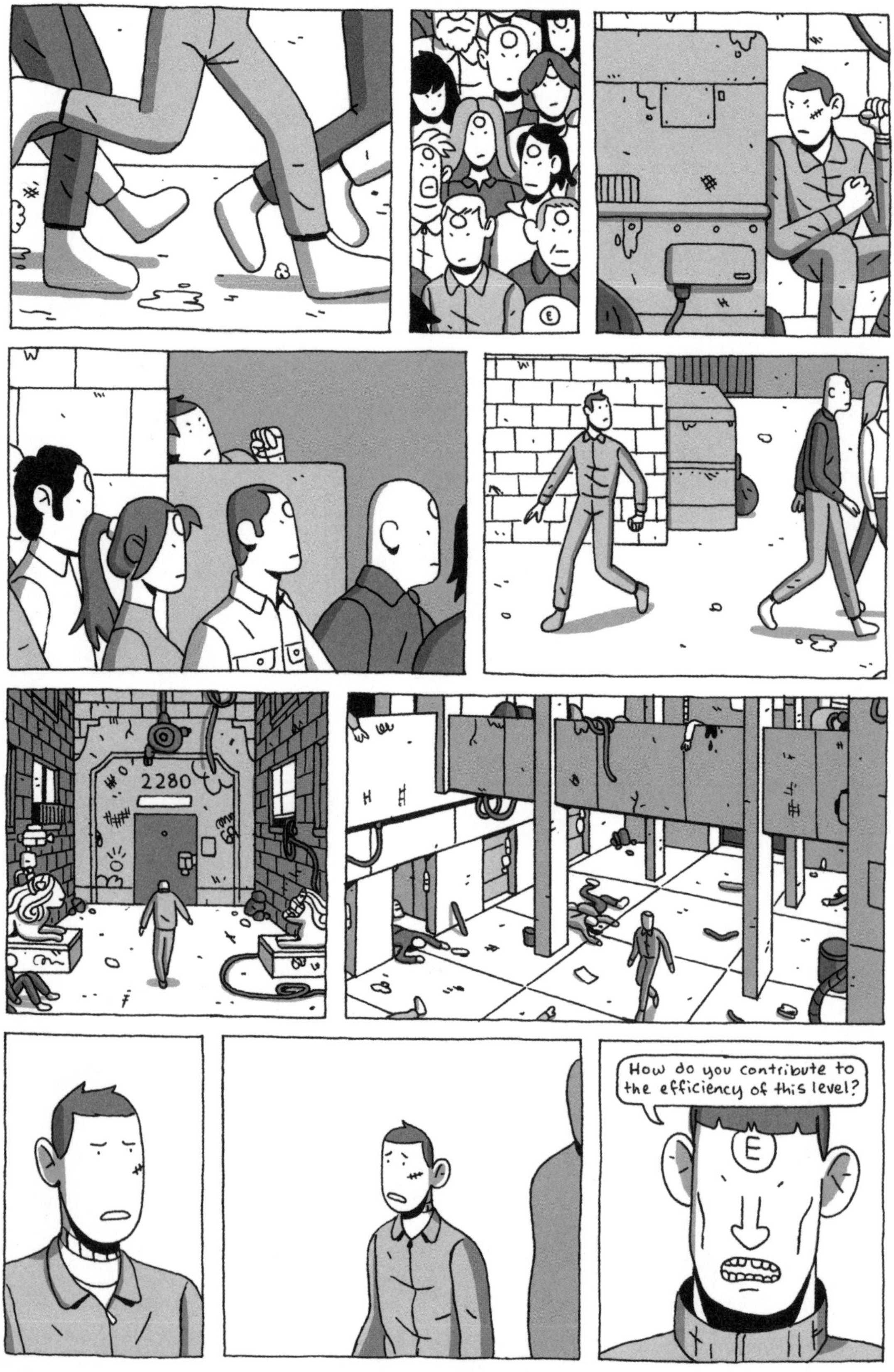
2280
How do you contribute to the efficiency of this level?

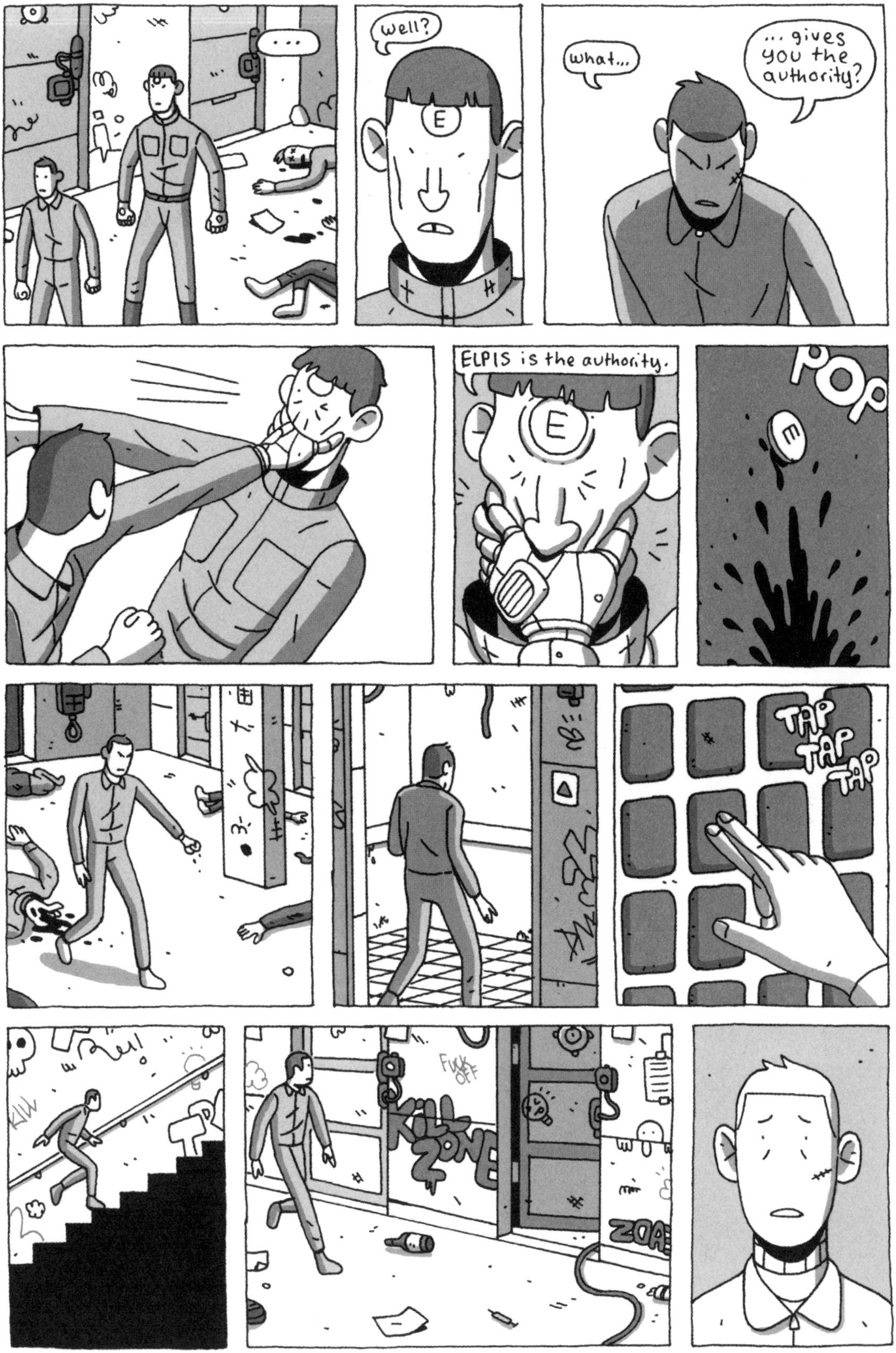
...
well?
what...
...gives you the authority?
ELPIS is the authority.
POP
TAP
TAP
TAP
FUCK OFF
KILL ZONE
ZOA

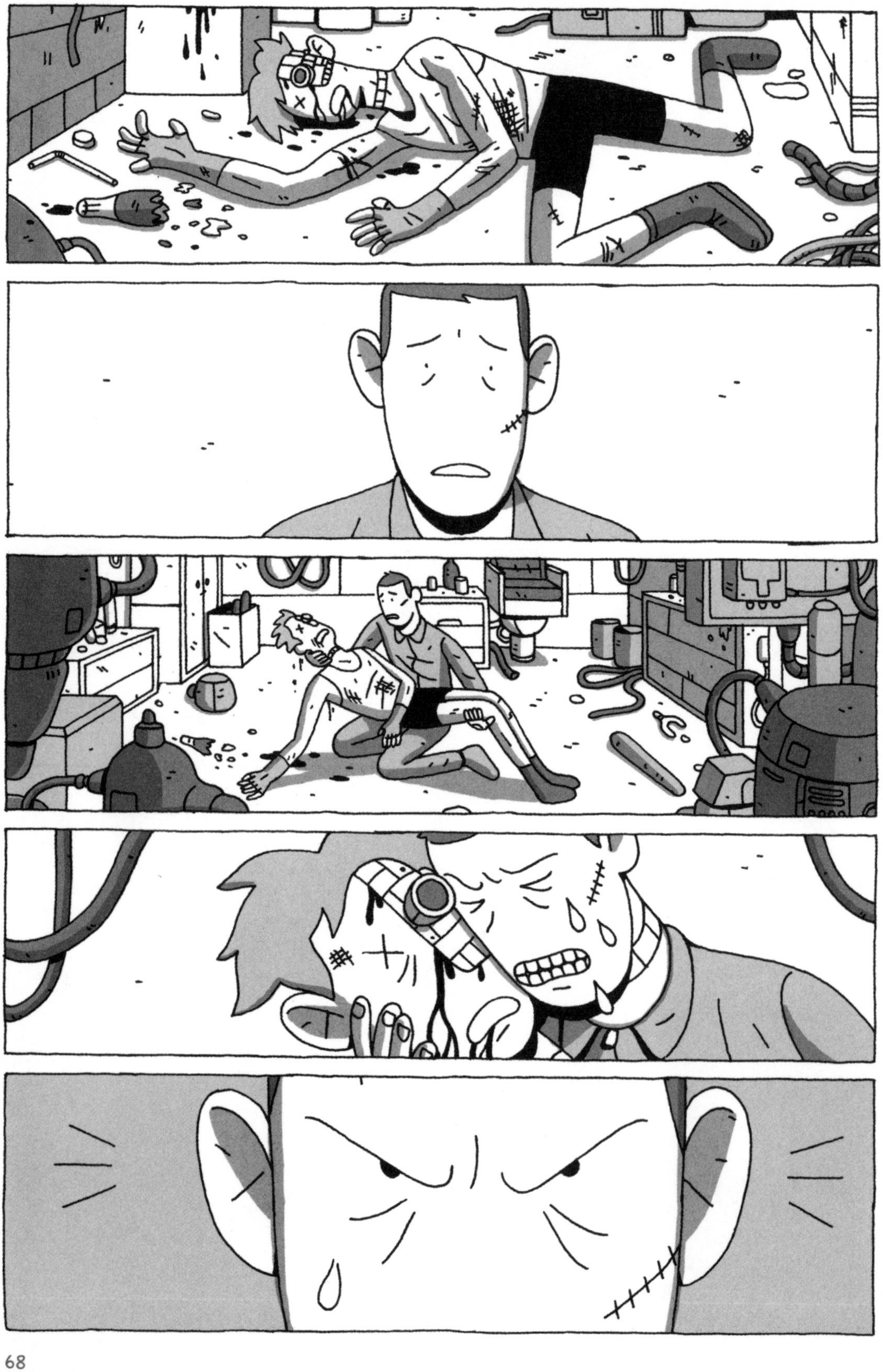

00:59 29
DOOM!

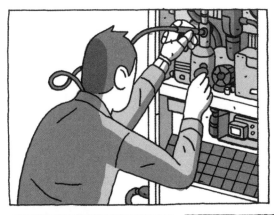

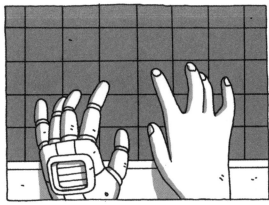

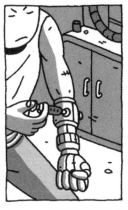

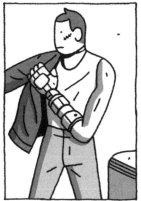

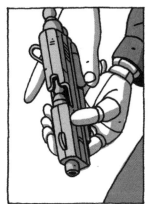

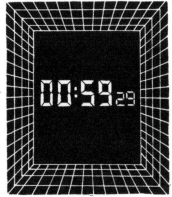

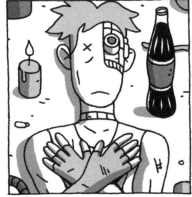

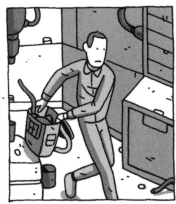

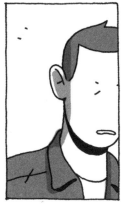

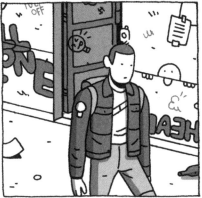

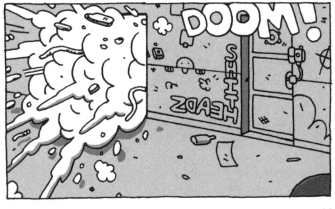

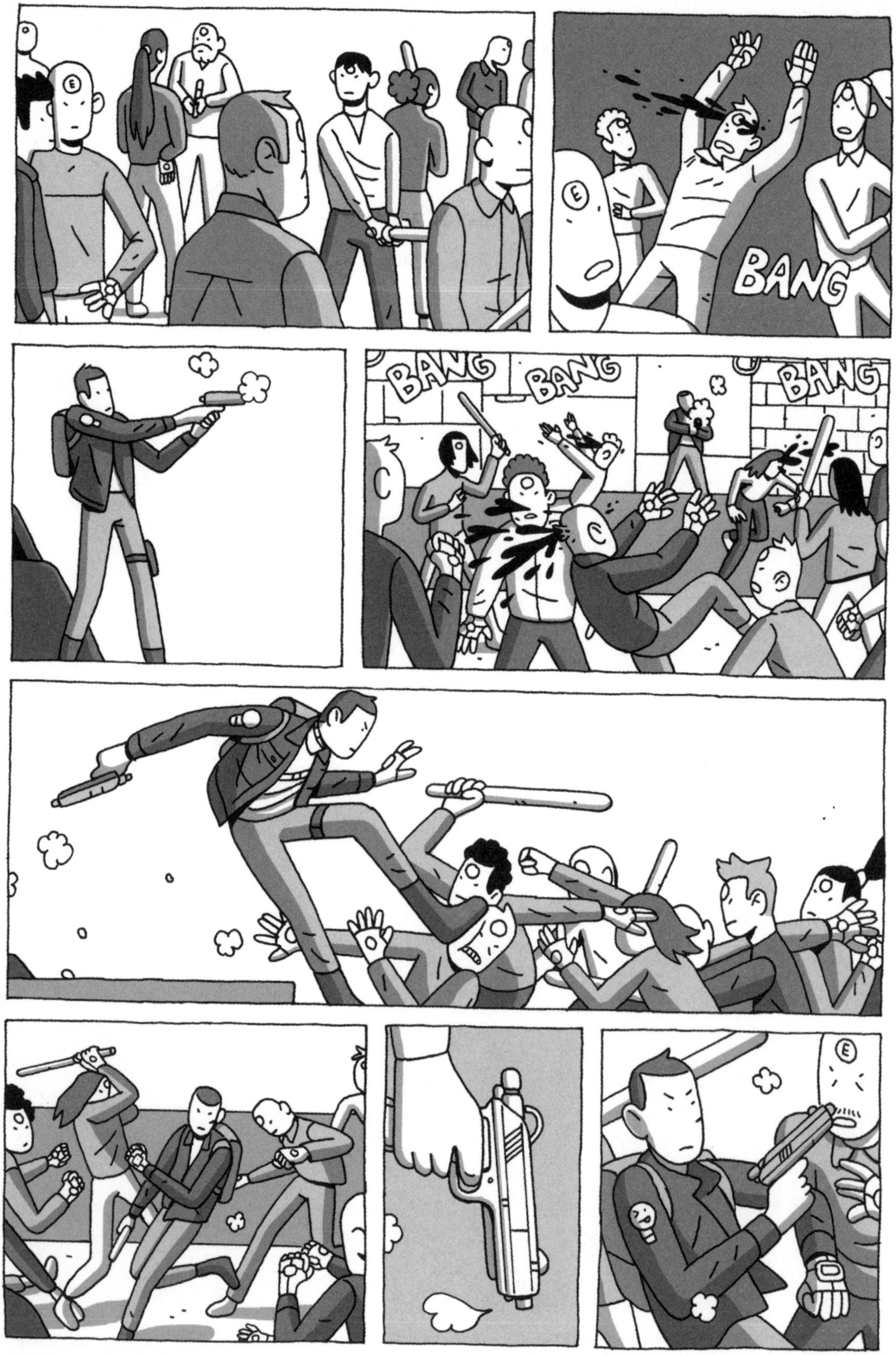
BANG
BANG
BANG
BANG

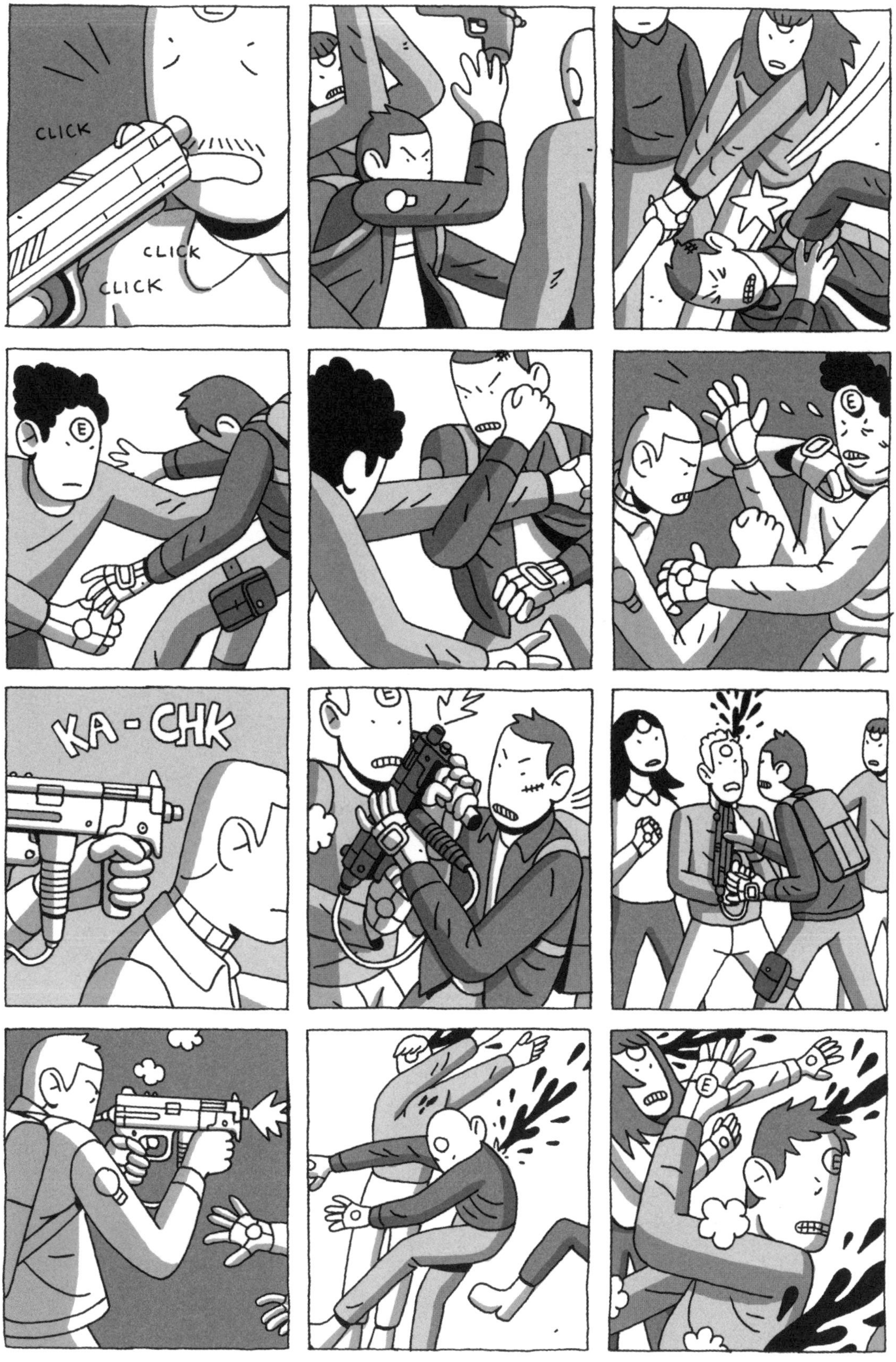
CLICK
CLICK
CLICK
KA-CHK

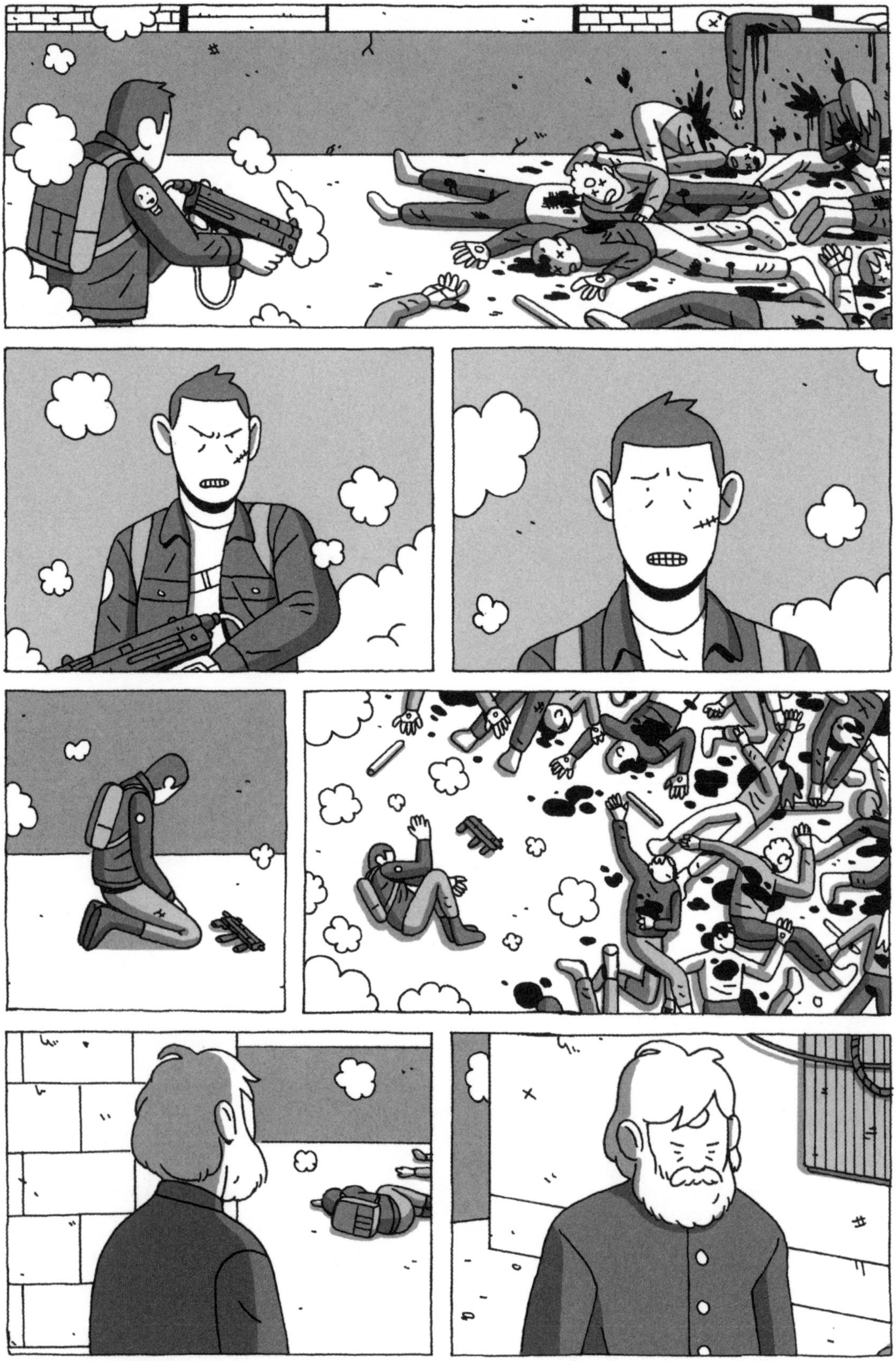

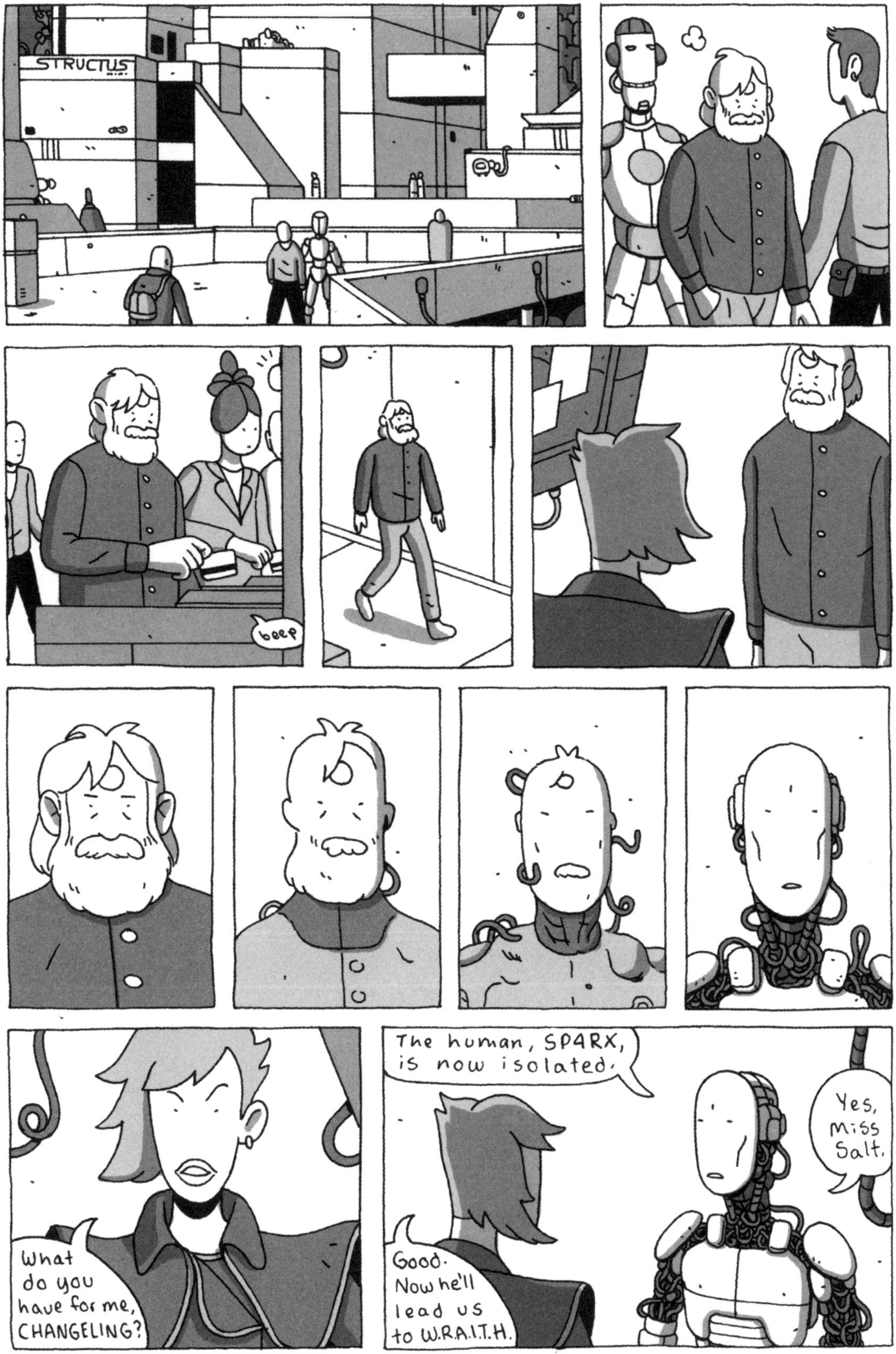
STRUCTUS
beep
What do you have for me, CHANGELING?
The human, SP4RX, is now isolated.
Yes, miss Salt.
Good. Now he'll lead us to W.R.A.I.T.H.

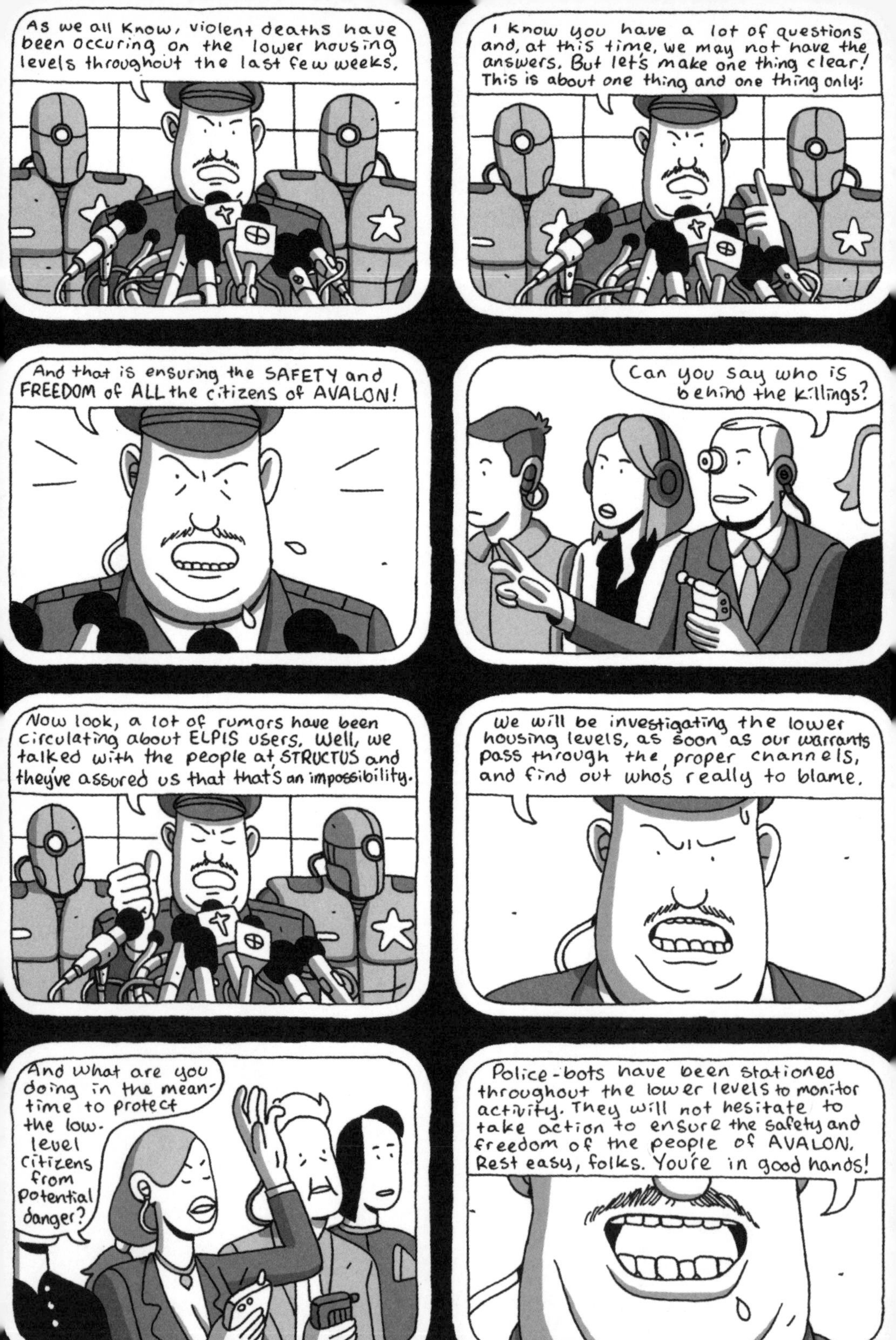
As we all know, violent deaths have been occuring on the lower housing levels throughout the last few weeks.
I know you have a lot of questions and, at this time, we may not have the answers. But let's make one thing clear! This is about one thing and one thing only:
And that is ensuring the SAFETY and FREEDOM of ALL the citizens of AVALON!
Can you say who is behind the killings?
Now look, a lot of rumors have been circulating about ELPIS users. Well, we talked with the people at STRUCTUS and they've assured us that that's an impossibility.
We will be investigating the lower housing levels, as soon as our warrants pass through the proper channels, and find out who's really to blame.
And what are you doing in the mean-time to protect the low-level citizens from potential danger?
Police-bots have been stationed throughout the lower levels to monitor activity. They will not hesitate to take action to ensure the safety and freedom of the people of AVALON. Rest easy, folks. You're in good hands!

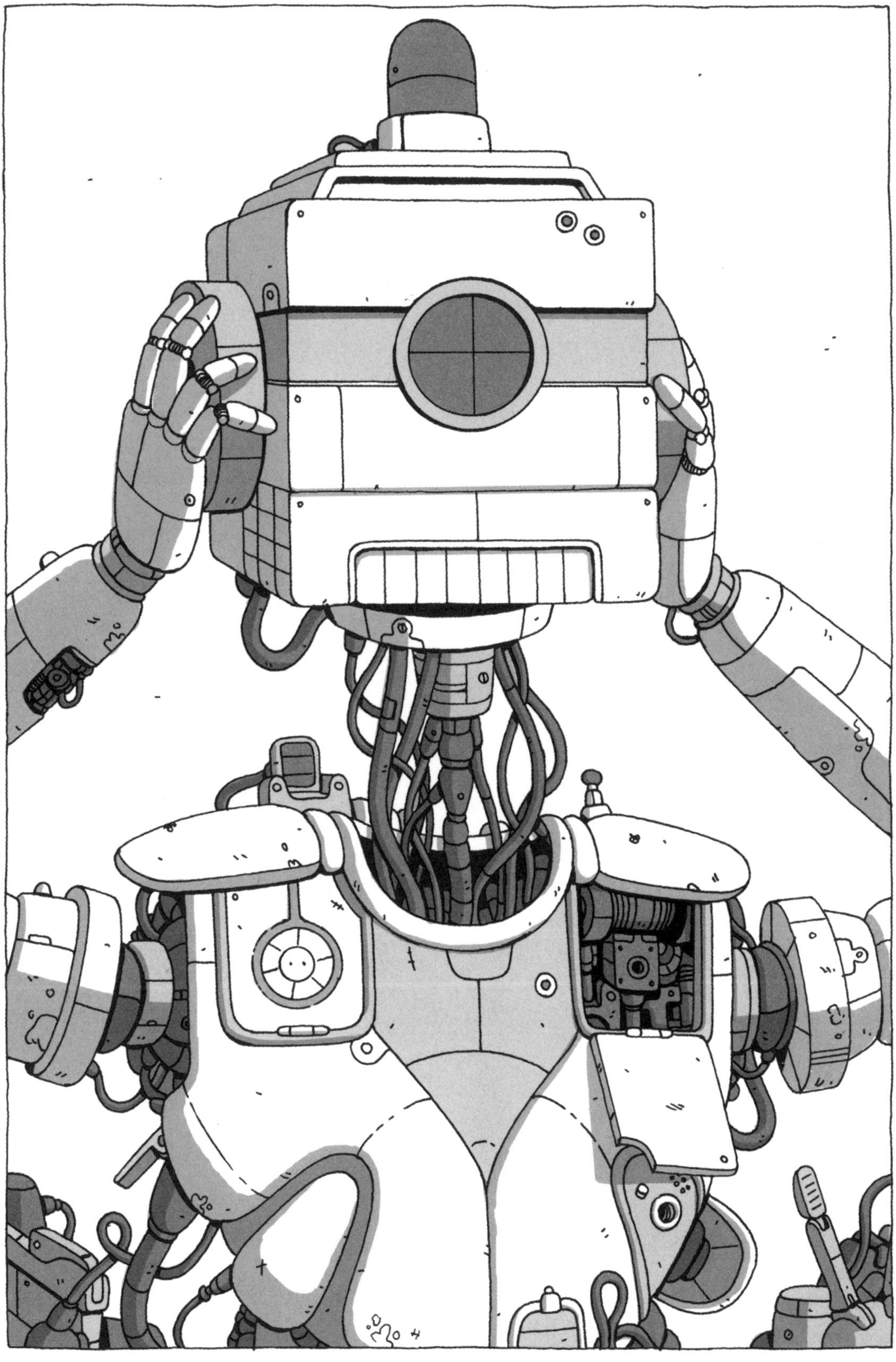

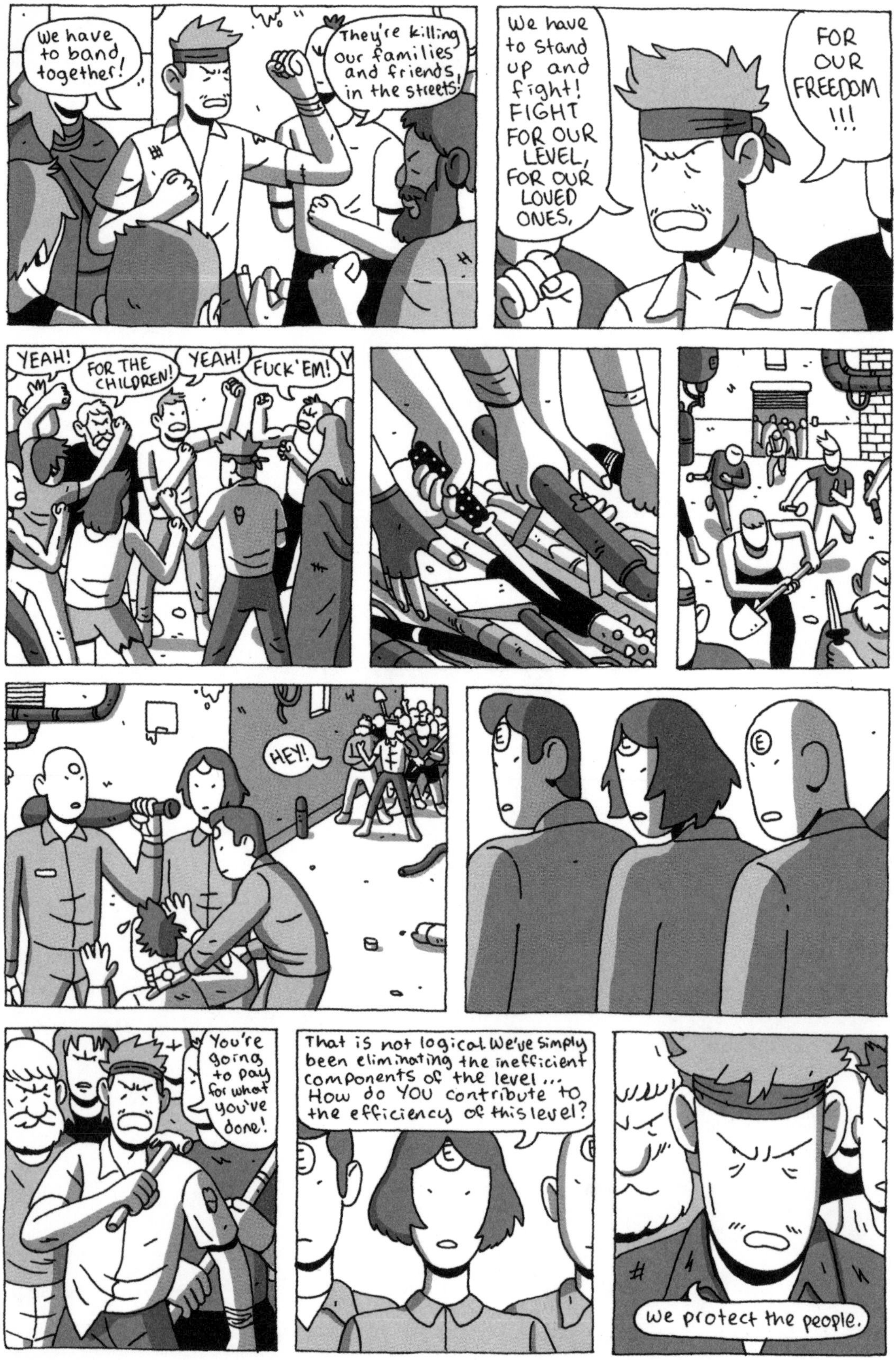
We have to band together!
They're killing our families and friends in the streets!
We have to stand up and fight! FIGHT FOR OUR LEVEL, FOR OUR LOVED ONES,
FOR OUR FREEDOM !!!
YEAH!
FOR THE CHILDREN!
YEAH!
FUCK 'EM!
HEY!
You're going to pay for what you've done!
That is not logical. We've simply been eliminating the inefficient components of the level... How do YOU contribute to the efficiency of this level?
We protect the people.

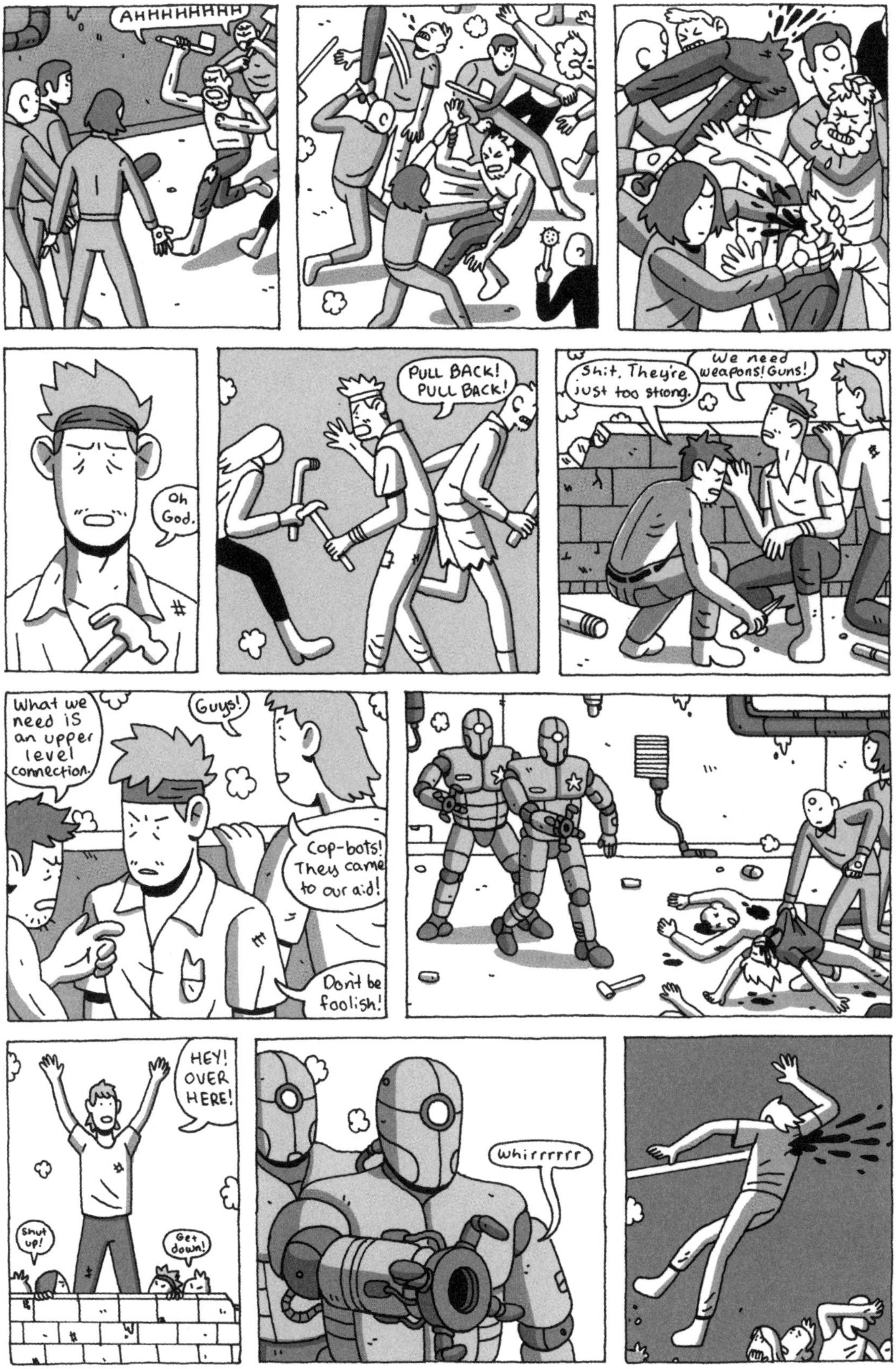
AHHHHHHHH
Oh God.
PULL BACK! PULL BACK!
Shit. They're just too strong.
We need weapons! Guns!
What we need is an upper level connection.
Guys!
Cop-bots! They came to our aid!
Don't be foolish!
HEY! OVER HERE!
Shut up!
Get down!
Whirrrrrr

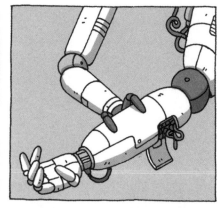
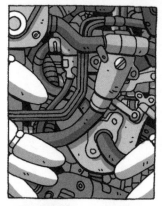
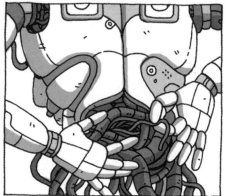
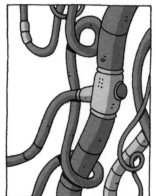

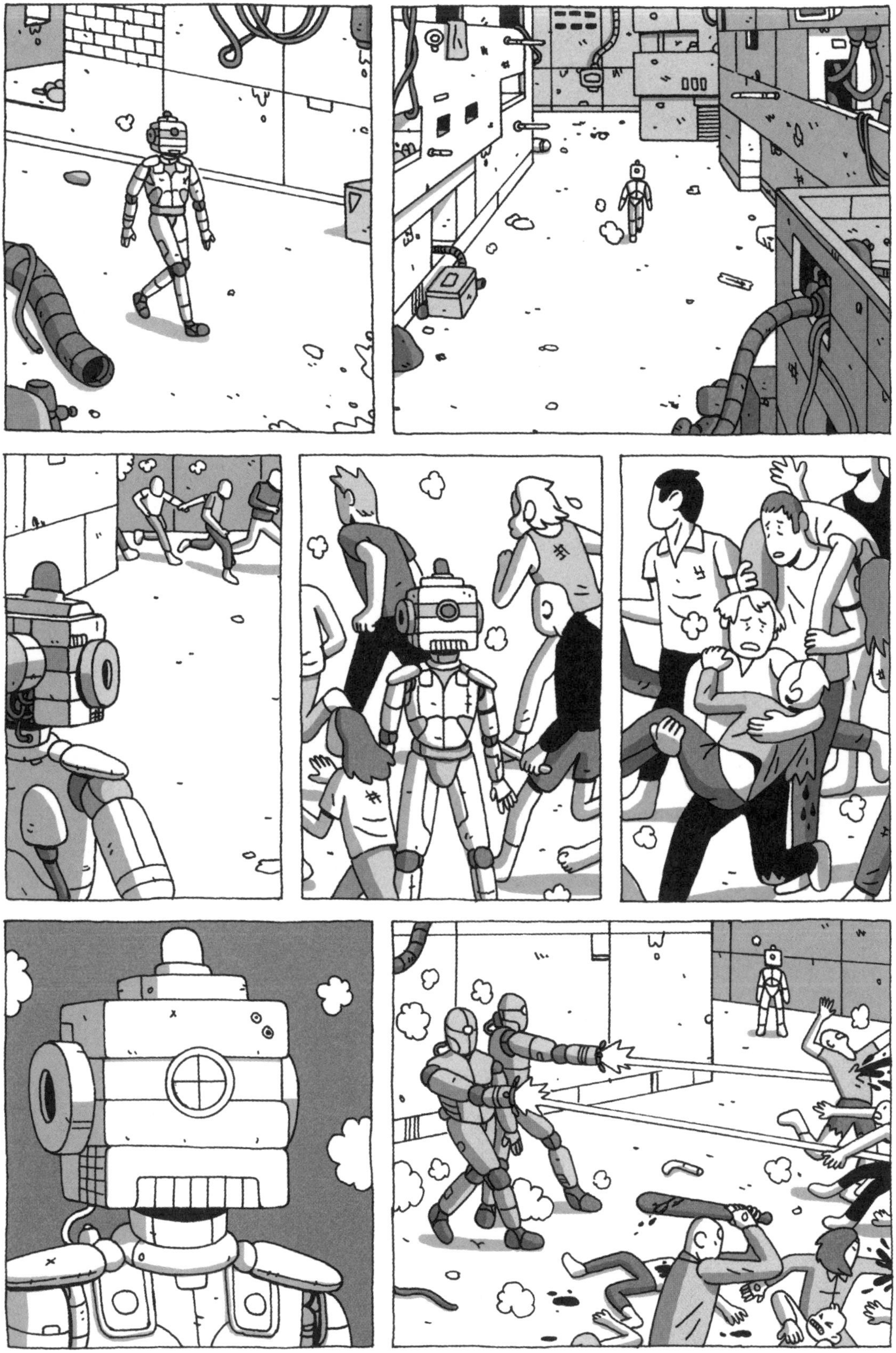

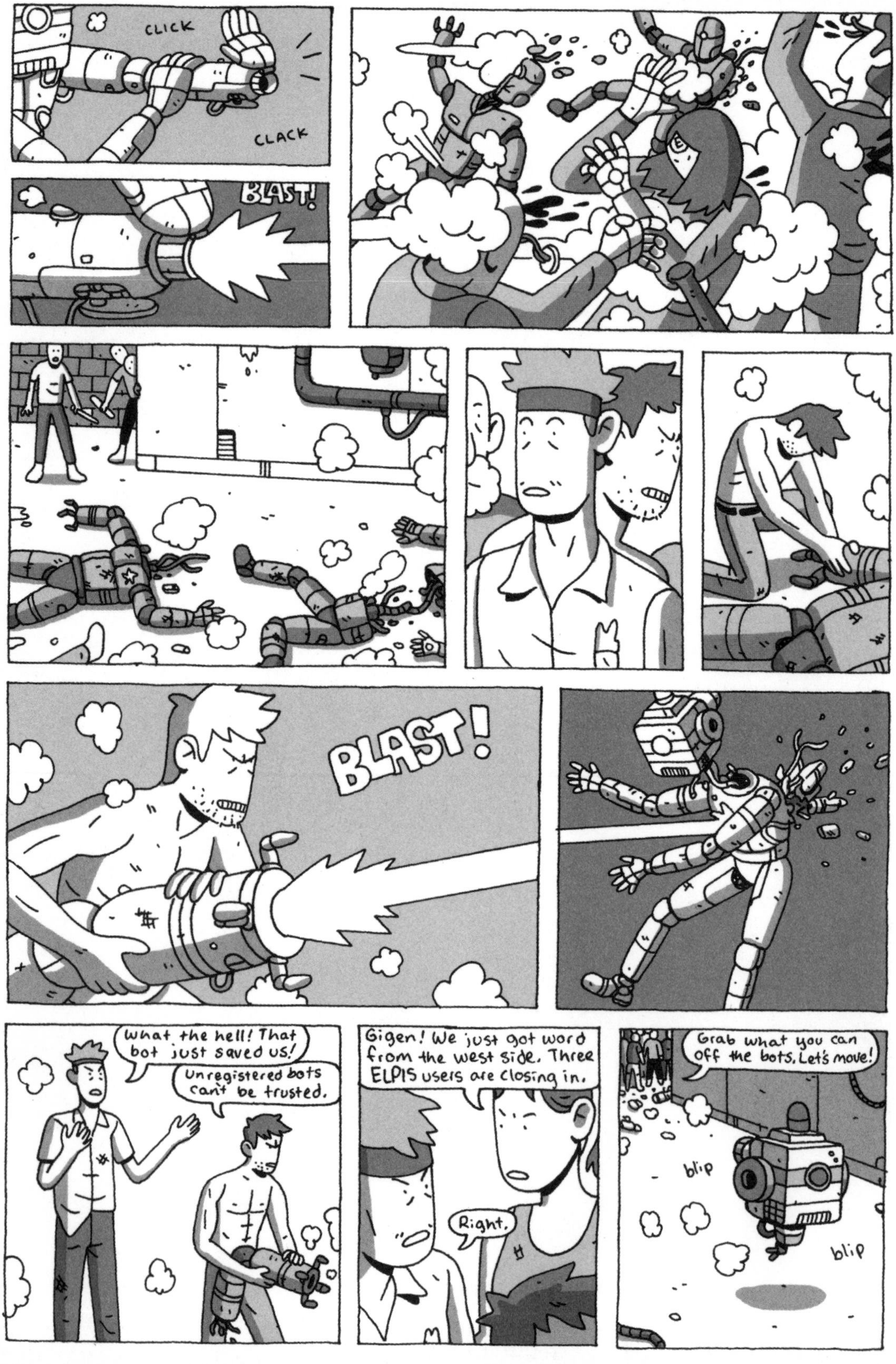
CLICK
CLACK
BLAST!
BLAST!
What the hell! That bot just saved us!
Unregistered bots can't be trusted.
Gigen! We just got word from the west side. Three ELPIS users are closing in.
Right.
Grab what you can off the bots. Let's move!
blip
blip

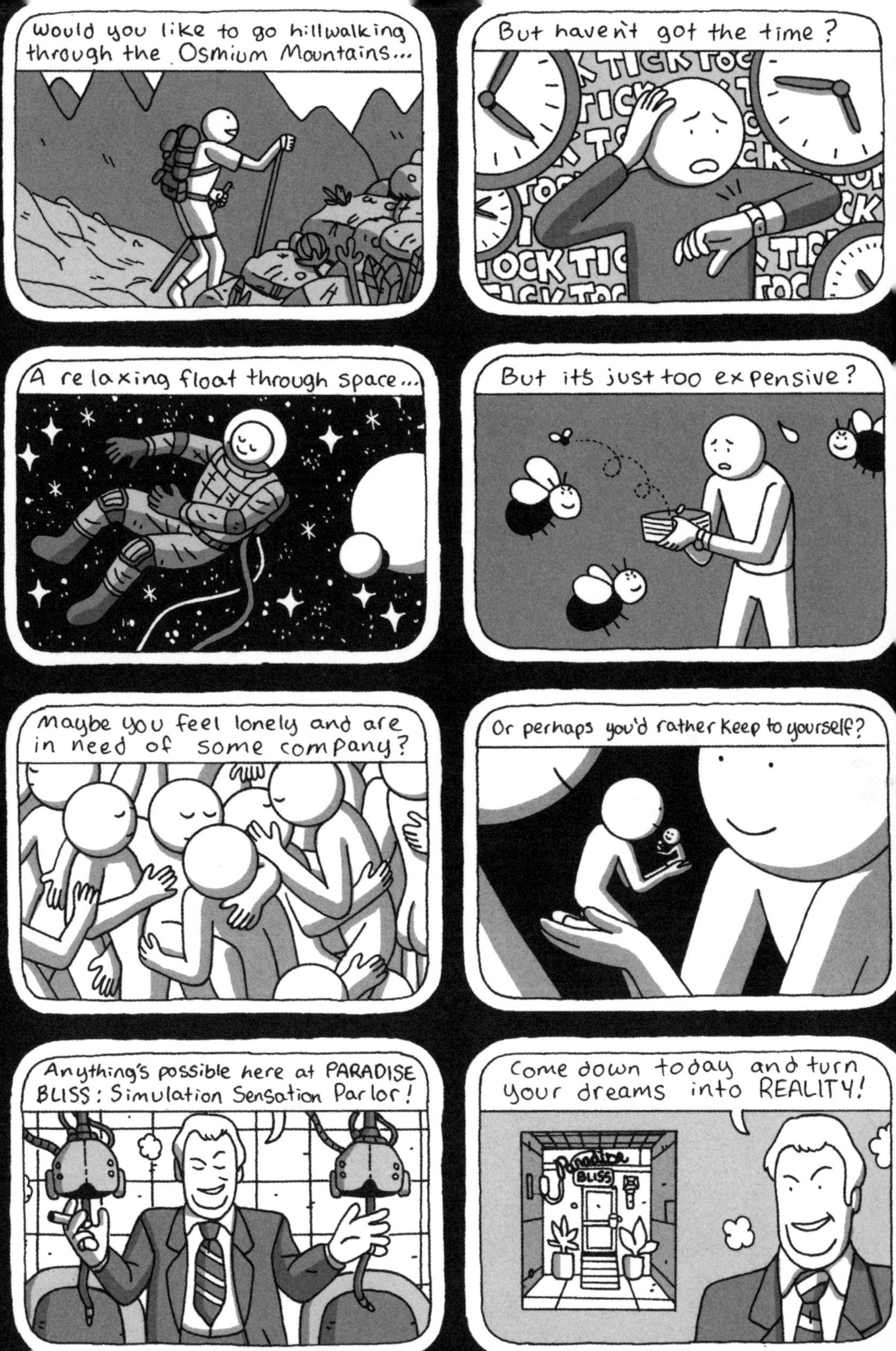
Would you like to go hillwalking through the Osmium Mountains...
But haven't got the time?
TICK TOCK
A relaxing float through space...
But it's just too expensive?
Maybe you feel lonely and are in need of some company?
Or perhaps you'd rather keep to yourself?
Anything's possible here at PARADISE BLISS: Simulation Sensation Parlor!
Come down today and turn your dreams into REALITY!
Paradise
BLISS

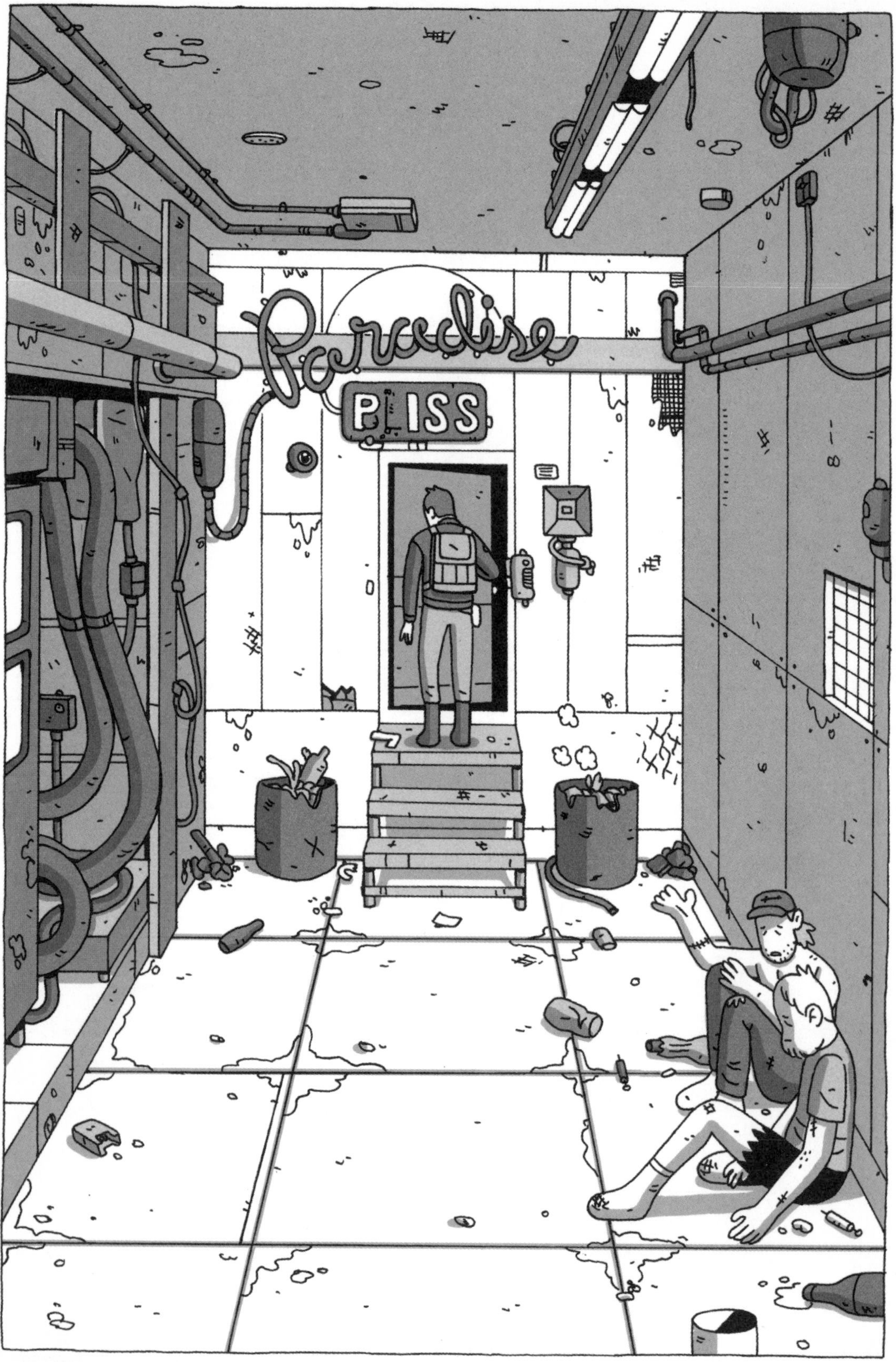
Paradise
P ISS

SNAG!
disconnect!
Oh shit ... neheh
DOMP!
Watch where you're FUCKING going, ASSHOLE!

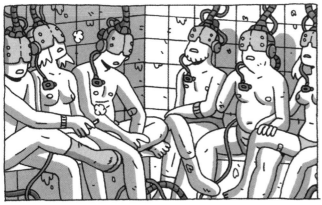

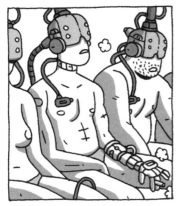

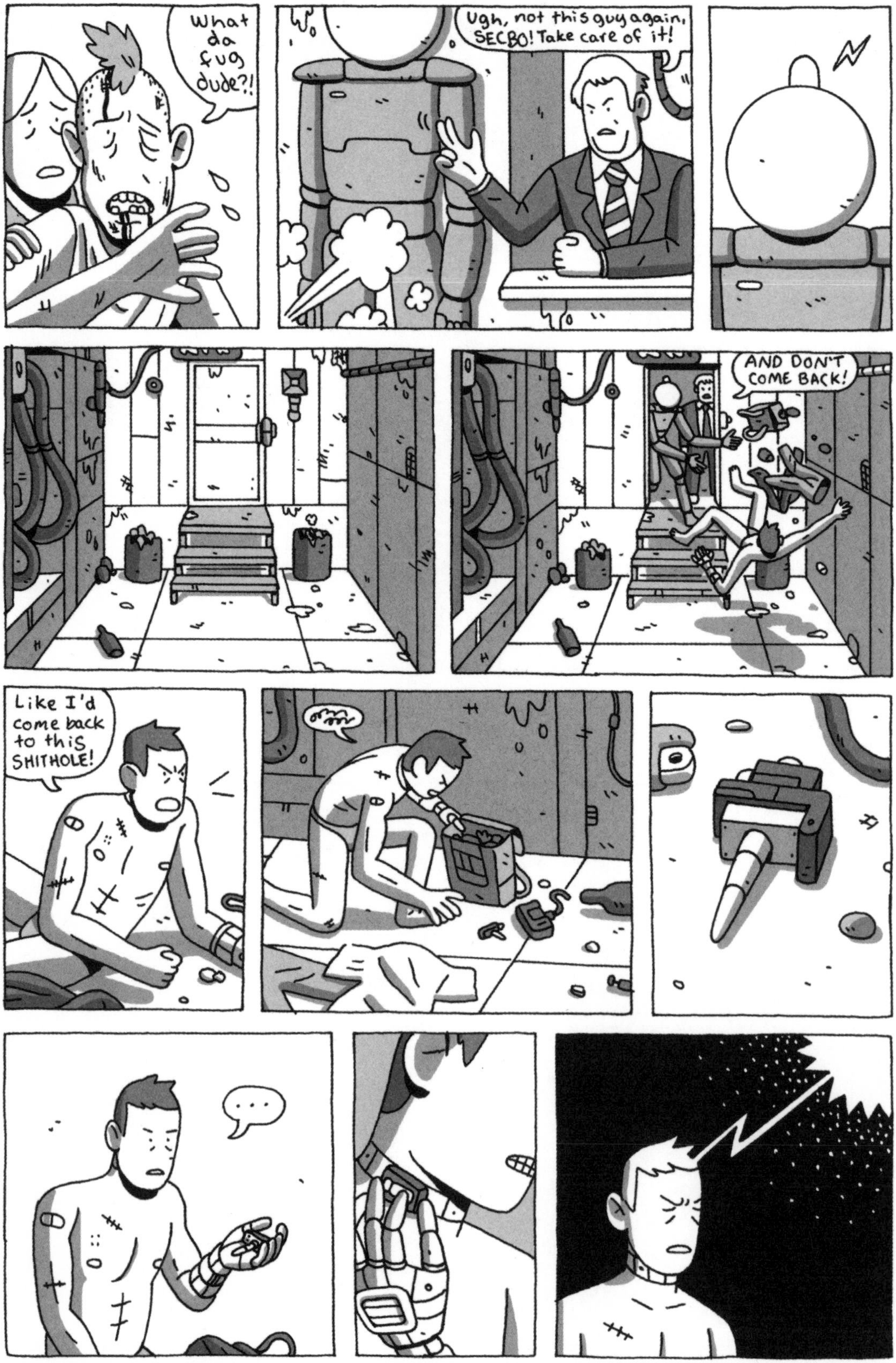
What da fug dude?!
Ugh, not this guy again, SECBO! Take care of it!
AND DON'T COME BACK!
Like I'd come back to this SHITHOLE!
...

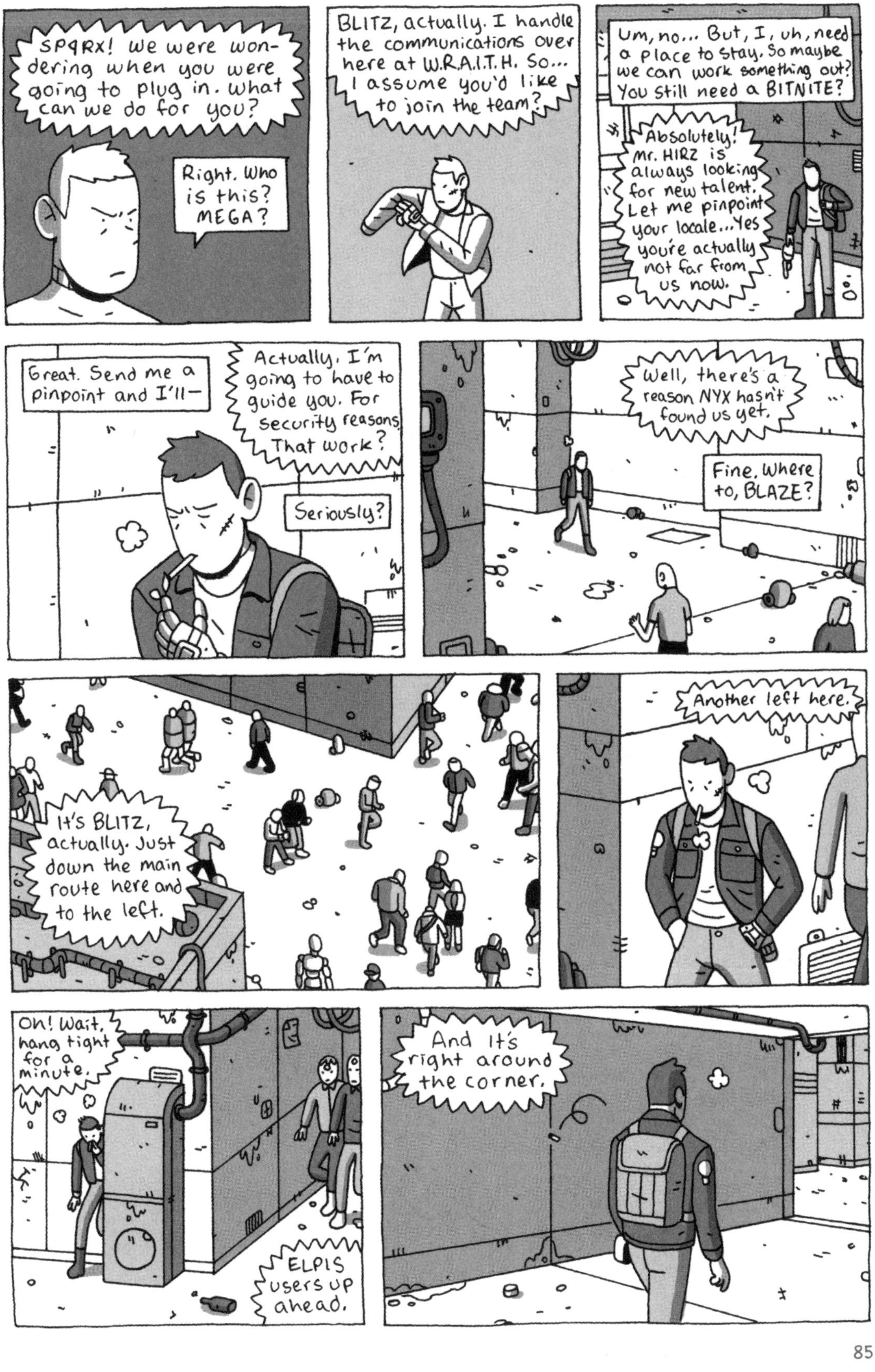
SP4RX! We were wondering when you were going to plug in. What can we do for you?
Right. Who is this? MEGA?
BLITZ, actually. I handle the communications over here at W.R.A.I.T.H. So... I assume you'd like to join the team?
Um, no... But, I, uh, need a place to stay. So maybe we can work something out? You still need a BITNITE?
Absolutely! Mr. HIRZ is always looking for new talent. Let me pinpoint your locale... Yes you're actually not far from us now.
Great. Send me a pinpoint and I'll—
Actually, I'm going to have to guide you. For security reasons. That work?
Seriously?
Well, there's a reason NYX hasn't found us yet.
Fine. Where to, BLAZE?
It's BLITZ, actually. Just down the main route here and to the left.
Another left here.
Oh! Wait, hang tight for a minute.
ELPIS users up ahead.
And it's right around the corner.

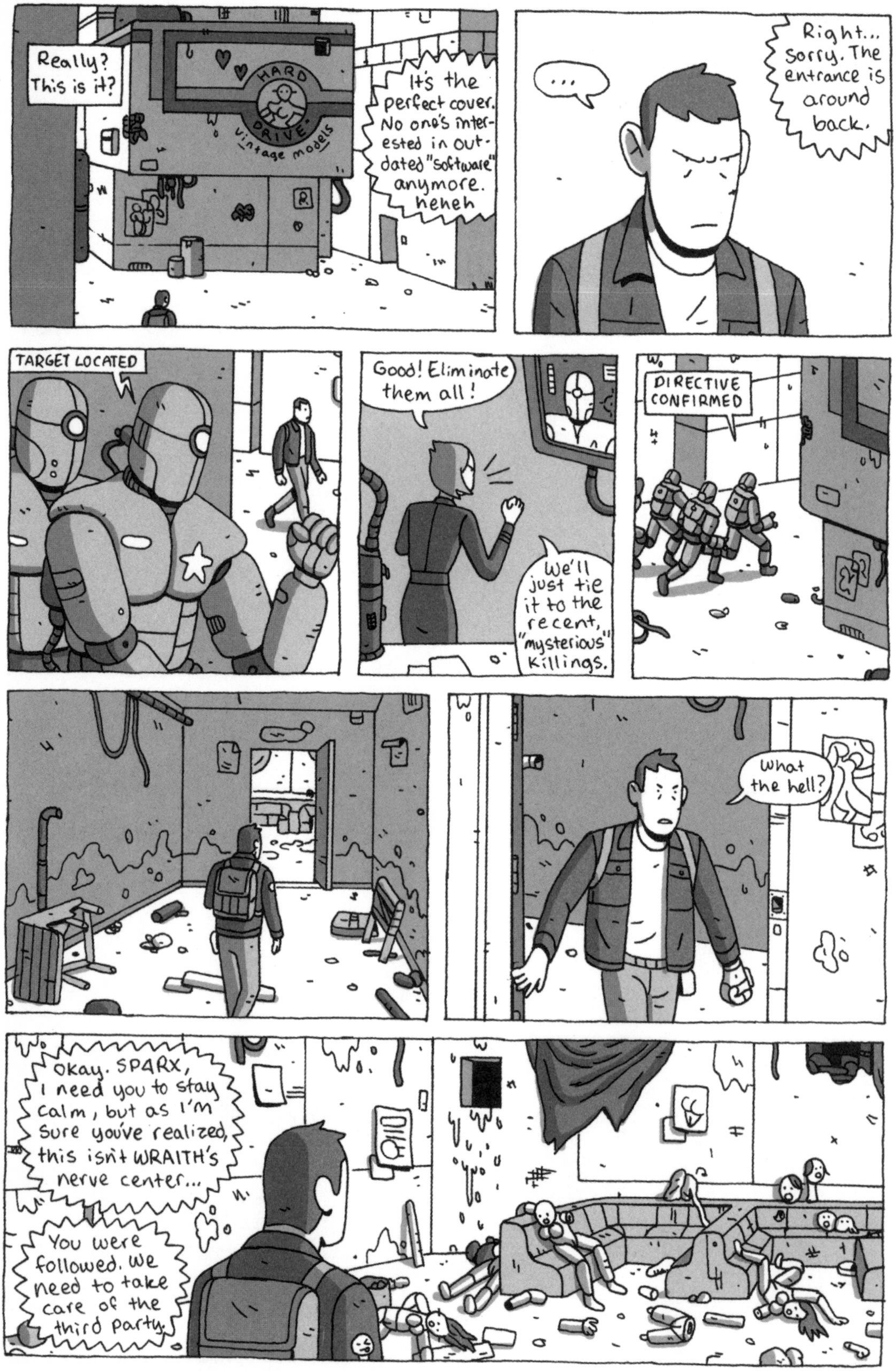
Really? This is it?
HARD DRIVE
Vintage models
It's the perfect cover. No one's interested in outdated "software" anymore. heheh
...
Right... Sorry. The entrance is around back.
TARGET LOCATED
Good! Eliminate them all!
We'll just tie it to the recent, "mysterious" killings.
DIRECTIVE CONFIRMED
What the hell?
Okay. SPARX, I need you to stay calm, but as I'm sure you've realized, this isn't WRAITH's nerve center...
You were followed. We need to take care of the third party.

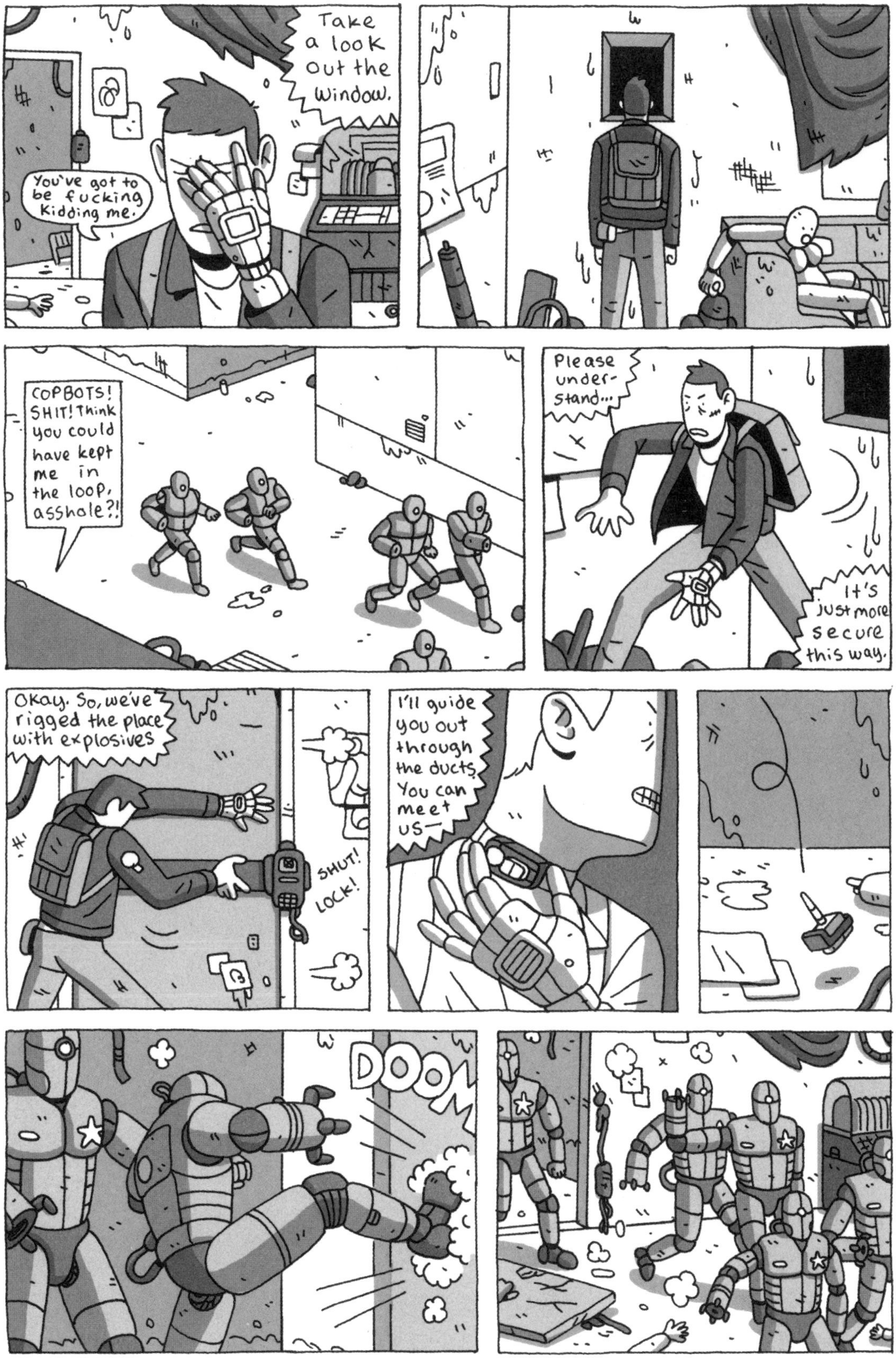
Take a look out the window.
You've got to be fucking kidding me.
COPBOTS! SHIT! Think you could have kept me in the loop, asshole?!
Please under-stand...
It's just more secure this way.
Okay. So, we've rigged the place with explosives
SHUT! LOCK!
I'll guide you out through the ducts. You can meet us—
DOOM

OBSOLETE SEXBOTS.

THERMOGRAPHICS PROCESSING. PROBE THE AREA.

NEURAL COMMUNICATION UNIT DISCOVERED.

HEAT SOURCE LOCATED. COMMENCE EVACUATION IMMEDIAT—

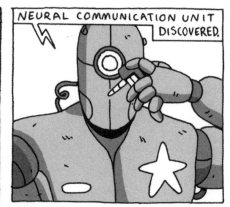

DOOM

GODDAMMIT! THAT USELESS HORDE OF TITANIUM EXCREMENT!

LEVI!

Discharge all the police bots in our service! Have them replaced with ELPIS USERS!

We need an assembly that can be properly controlled!

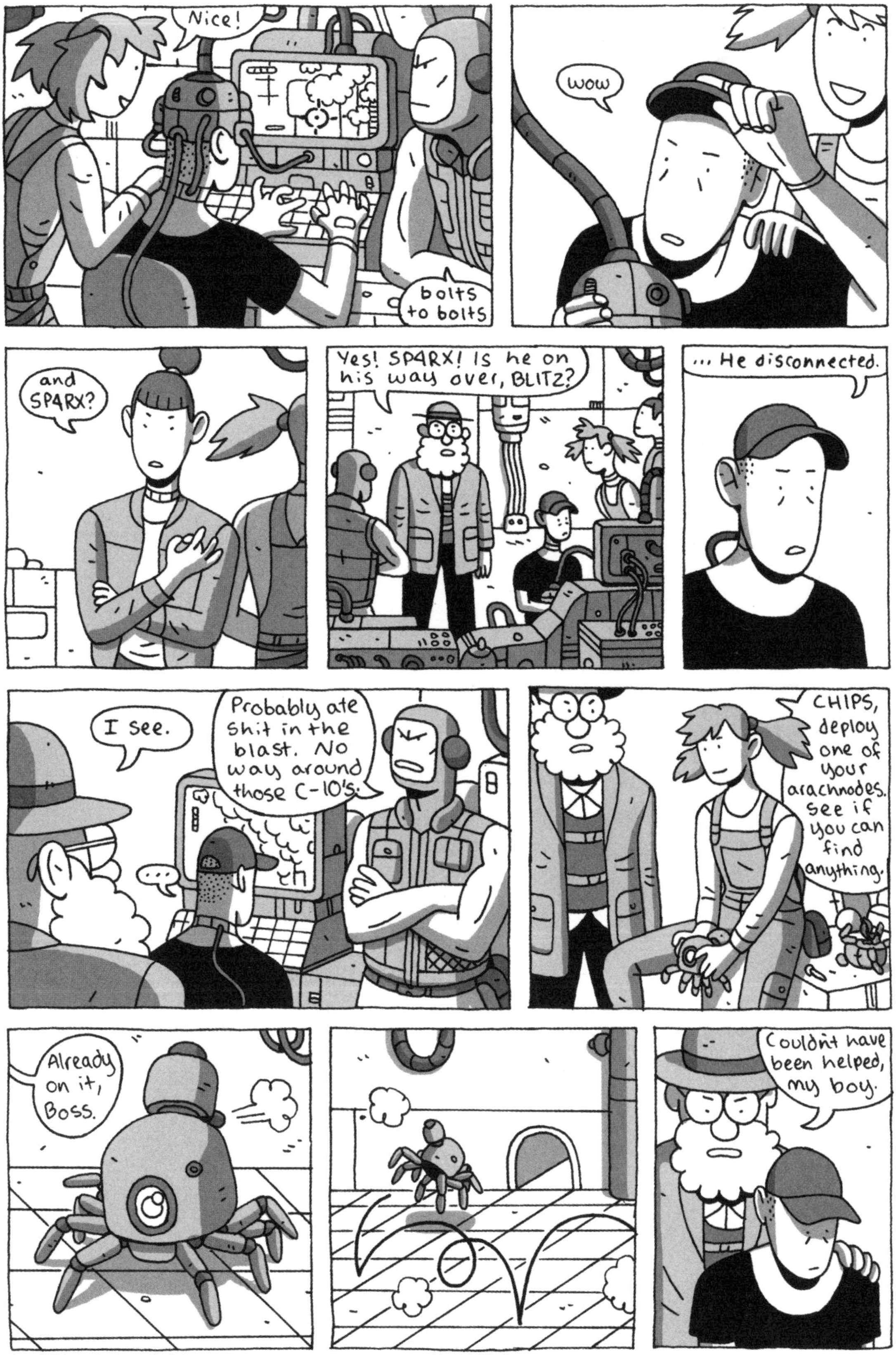
Nice!
bolts to bolts
wow
and SP4RX?
Yes! SP4RX! Is he on his way over, BLITZ?
... He disconnected.
I see.
...
Probably ate shit in the blast. No way around those C-10's.
CHIPS, deploy one of your arachnodes. See if you can find anything.
Already on it, Boss.
Couldn't have been helped, my boy.

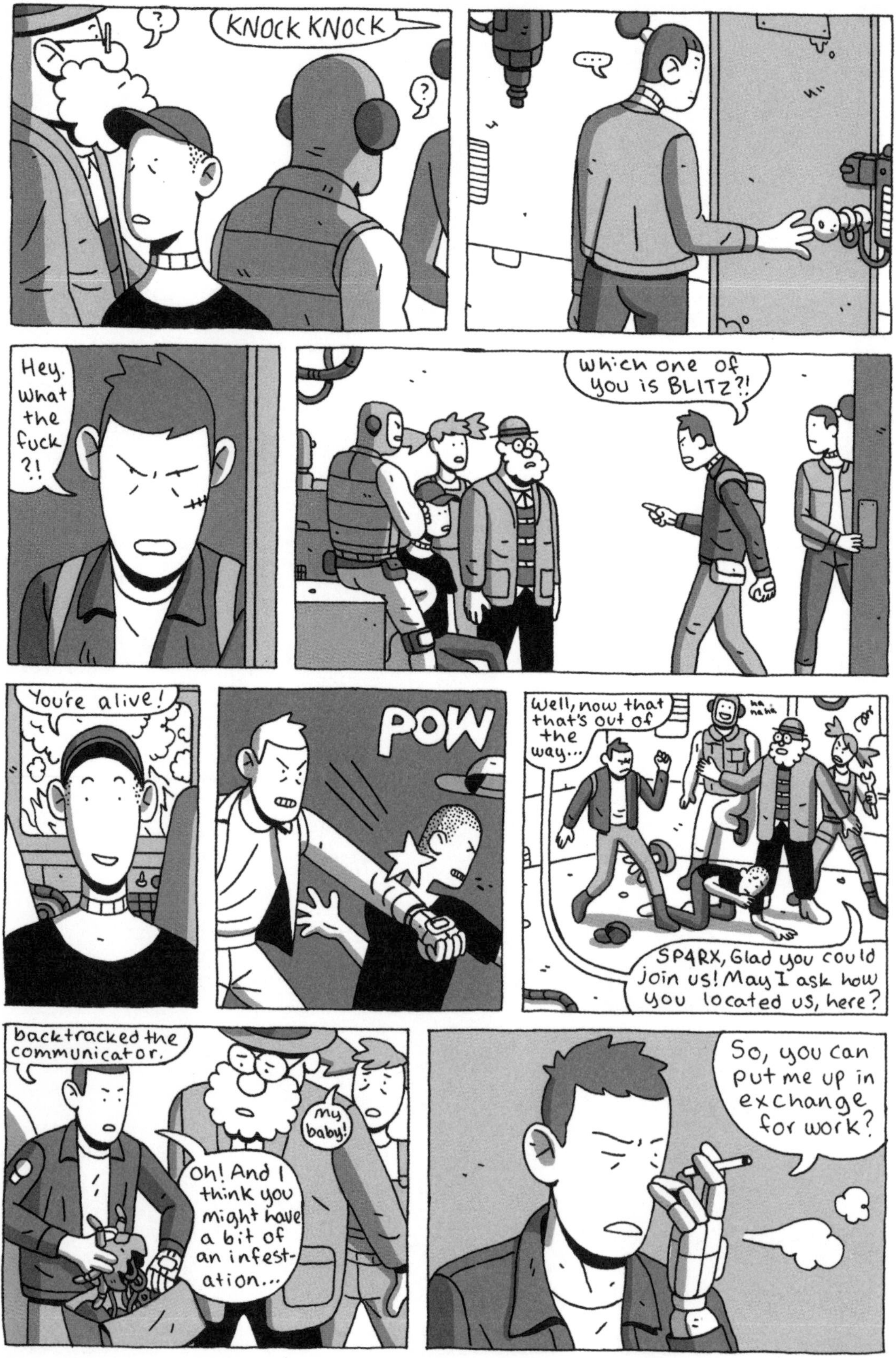
?
KNOCK KNOCK
?
...
Hey. What the fuck ?!
Which one of you is BLITZ?!
You're alive!
POW
Well, now that that's out of the way...
SP4RX, Glad you could join us! May I ask how you located us, here?
backtracked the communicator.
my baby!
Oh! And I think you might have a bit of an infestation...
So, you can put me up in exchange for work?

Not only that, SP4RX, but we can offer you an opportunity to put free- dom back in the hands of the people to squash the bureau- cratic ministry lording over AVA LON to deliv er the pe just

That asshole better be good.

Haha He's okay by me.

Yeah, look, I don't really care about any of that.

I'll do whatever you want. I just need a place to crash.

Very well.

Let me give you a proper intro- duction to every- one.

CHIPS mechanical engineer

BLITZ commun- ications & surveilance

MADDOG man-at -arms

MEGA systems engineer

MEGA, can you show SP4RX where he'll be working?

It's being used for storage right now, but if you just rearrange a little...

no, yeah, it's... it'll work.

So, we'll get to work in the morning.

yeah.

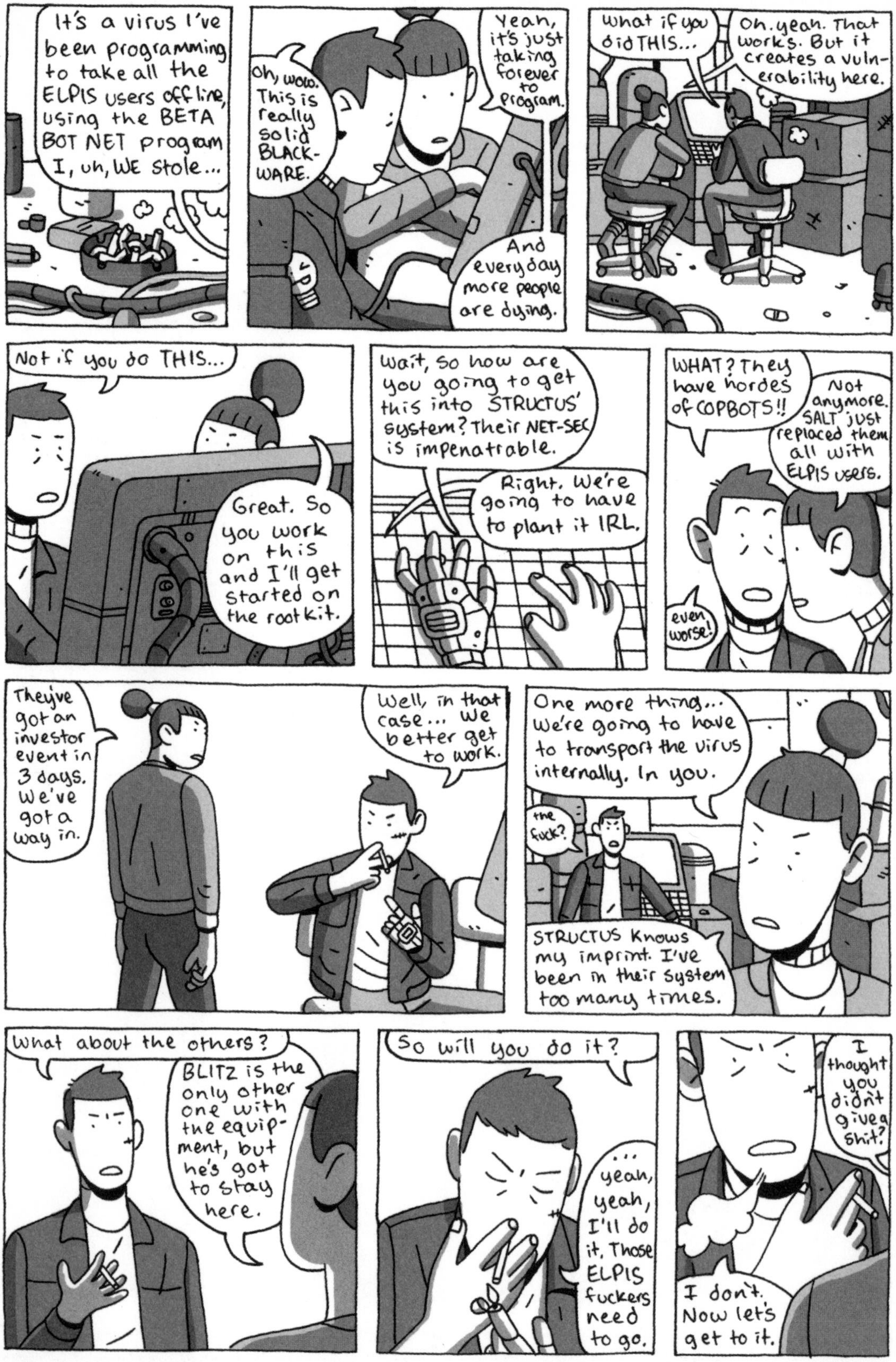
It's a virus I've been programming to take all the ELPIS users offline, using the BETA BOT NET program I, uh, WE stole...
Oh, wow. This is really solid BLACK-WARE.
Yeah, it's just taking forever to program.
And everyday more people are dying.
What if you did THIS...
Oh. yeah. That works. But it creates a vulnerability here.
Not if you do THIS...
Great. So you work on this and I'll get started on the rootkit.
Wait, so how are you going to get this into STRUCTUS' system? Their NET-SEC is impenatrable.
Right. We're going to have to plant it IRL.
WHAT? They have hordes of COPBOTS!!
Not anymore. SALT just replaced them all with ELPIS users.
even worse!
They've got an investor event in 3 days. We've got a way in.
Well, in that case... we better get to work.
One more thing... We're going to have to transport the virus internally. In you.
the fuck?
STRUCTUS knows my imprint. I've been in their system too many times.
What about the others?
BLITZ is the only other one with the equipment, but he's got to stay here.
So will you do it?
... yeah, yeah, I'll do it. Those ELPIS fuckers need to go.
I thought you didn't give a shit?
I don't. Now let's get to it.

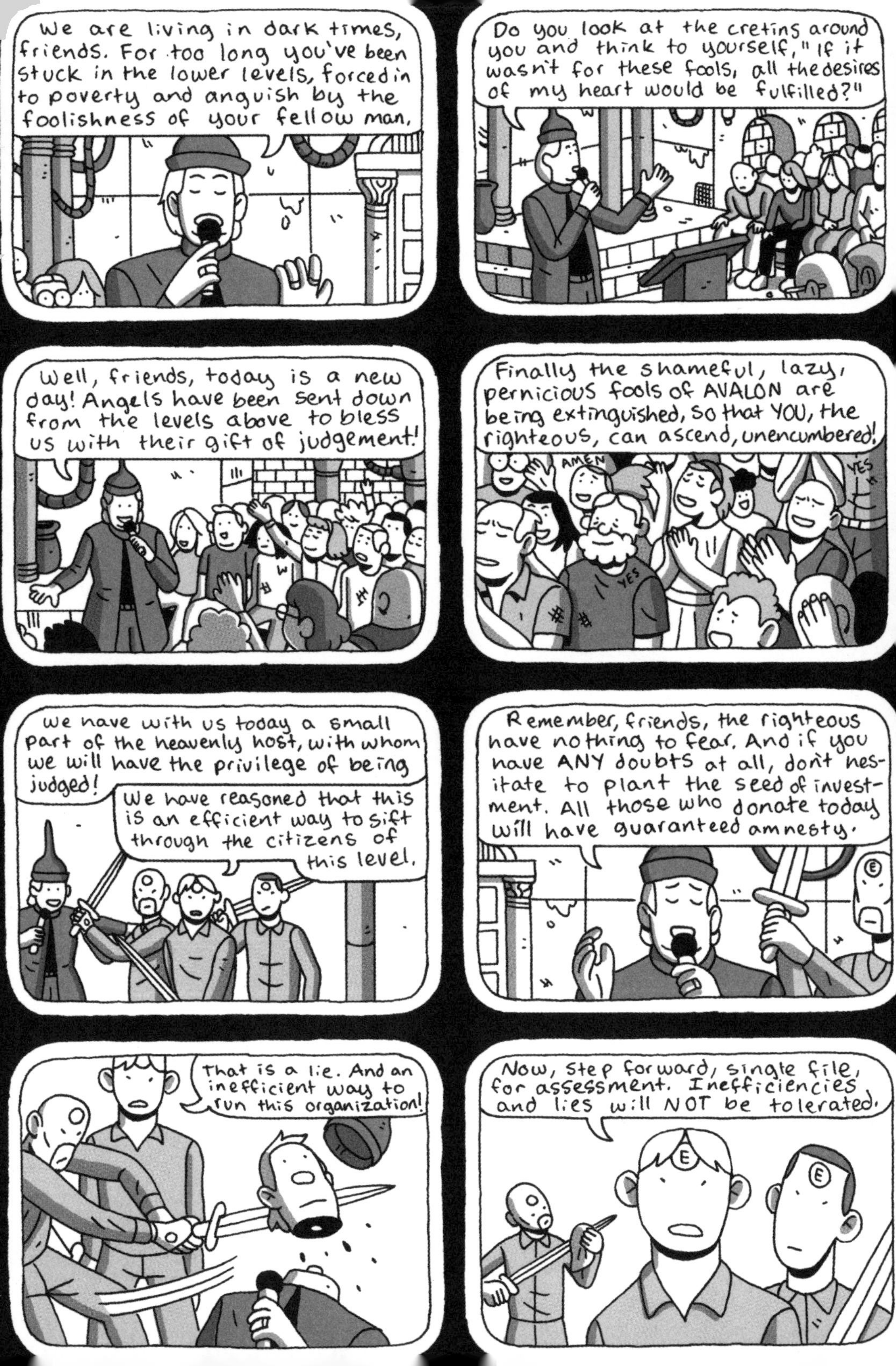
We are living in dark times, friends. For too long you've been stuck in the lower levels, forced in to poverty and anguish by the foolishness of your fellow man,
Do you look at the cretins around you and think to yourself, "If it wasn't for these fools, all the desires of my heart would be fulfilled?"
Well, friends, today is a new day! Angels have been sent down from the levels above to bless us with their gift of judgement!
Finally the shameful, lazy, pernicious fools of AVALON are being extinguished, so that YOU, the righteous, can ascend, unencumbered!
AMEN
YES
YES
We have with us today a small part of the heavenly host, with whom we will have the privilege of being judged!
We have reasoned that this is an efficient way to sift through the citizens of this level.
Remember, friends, the righteous have nothing to fear. And if you have ANY doubts at all, don't hesitate to plant the seed of investment. All those who donate today will have guaranteed amnesty.
That is a lie. And an inefficient way to run this organization!
Now, step forward, single file, for assessment. Inefficiencies and lies will NOT be tolerated.

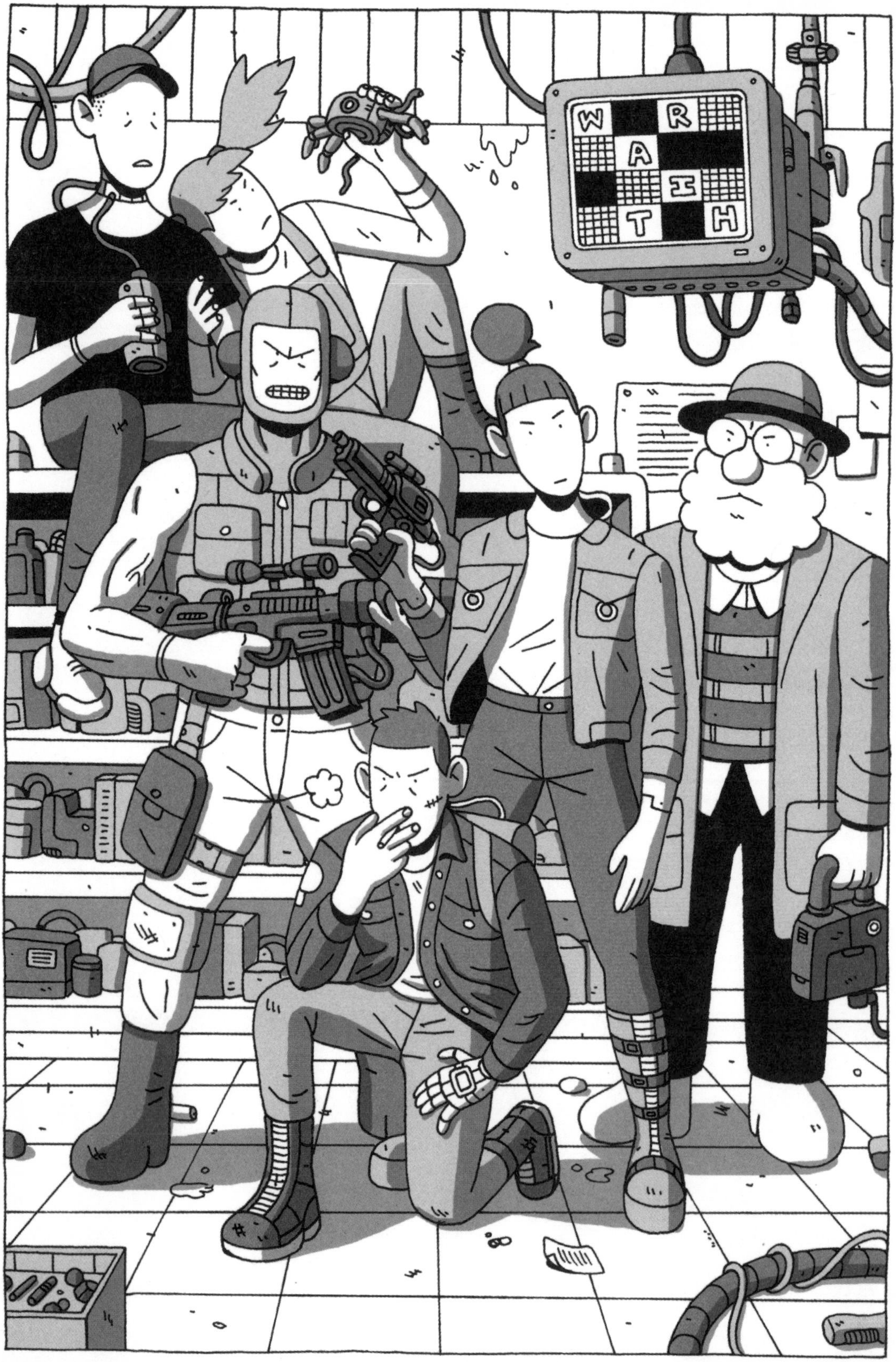
W R
A
I
T H

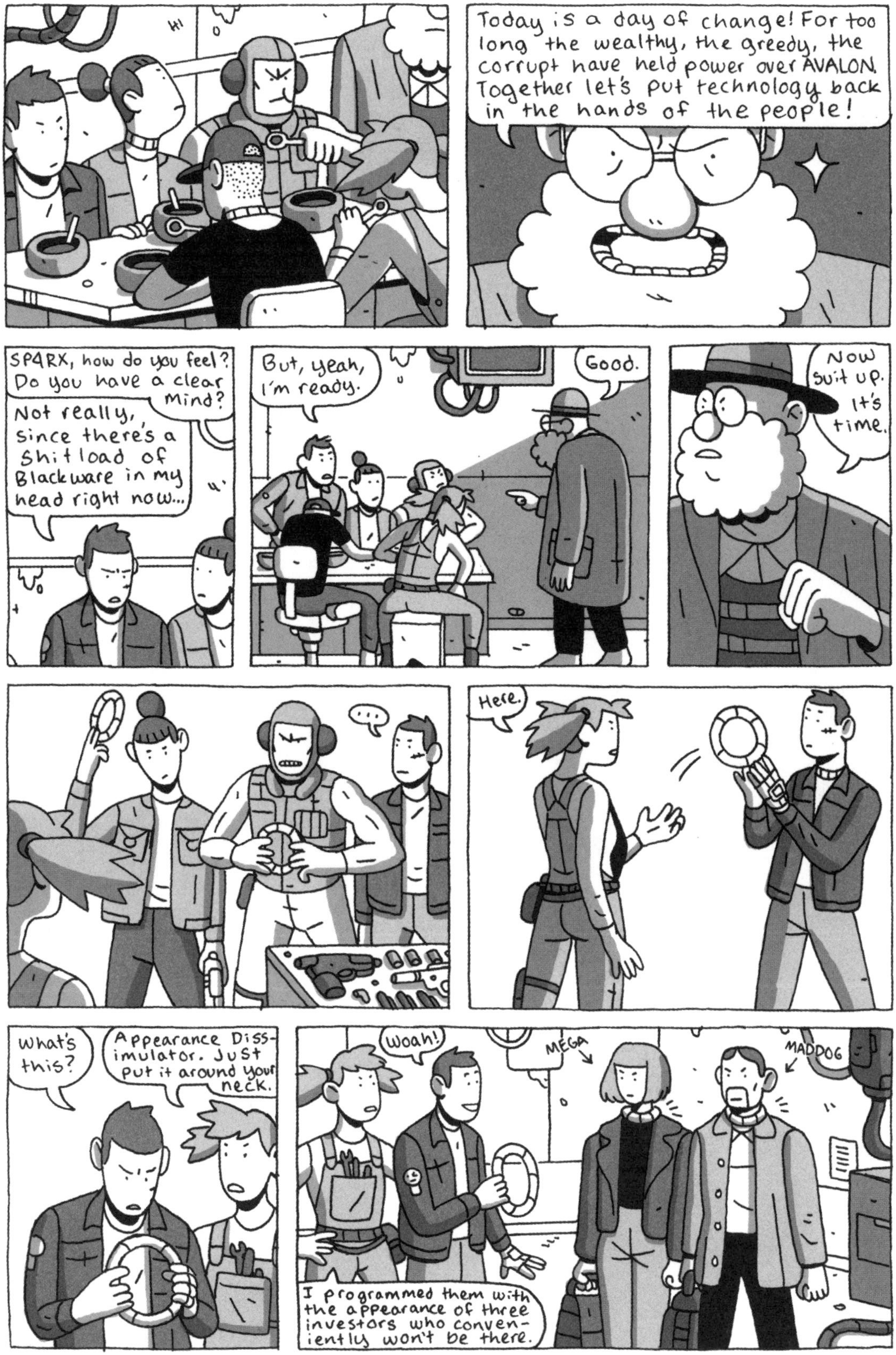

Hi
Today is a day of change! For too long the wealthy, the greedy, the corrupt have held power over AVALON. Together let's put technology back in the hands of the people!
SP4RX, how do you feel? Do you have a clear mind?
Not really, since there's a shitload of Blackware in my head right now...
But, yeah, I'm ready.
Good.
Now suit up. It's time.
Here.
What's this?
Appearance Dissimulator. Just put it around your neck.
Woah!
MEGA
MADDOG
I programmed them with the appearance of three investors who conveniently won't be there.

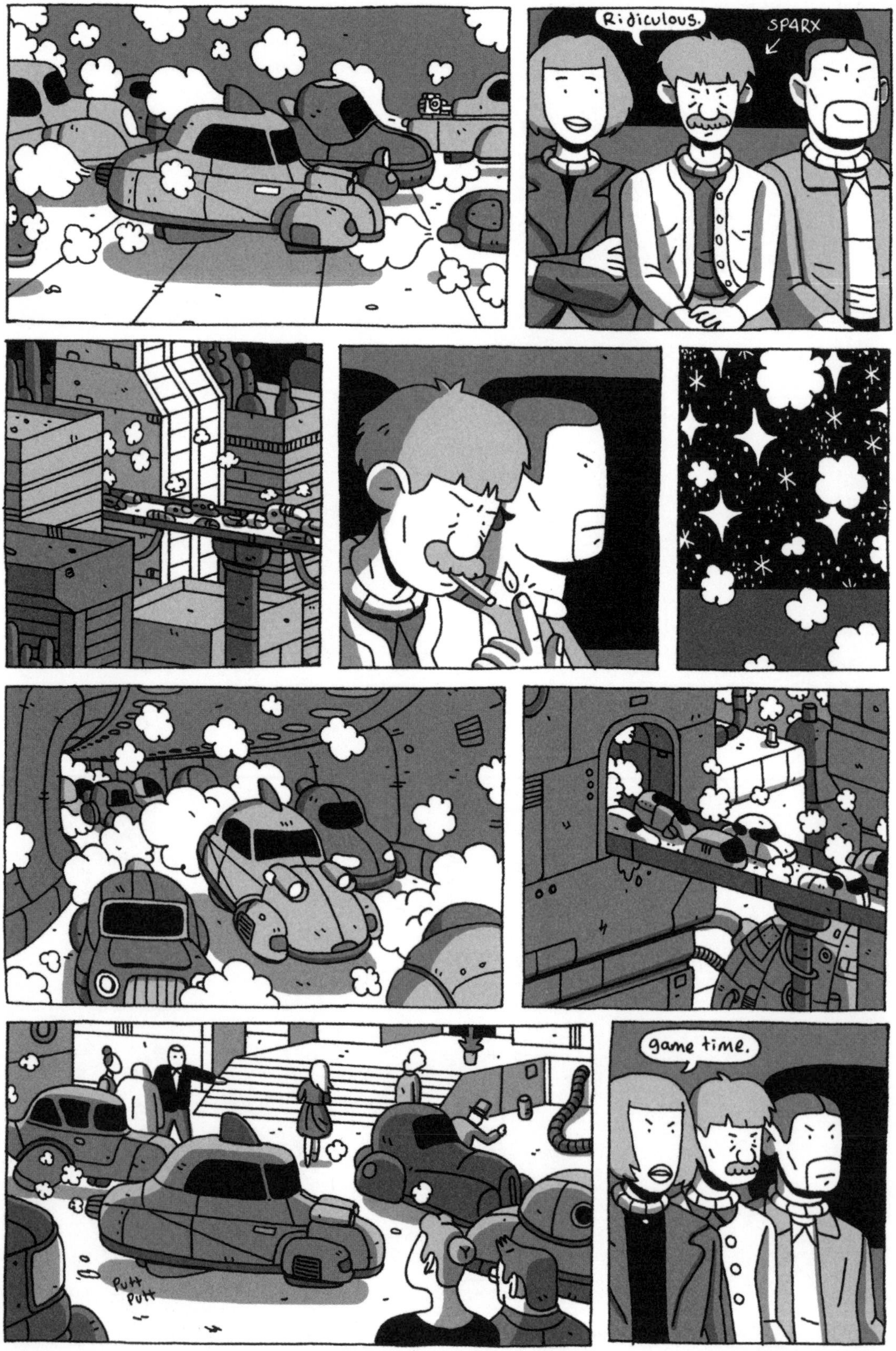
Ridiculous.
SPARX
game time.
Putt Putt

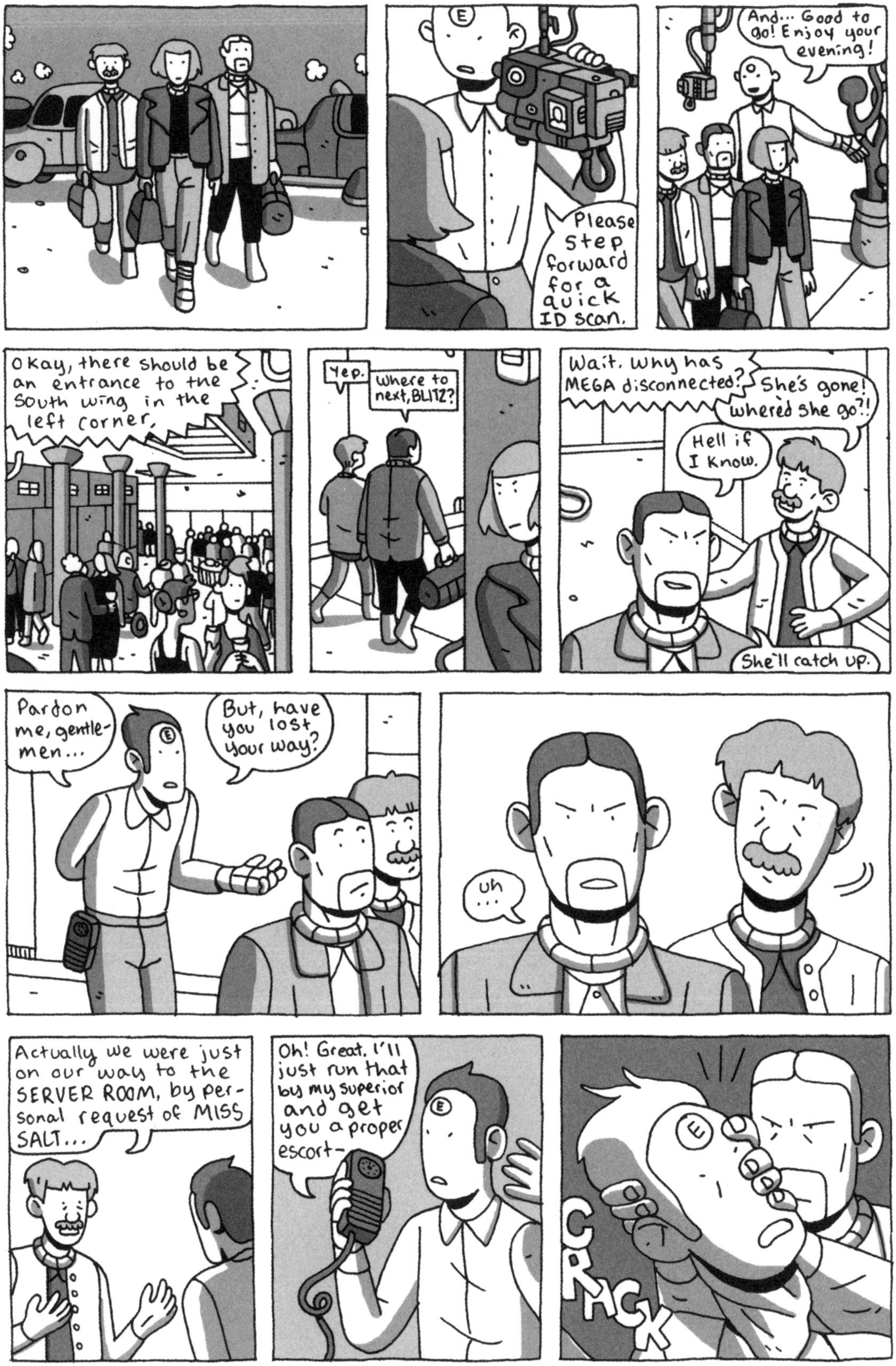
Please step forward for a quick ID scan.
And... Good to go! Enjoy your evening!
Okay, there should be an entrance to the South wing in the left corner,
Yep.
Where to next, BLITZ?
Wait. Why has MEGA disconnected?
She's gone! where'd she go?!
Hell if I know.
She'll catch up.
Pardon me, gentlemen...
But, have you lost your way?
uh ...
Actually we were just on our way to the SERVER ROOM, by personal request of MISS SALT...
Oh! Great. I'll just run that by my superior and get you a proper escort-
CRACK

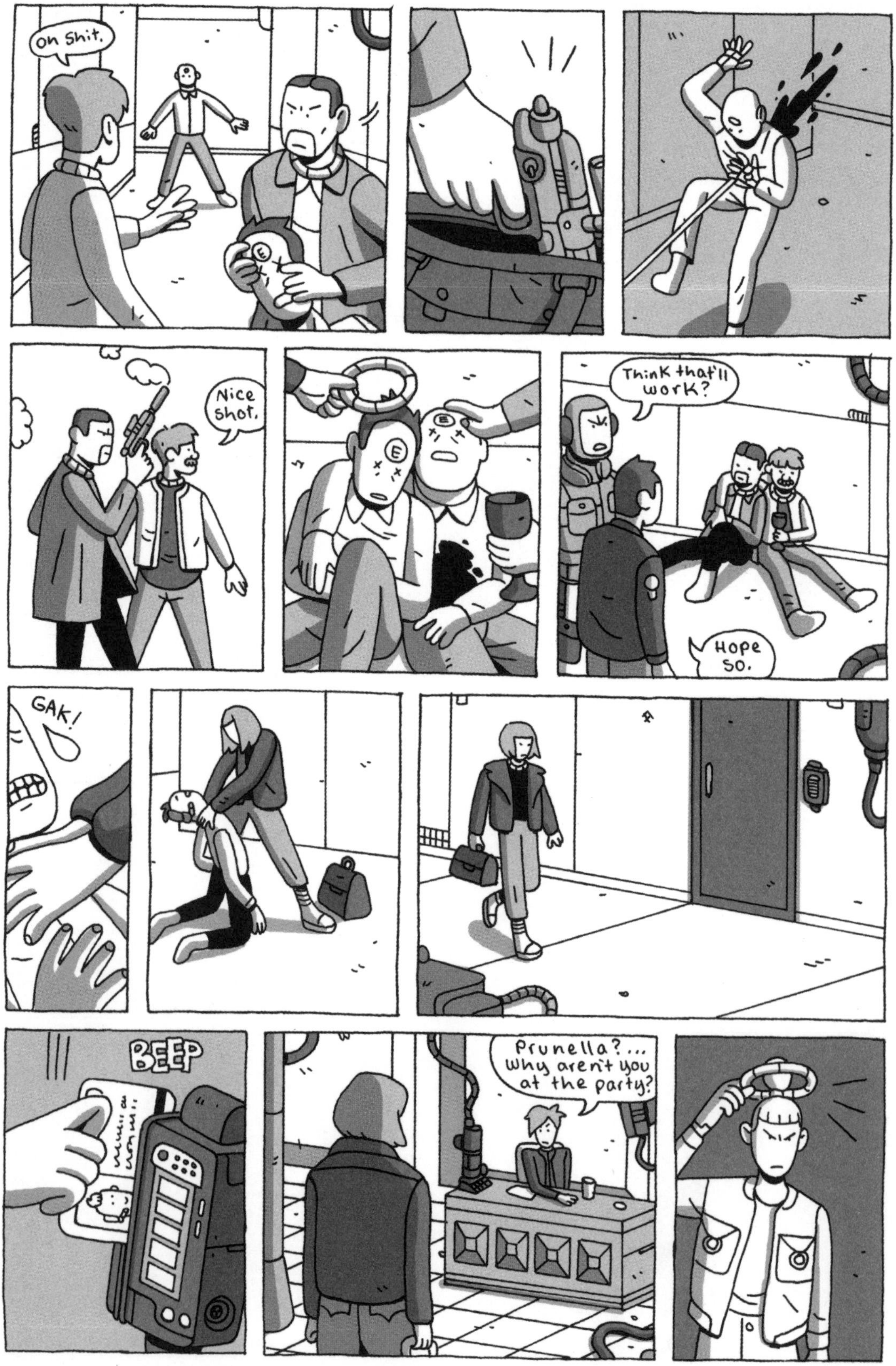
Oh Shit.
Nice shot.
Think that'll work?
Hope so.
GAK!
BEEP
Prunella?... Why aren't you at the party?

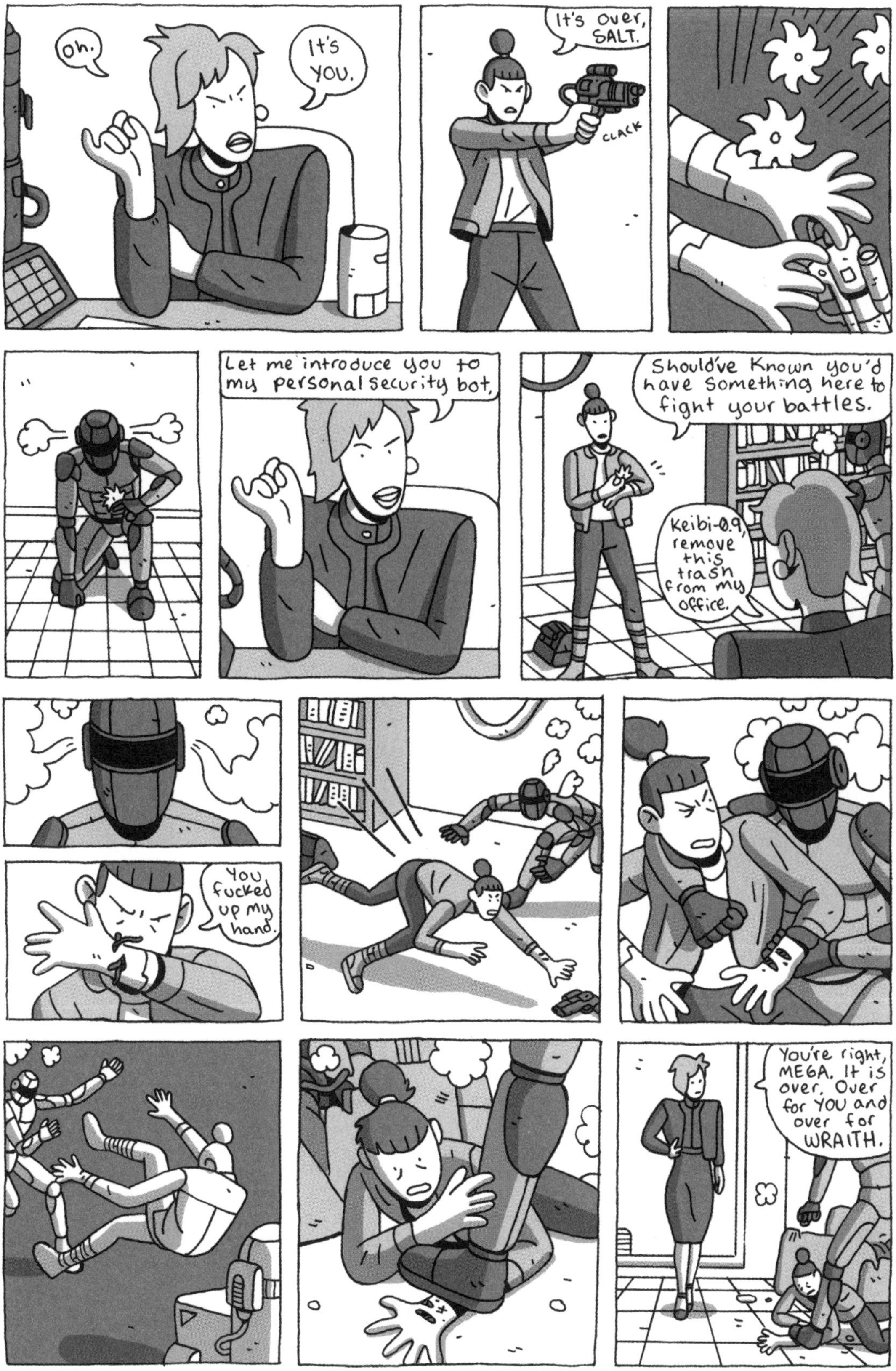
Oh.
It's you.
It's over, SALT.
CLACK
Let me introduce you to my personal security bot,
Should've Known you'd have Something here to fight your battles.
Keibi-0.9, remove this trash from my office.
You fucked up my hand.
You're right, MEGA. It is over. Over for YOU and over for WRAITH.

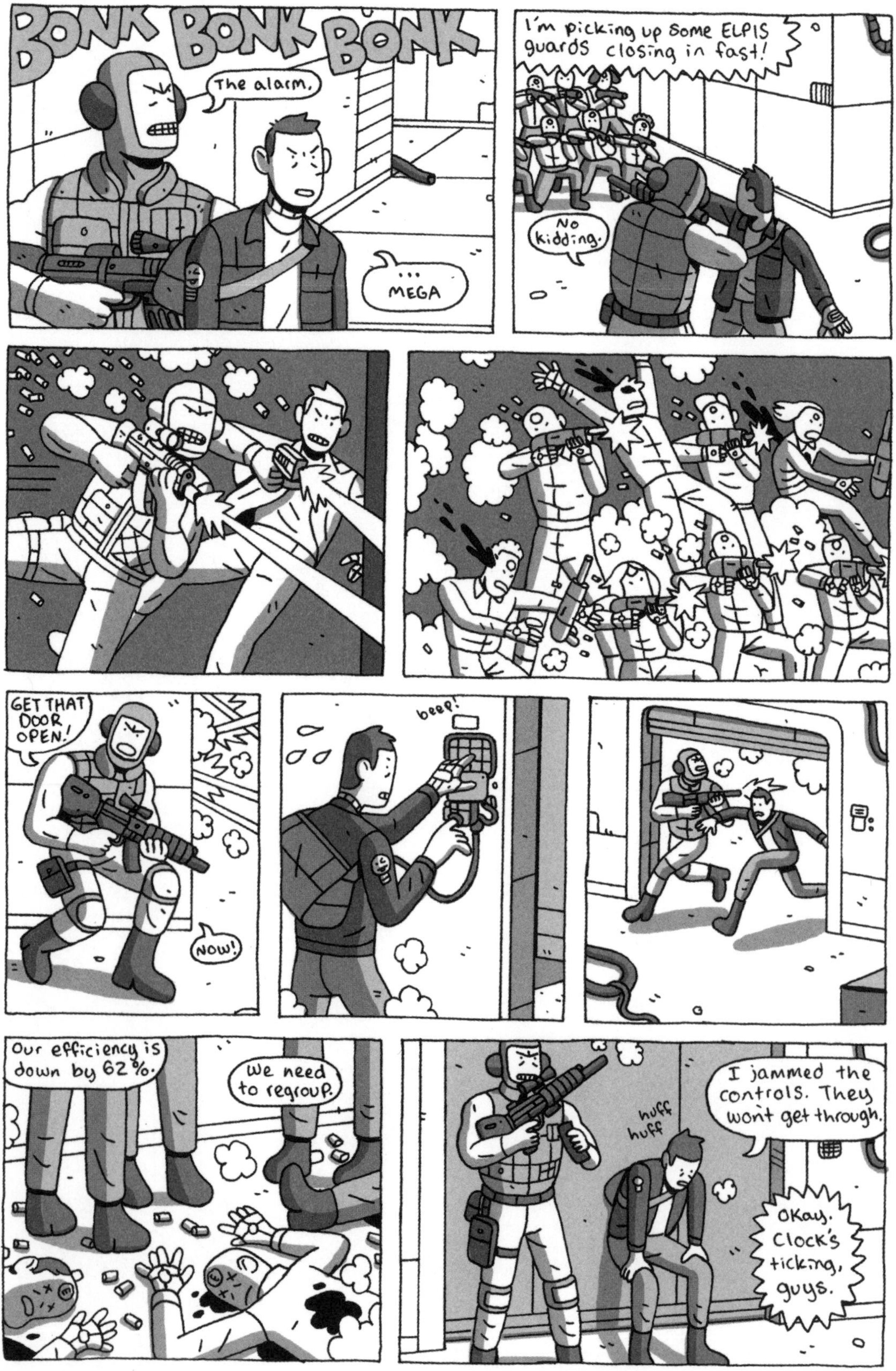
BONK BONK BONK
The alarm.
... MEGA
I'm picking up some ELPIS guards closing in fast!
No kidding.
GET THAT DOOR OPEN!
NOW!
beep!
Our efficiency is down by 62%.
We need to regroup.
huff huff
I jammed the controls. They won't get through.
Okay. Clock's ticking, guys.

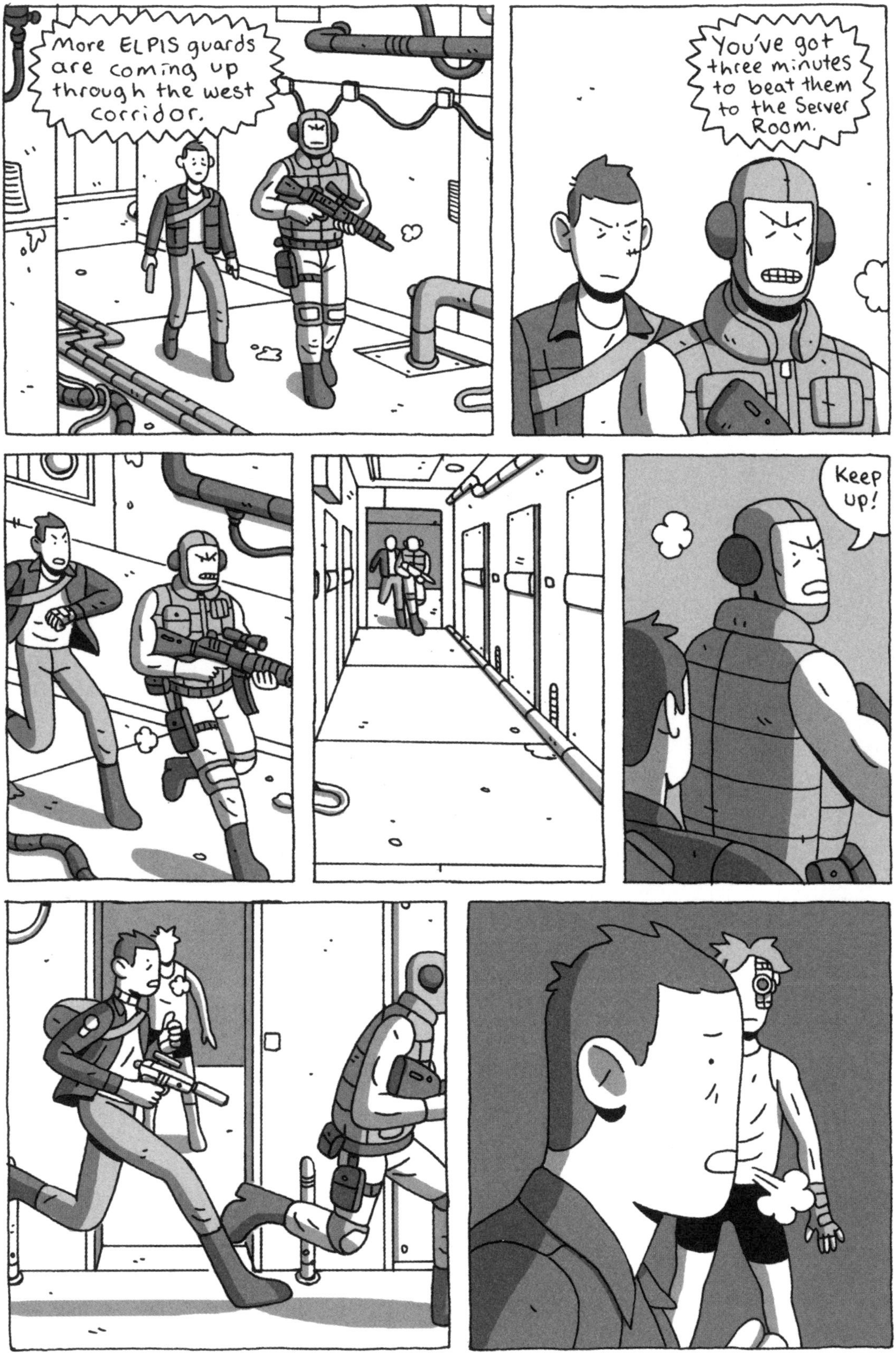
More ELPIS guards are coming up through the west corridor.
You've got three minutes to beat them to the Server Room.
Keep up!

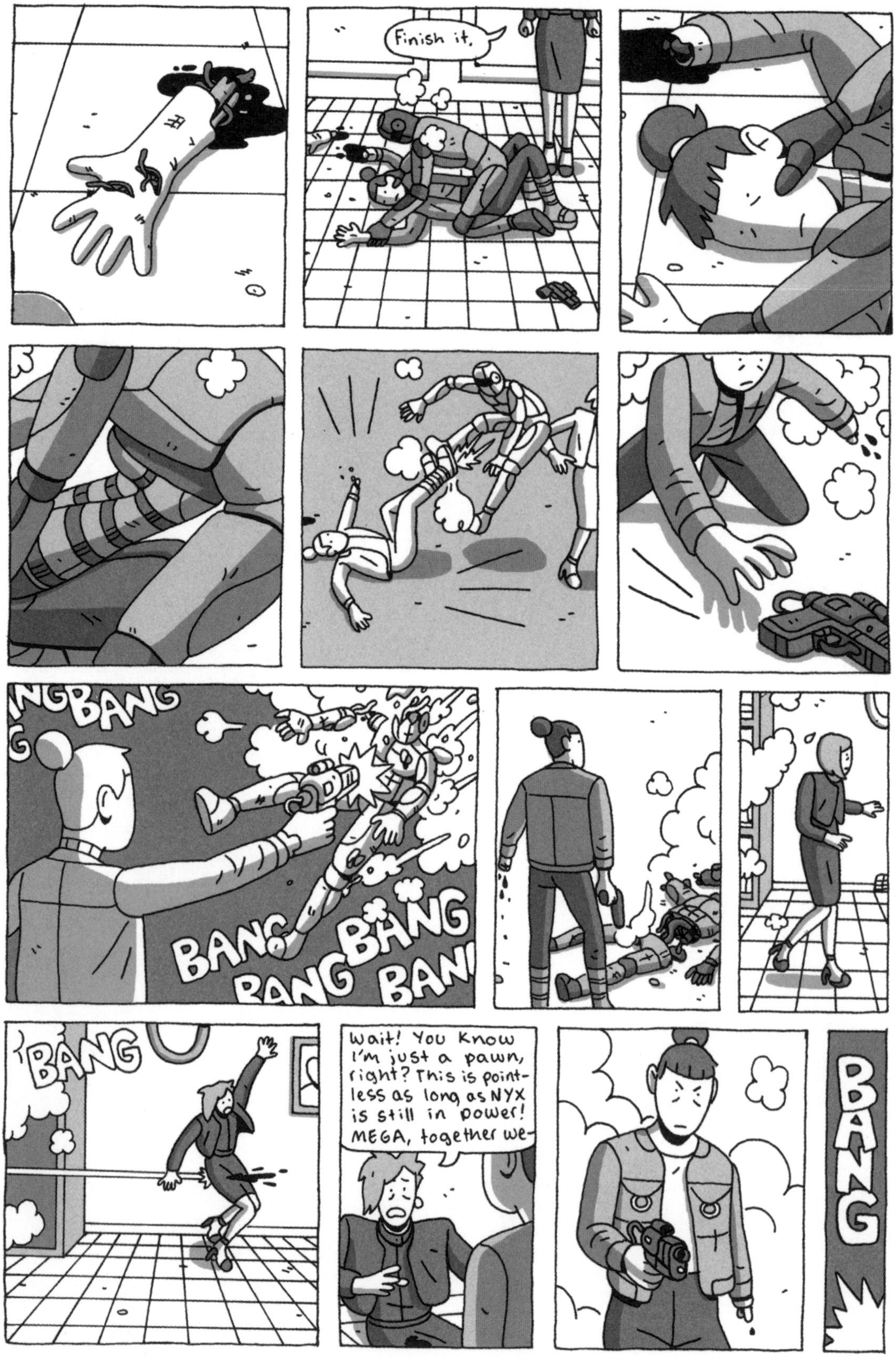
Finish it.
BANG BANG
BANG BANG
BANG BANG BAN
BANG
Wait! You know I'm just a pawn, right? This is pointless as long as NYX is still in power! MEGA, together we-
BANG

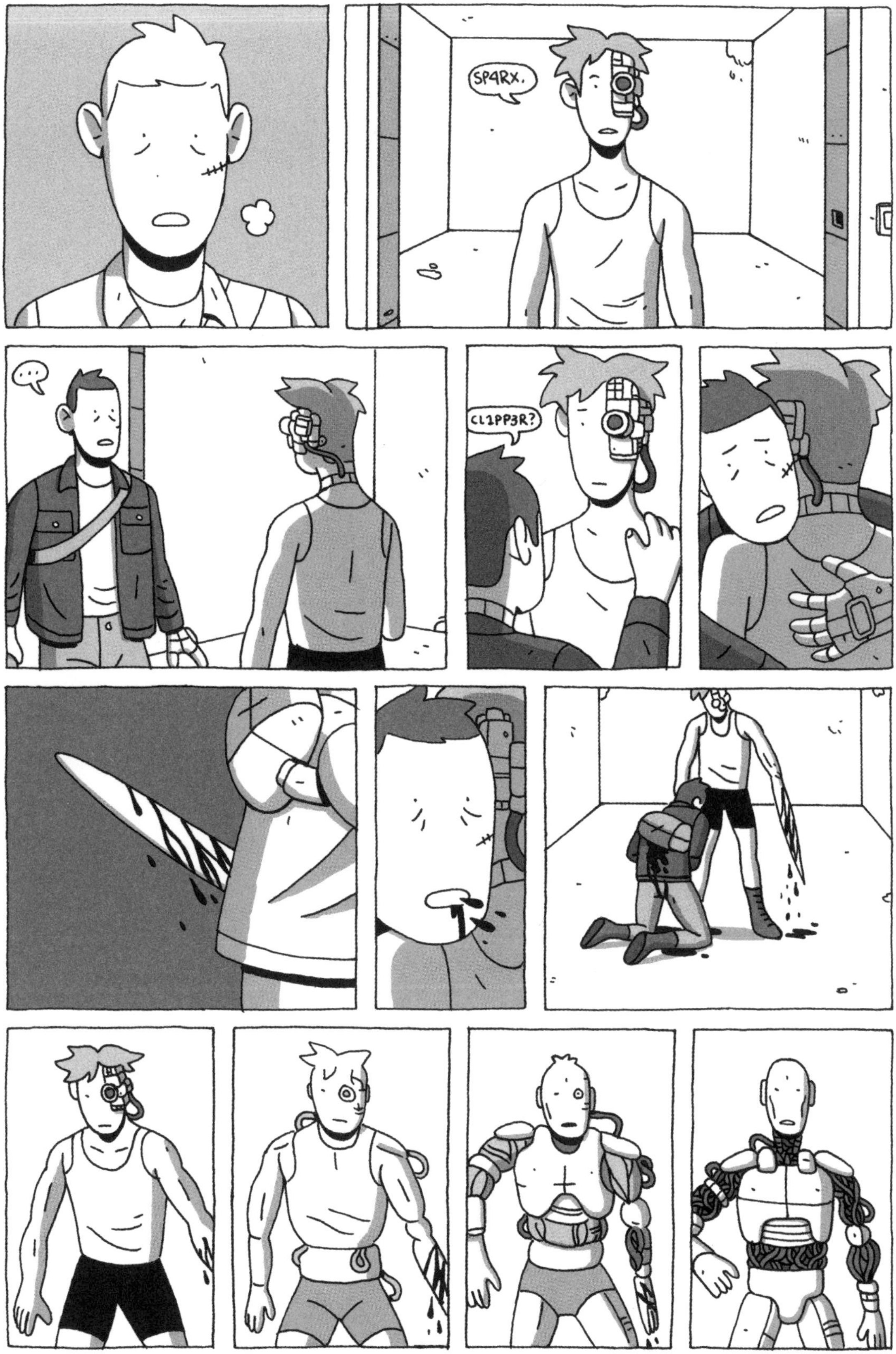
SP4RX.
CL1PP3R?

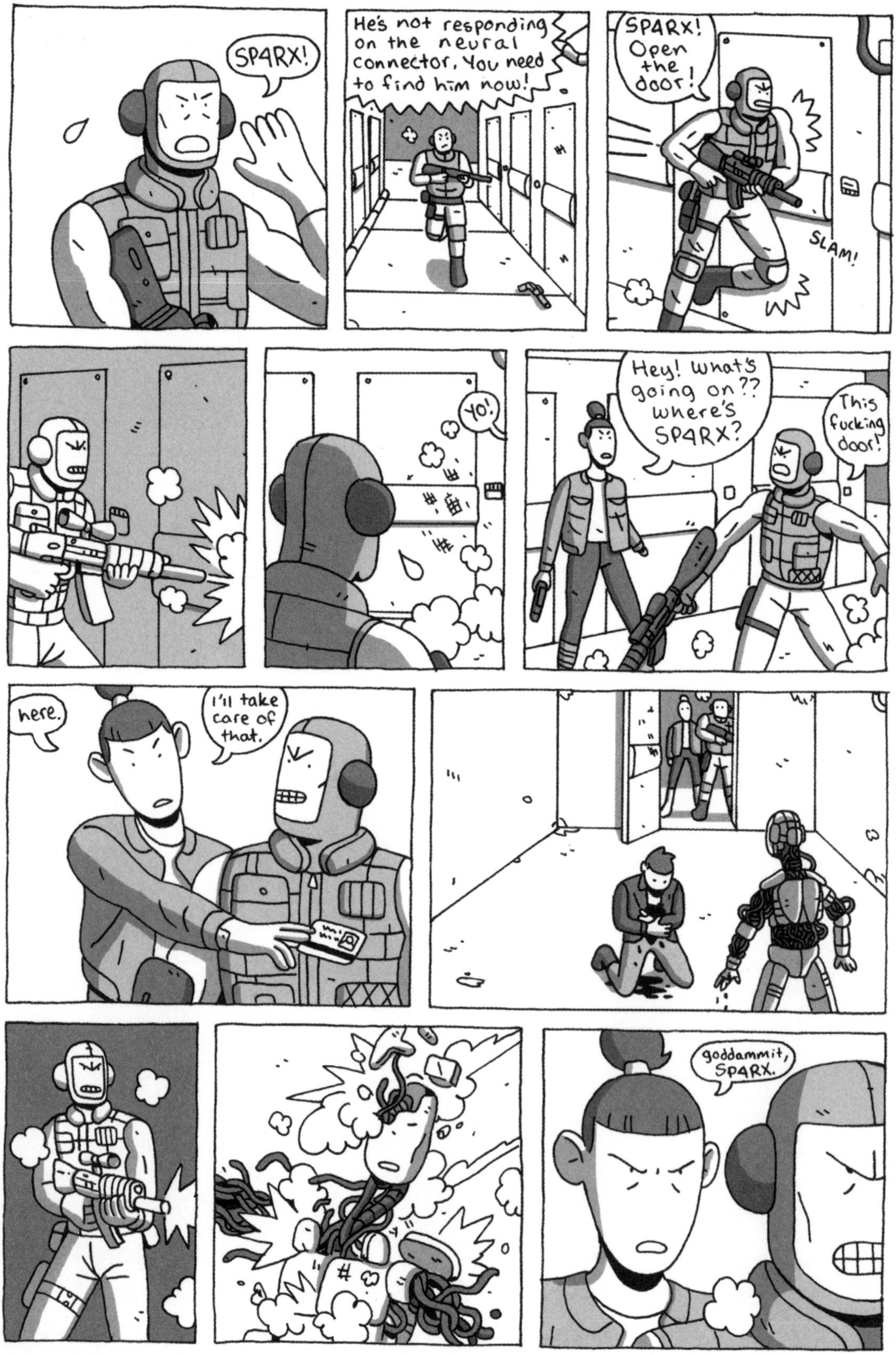

SP4RX!
He's not responding on the neural connector. You need to find him now!
SP4RX! Open the door!
SLAM!
YO!
Hey! What's going on?? Where's SP4RX?
This fucking door!
here.
I'll take care of that.
goddammit, SP4RX.

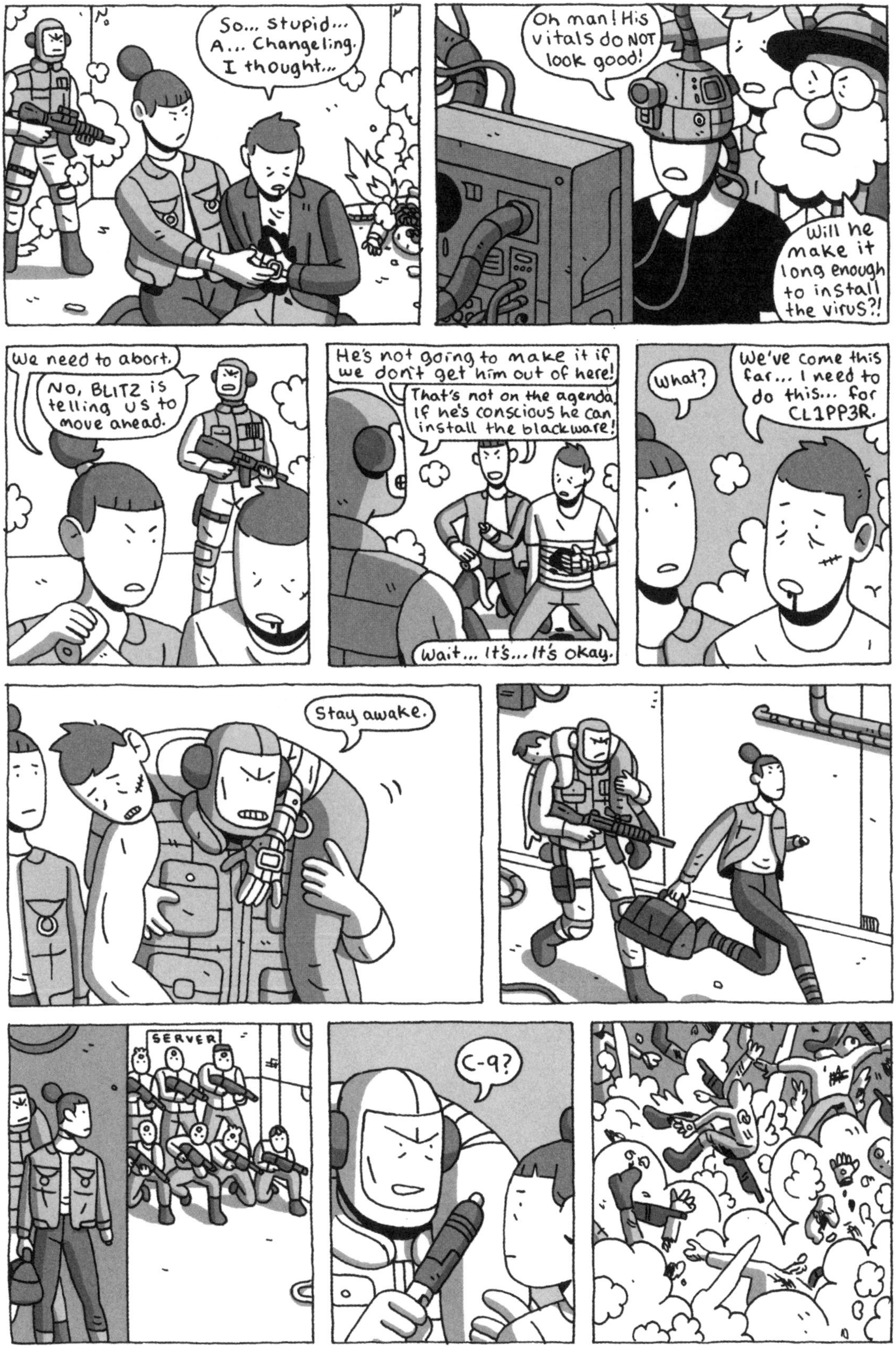

So... stupid... A... Changeling. I thought...
Oh man! His vitals do NOT look good!
Will he make it long enough to install the virus?!
We need to abort.
No, BLITZ is telling us to move ahead.
He's not going to make it if we don't get him out of here!
That's not on the agenda. If he's conscious he can install the blackware!
Wait... It's... It's okay.
What?
We've come this far... I need to do this... for CL1PP3R.
Stay awake.
SERVER
C-9?

I'll help him plug in. You stand guard

Roger.

Ready?

As I'll ever be, ... I guess

heh.

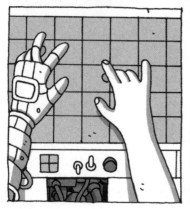

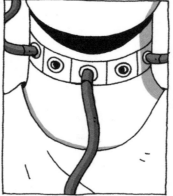

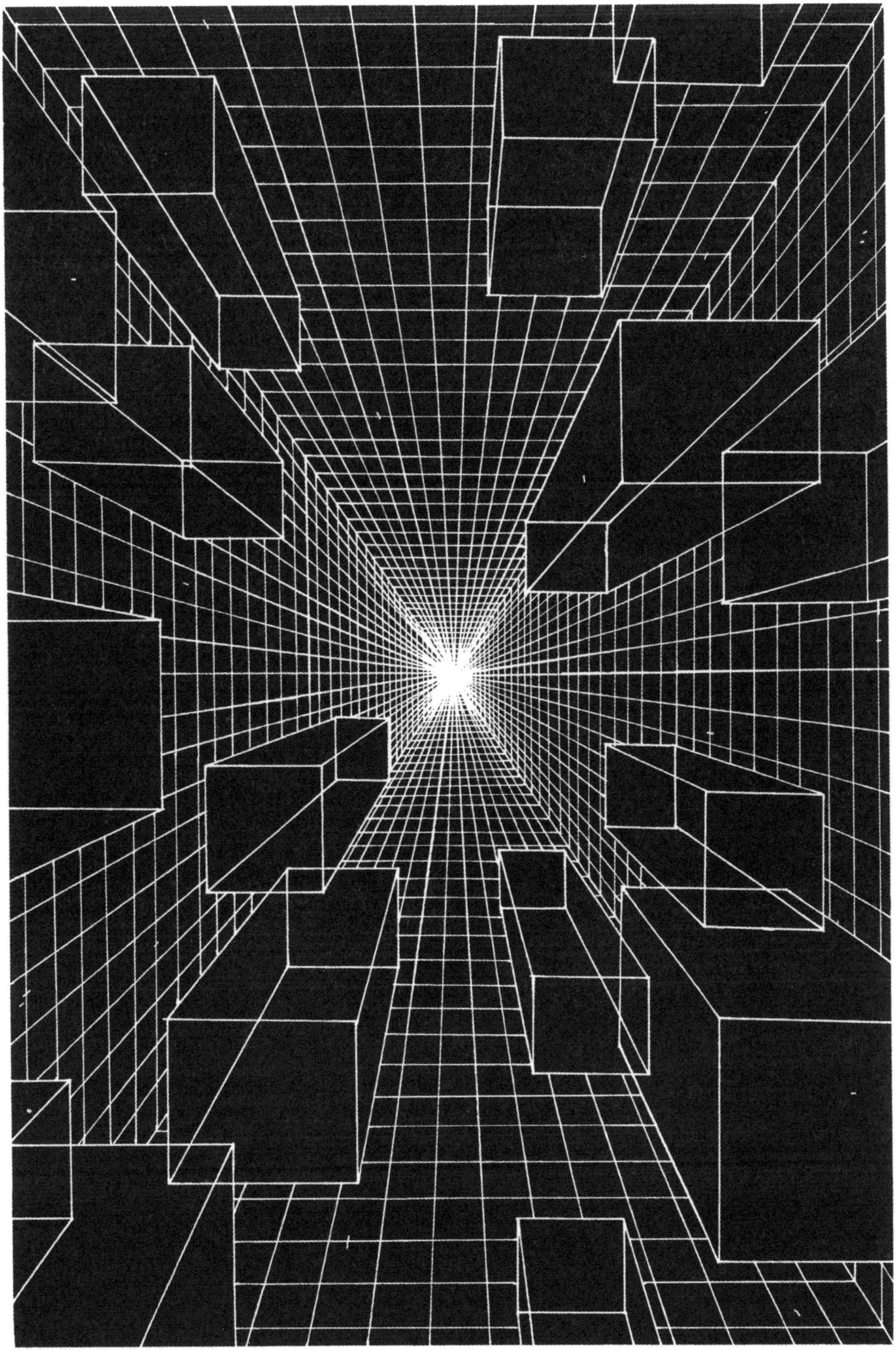

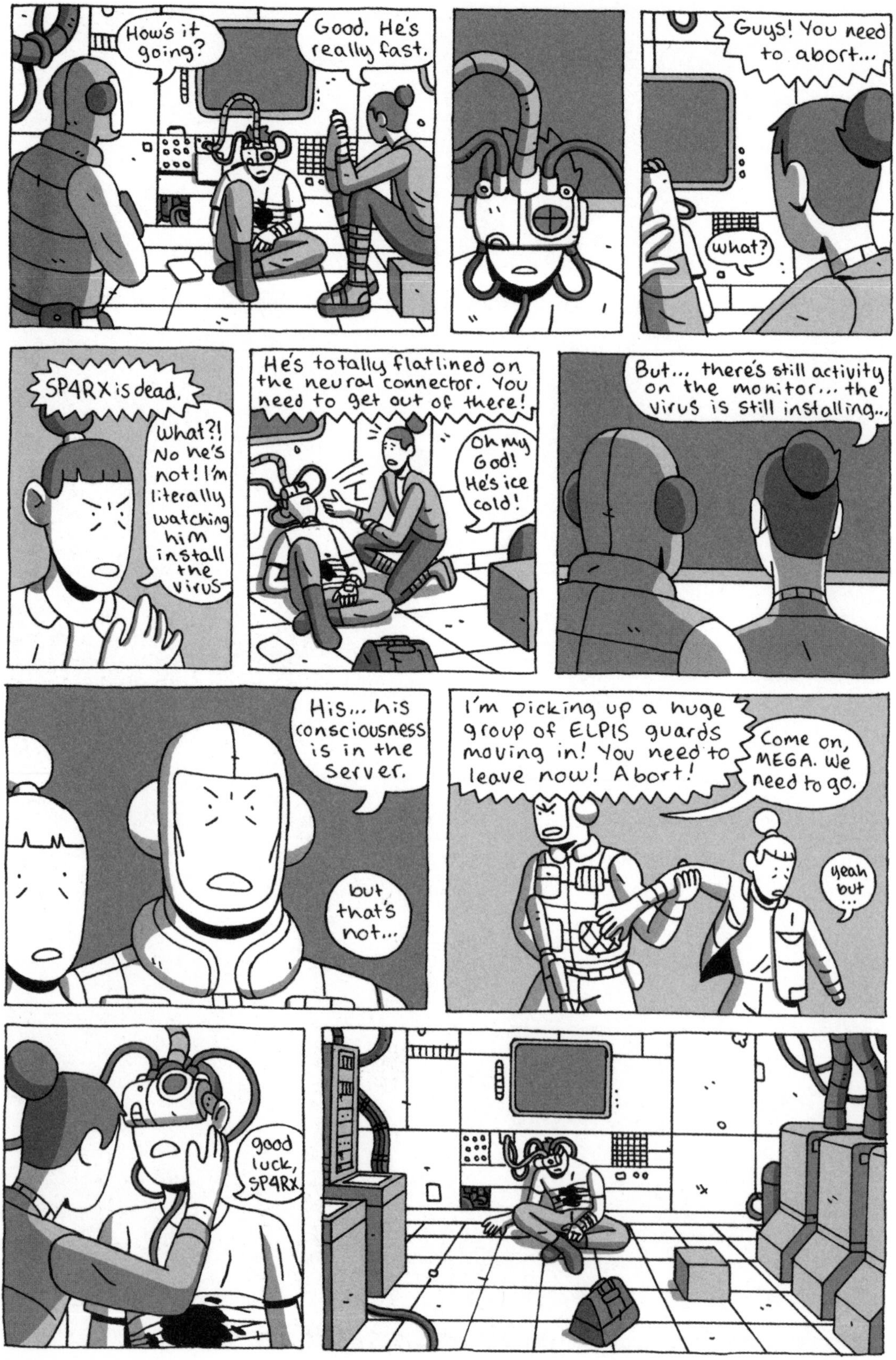

How's it going?
Good. He's really fast.
Guys! You need to abort...
what?
SP4RX is dead.
What?! No he's not! I'm literally watching him install the virus
He's totally flatlined on the neural connector. You need to get out of there!
Oh my God! He's ice cold!
But... there's still activity on the monitor... the virus is still installing...
His... his consciousness is in the server.
but that's not...
I'm picking up a huge group of ELPIS guards moving in! You need to leave now! Abort!
Come on, MEGA. We need to go.
yeah but ...
good luck, SP4RX

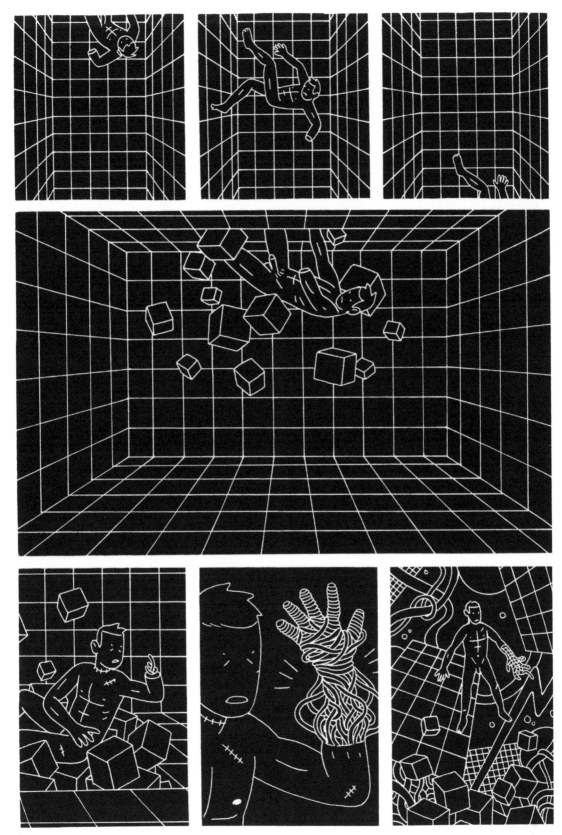

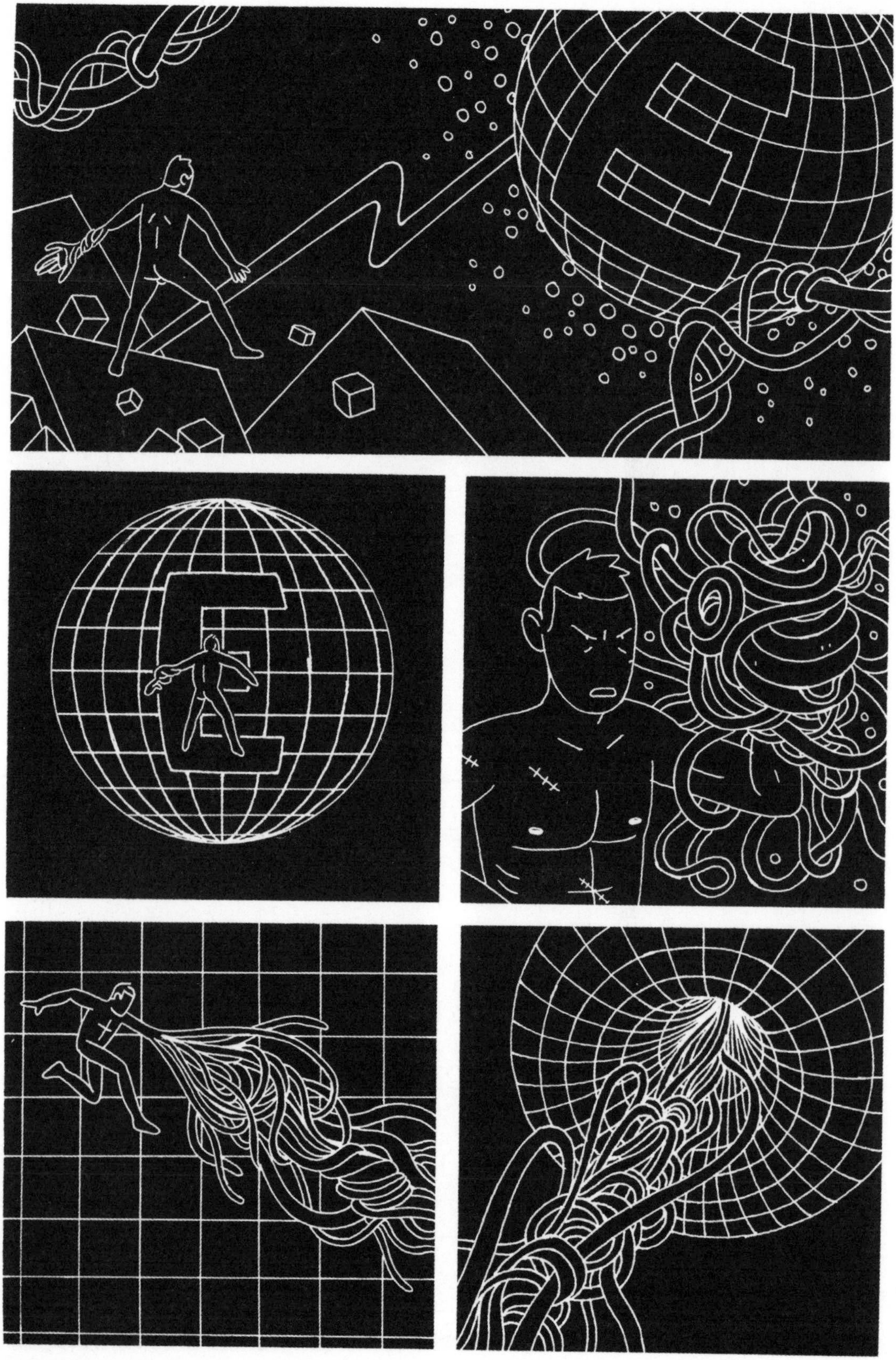

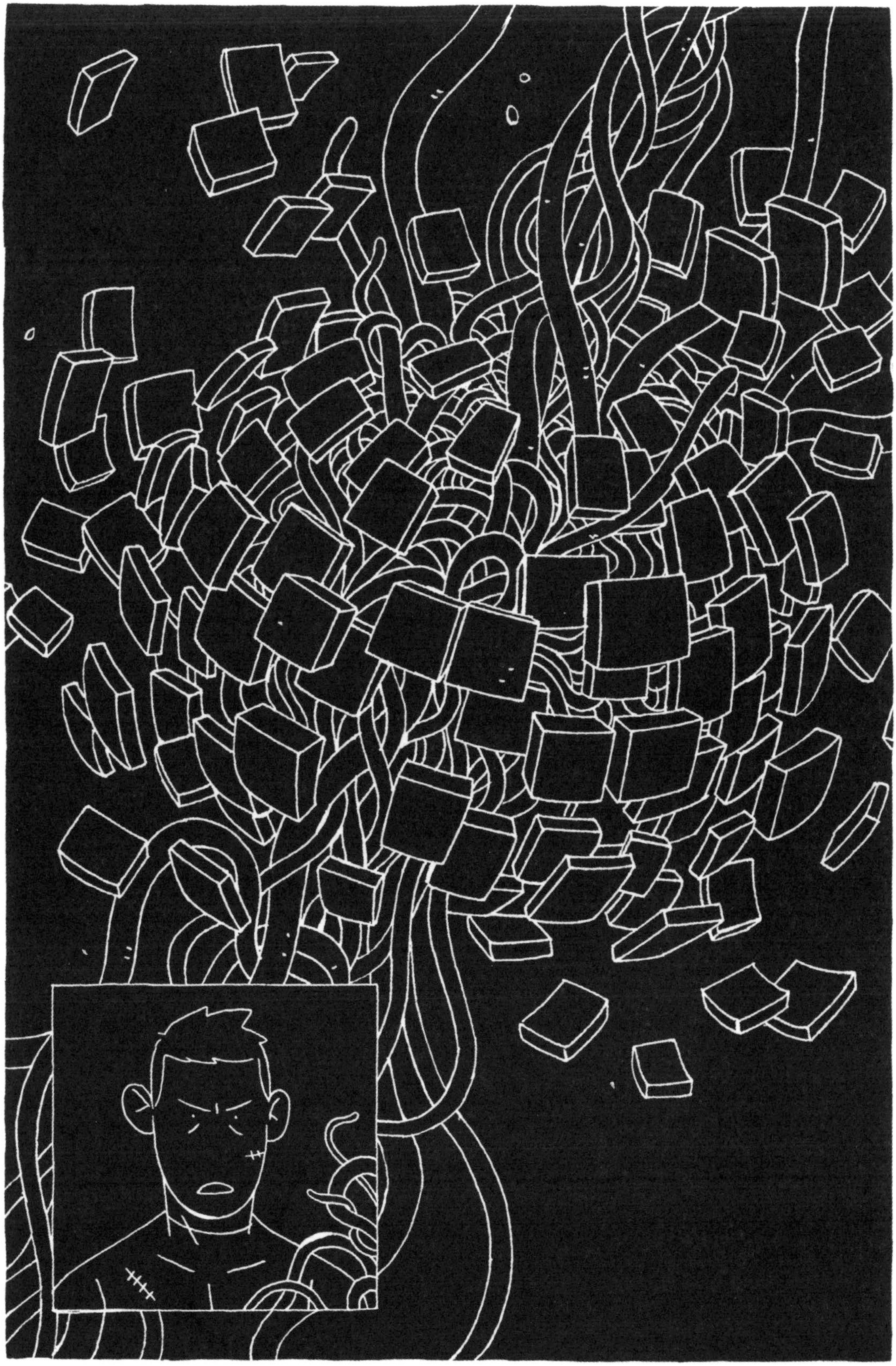

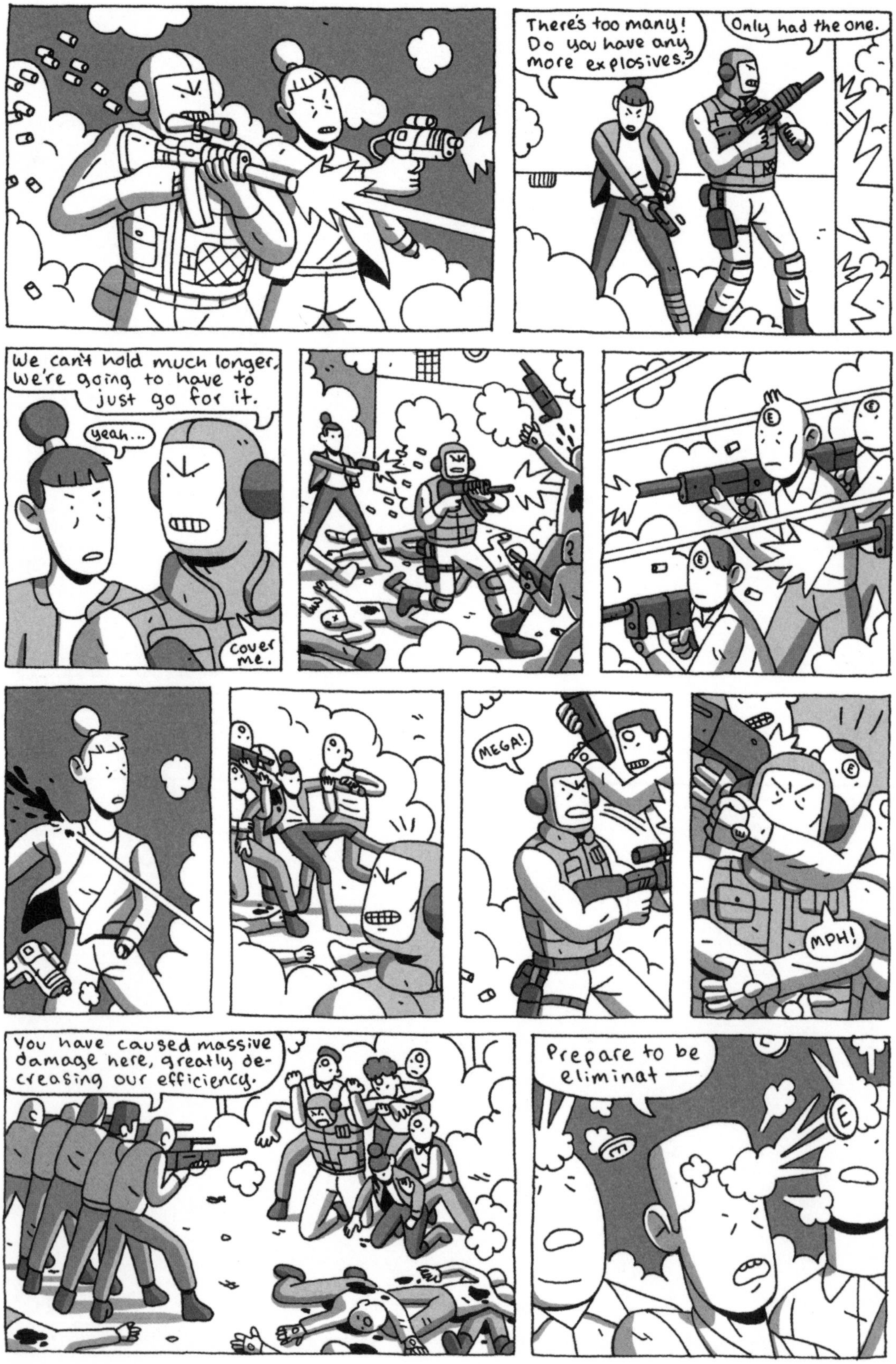
There's too many! Do you have any more explosives?
Only had the one.
We can't hold much longer, we're going to have to just go for it.
yeah...
cover me.
MEGA!
MPH!
You have caused massive damage here, greatly decreasing our efficiency.
Prepare to be eliminat—

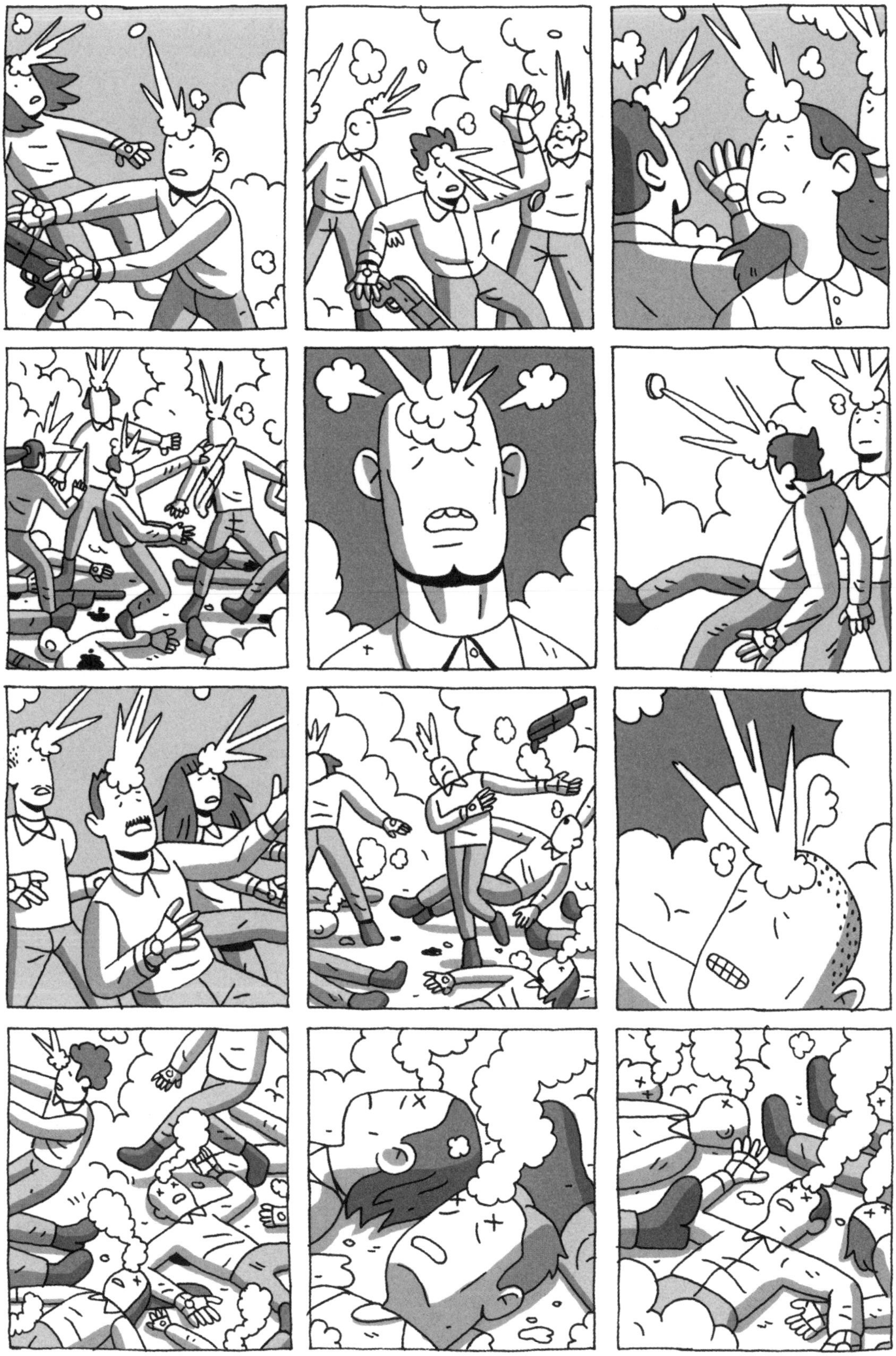

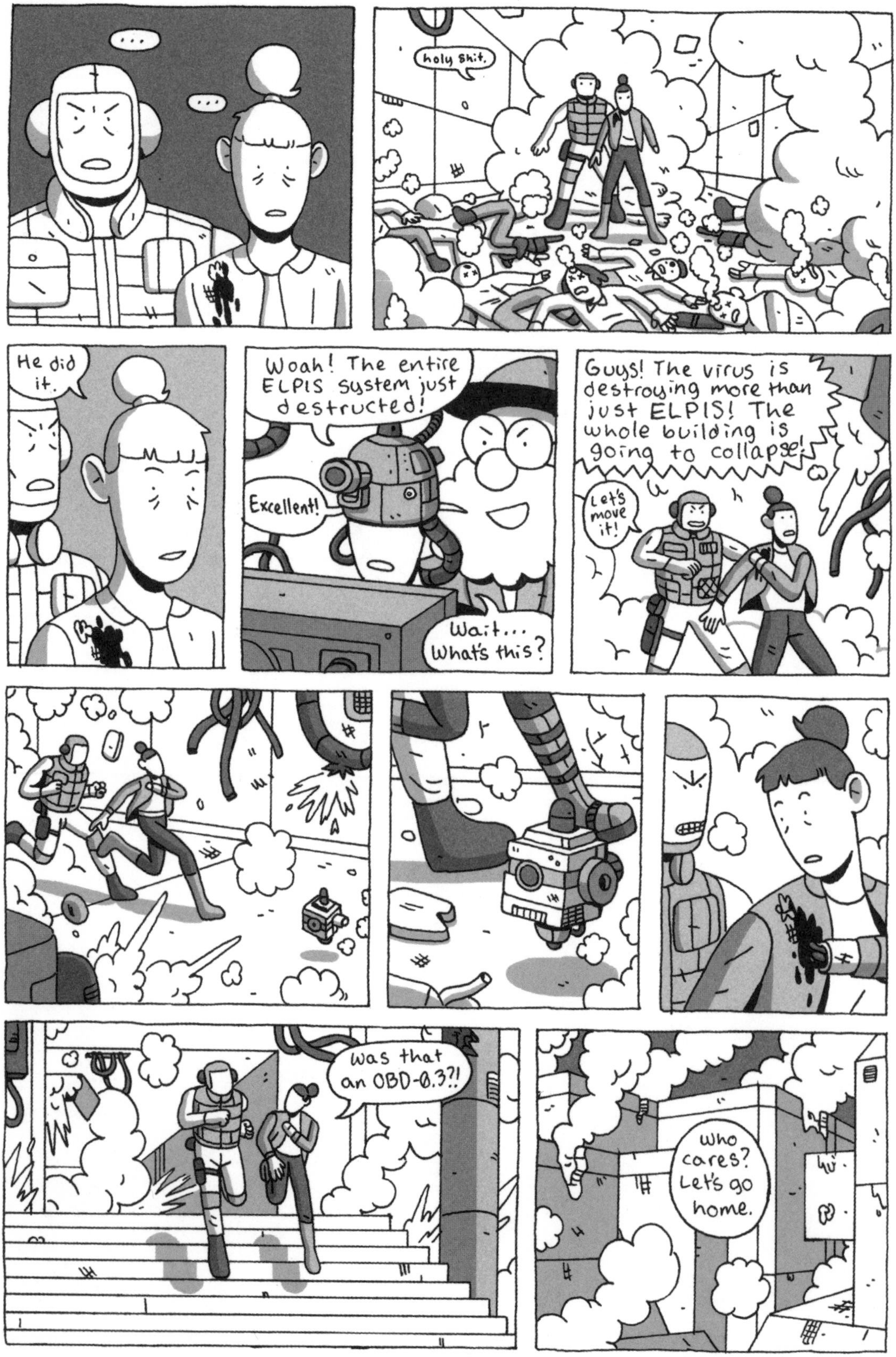
...
...
holy shit.
He did it.
Woah! The entire ELPIS system just destructed!
Excellent!
Wait... What's this?
Guys! The virus is destroying more than just ELPIS! The whole building is going to collapse!
Let's move it!
Was that an OBD-0.3?!
Who cares? Let's go home.

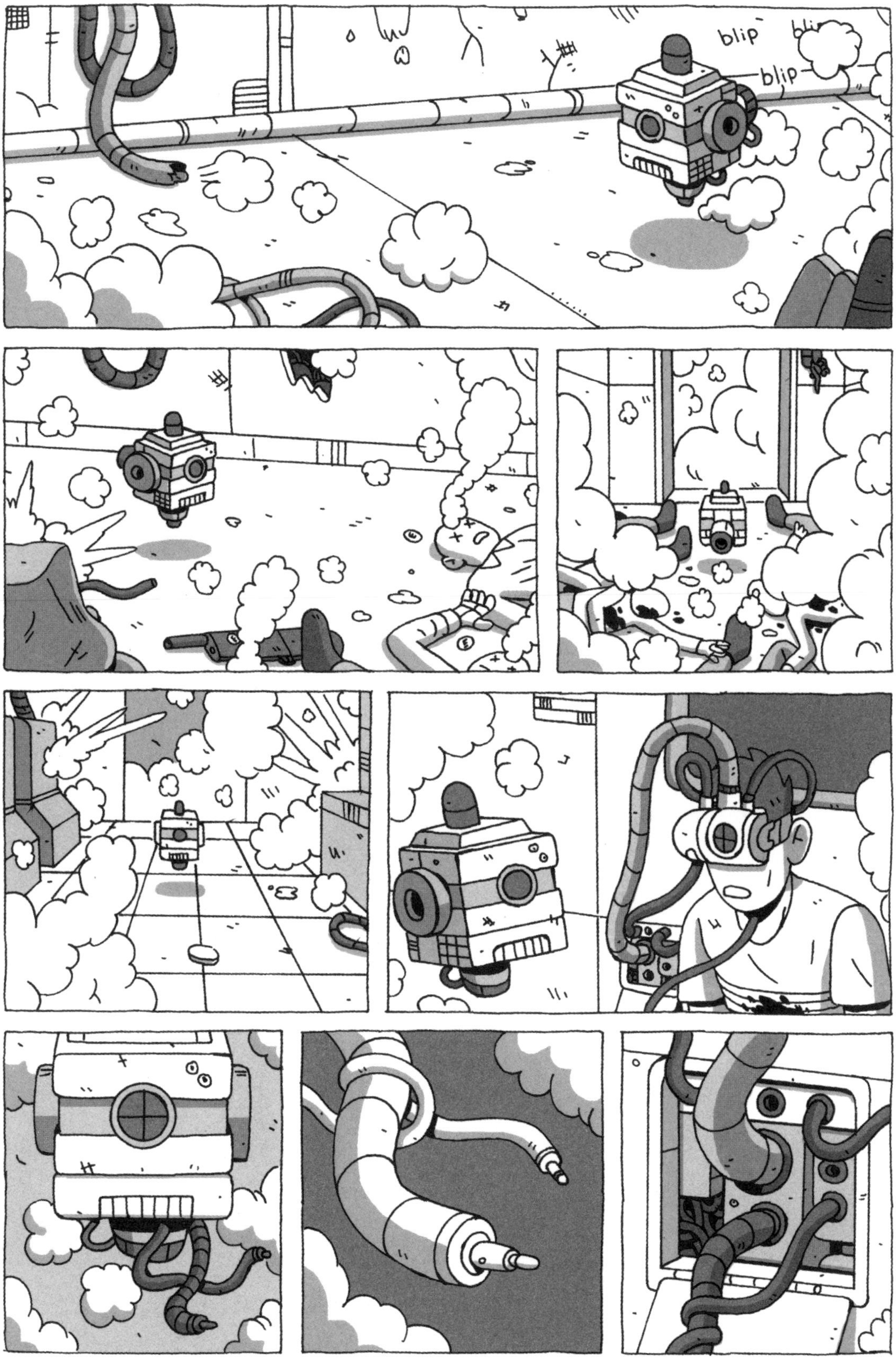
blip
blip
blip

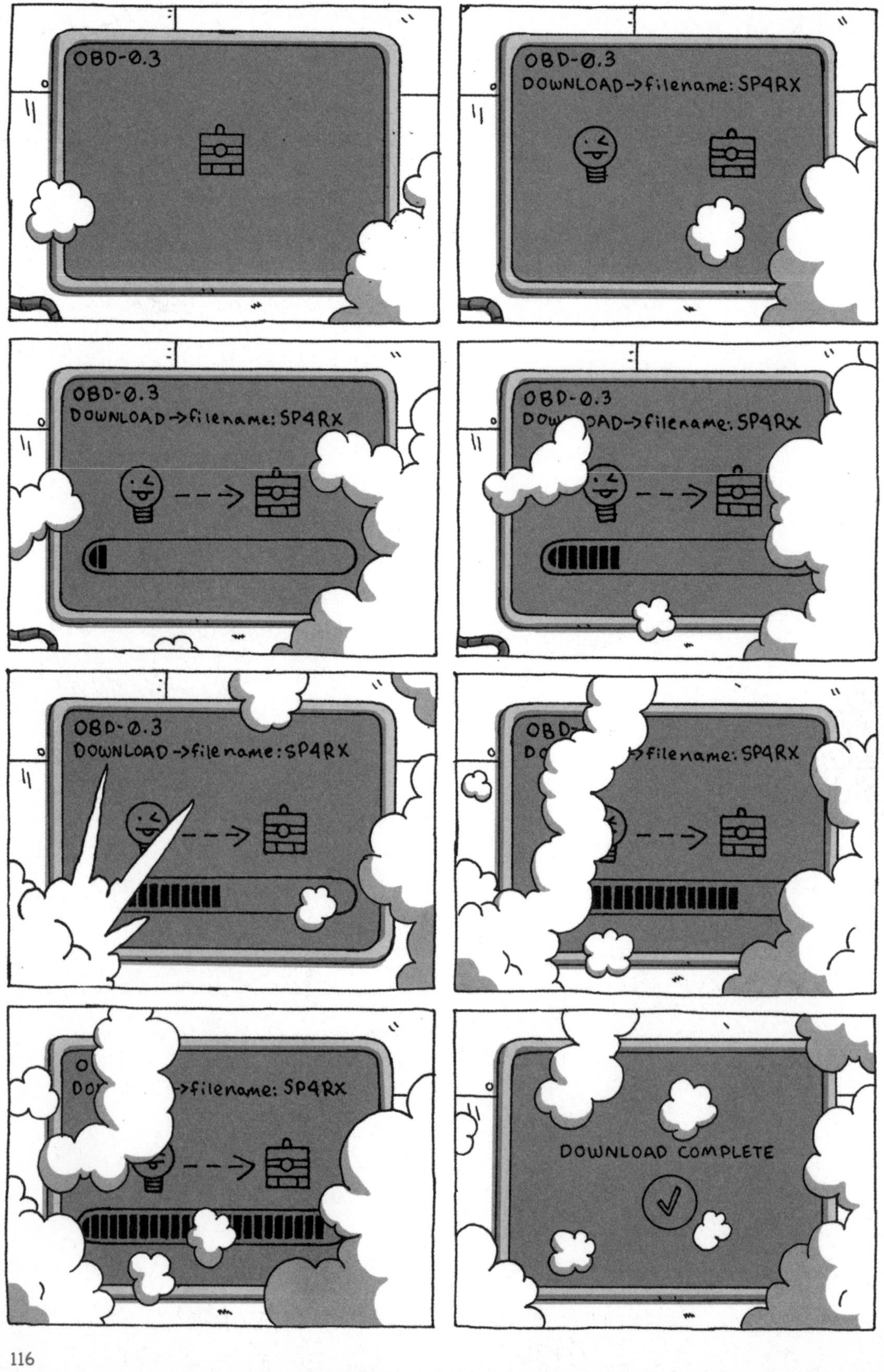

OBD-0.3
OBD-0.3
DOWNLOAD->filename: SP4RX
OBD-0.3
DOWNLOAD->filename: SP4RX
OBD-0.3
AD->filename: SP4RX
OBD-0.3
DOWNLOAD->filename: SP4RX
->filename: SP4RX
->filename: SP4RX
DOWNLOAD COMPLETE